The Crimes of Others

Recent Titles in

Studies in Penal Theory and Philosophy
R.A. Duff, General Editor

Just Sentencing
Principles and Procedures for a Workable System
Richard S. Frase

Popular Punishment
On the Normative Significance of Public Opinion
Jesper Ryberg and Julian V. Roberts

Taming the Presumption of Innocence
Richard Lippke

Sentencing Multiple Crimes
Edited by Jesper Ryberg, Julian V. Roberts and Jan W. de Keijser

Playing Fair
Political Obligation and the Problems of Punishment
Richard Dagger

Hate, Politics, Law
Critical Perspectives on Combating Hate
Edited by Thomas Brudholm and Birgitte Schepelern Johansen

Criminal Law in the Age of the Administrative State
Vincent Chiao

Punishment and Citizenship
A Theory of Criminal Disenfranchisement
Milena Tripkovic

Beyond Punishment?
A Normative Account of Collateral Restrictions on Offenders
Zachary Hoskins

Neurointerventions, Crime, and Punishment Ethical Considerations
Jesper Ryberg

The Metamorphosis of Criminal Justice
A Comparative Account
Jacqueline S. Hodgson

Guilty Acts, Guilty Minds
Stephen P. Garvey

Sentencing and Artificial Intelligence
Jesper Ryberg and Julian V. Roberts

Punishment for the Greater Good
Adam J. Kolber

The Crimes of Others

Criminal Records, Publicity, and Crimes of Abuse

KATERINA HADJIMATHEOU

Senior Lecturer, Department of Sociology and Criminology, University of Essex, UK

OXFORD
UNIVERSITY PRESS

OXFORD
UNIVERSITY PRESS

Great Clarendon Street, Oxford, OX2 6DP,
United Kingdom

Oxford University Press is a department of the University of Oxford.
It furthers the University's objective of excellence in research, scholarship,
and education by publishing worldwide. Oxford is a registered trade mark of
Oxford University Press in the UK and in certain other countries.

Published in the United States of America by Oxford University Press
198 Madison Avenue, New York, NY 10016, United States of America.

British Library Cataloguing in Publication Data
Data available

Library of Congress Control Number: 2025947848

ISBN 9780198925118

DOI: 10.1093/9780198925149.001.0001

Printed and bound by
CPI Group (UK) Ltd., Croydon, CR0 4YY

MIX
Paper | Supporting responsible forestry
FSC® C013604

The manufacturer's authorised representative in the EU for product safety is
Oxford University Press España S.A. of Parque Empresarial San Fernando de Henares,
Avenida de Castilla, 2 – 28830 Madrid (www.oup.es/en or product.safety@oup.com).
OUP España S.A. also acts as importer into Spain of products made by the manufacturer.

Contents

Acknowledgements vii

1. The Right to Know and Criminal Records 1
   Introduction 1
   Part I: Why We Should Re-examine Access to Criminal Records 1
   Part II: The Scope of Inquiry: What Are Criminal Records? 8
   Conclusion and outline of the book 21
2. The Harms and Wrongs of Public Criminal Records: A Matter of Human Flourishing 23
   Introduction 23
   Part I: The Consequences of Visible Criminal Records 25
   Part II: The Moral Harms of a Public Criminal Record 42
   Conclusion 47
3. Are Criminal Records an Intrinsically Public Matter? Political Theory and The Publicness of Crime 49
   Introduction 49
   Does the Idea of the Social Contract Imply a Right to Know? 50
   Does the Idea of Crime as a 'public wrong' Imply a Right to Know? 57
   Conclusion 70
4. Transparency, Accountability, Open Justice, and Public Facts 73
   Introduction 73
   Democratic Accountability: The Public's Right to Scrutinize Actions Done in Its Name 75
   Sunlight Is the Best Disinfectant: Publicity to Reduce Corruption and the Abuse of Power 80
   Open Justice and the Criminal Court As the Ultimate Public Forum 82
   Openness in Courts but Confidentiality in Policing 94
   Conclusion 96
5. Public Criminal Records and Just Punishment 99
   Introduction 99
   Untangling Public Criminal Labelling, Stigmatization, and Censure 102
   The Communicative Justification for Public Labelling as Punishment 107
   Public Criminal Labelling as a Deterrent to Crime 123
   Facilitating Punishment Through Exposure: The 'flypaper' Strategy 127
   Conclusion 130

6. Sharing Criminal Records to Prevent Harm 131
Introduction 131
The Proposal: A Harm-Prevention-Based Right to Know 135
A Defence of the Proposed Right to Know 136
The Kinds of Criminal History Information That Can Be Disclosed 144
The Right to Be Informed: 'upon request' and 'proactively' 145
The Rights of Subjects of Disclosure to Be Informed 146
Who Can Claim a Right to Know? 147
The Libertarian Objection 149
Conclusion 151

7. Disclosing Criminal Records to Protect People from Predatory Crimes and Crimes of Abuse 153
Introduction 153
The Distinctiveness of Dangerousness, Predation, and Abuse 154
Protecting Sex Workers from Predatory Offenders: 'Ugly Mug' and 'Dodgy Punter' Schemes 158
Domestic Abuse Disclosure Schemes 159
Objections from the Presumption of Innocence and of 'Harmlessness' 164
Conclusion 167

8. Defending a Limited Right to Know 169
Introduction 169
Lingering Lines of Objection to My Proposals 172
Broader Implications of My Proposal: #MeToo and the Informal Exposure of Wrongdoing 178
Conclusion 179

Bibliography 181
Index 197

Acknowledgements

I'd like to thank the following people, research groups, and organizations for their support. The British Academy's Mid-Career Fellowship Scheme, for funding my research into disclosure schemes and giving me the time to focus on this project. The European Society of Criminology's 'Collateral Consequences of Criminal Convictions Working Group', for giving me the chance to workshop both the proposal for this book and chapters of it. The research groups at the Centre for Applied Philosophy and Public Ethics (CAPPE) at the Australian National University, and the Centre for Ethics, Law, and Public Affairs (CELPA) at Warwick University for helpful feedback on early chapters. The Young European Research University Network (YERUN), for funding my visiting fellowship at Pompeu Fabre University, and Jose Luis Marti and Elena Larrauri for hosting me there and giving me the opportunity to present my work. Jonathan Jacobs and Maggie Smith and the Centre for Criminal Justice Ethics at John Jay College of Criminal Justice, for making my visiting fellowship in New York such a happy and productive experience. For helpful feedback on chapters and drafts, Nicola Collett, Antony Duff, Dorota Mokrosiniska, Chris Nathan, Marti Rovira, Milena Tripkovic, and Elina Zand-Kurtovic. For feedback and support with the application for the British Academy Mid-Career Fellowship, Sarak Kunz, Isabel Crowhurst, and Gary Williams. For funding open access to this book, the University of Essex. And special thanks to Saverio, Mario, and Aris for their patience and love.

1
The Right to Know and Criminal Records

Introduction	1
Part I: Why We Should Re-examine Access to Criminal Records	1
Changing stakes	1
Inconsistent practices	2
The limits of existing approaches	4
The value of an interdisciplinary approach to examining a right to know	6
Part II: The Scope of Inquiry: What Are Criminal Records?	8
Criminal records: an expansive category	8
Criminal records versus 'reputationally damaging information'	11
Analysing criminal records as a matter of criminal justice	13
The 'principle of less eligibility'	17
Conclusion and outline of the book	21

Introduction

Do we have a right to know about the criminality of others? That is the key question addressed by this book. The question is an abstract one, but the discussion seeks to make it concrete, focussing on laws and practices granting or withholding public access to criminal records. The aim is to propose a coherent, rigorous, and systematic analysis of the normative aspects of public access to criminal records which, in turn, provides the groundwork for fairer and more effective policies and practices for a digital age. We start that journey in this chapter by setting the scene, defining key terms and concepts, and explaining why the project is both worthwhile and timely.

Part I: Why We Should Re-examine Access to Criminal Records

Changing stakes

Today, criminal records are more accessible than ever before. Fast-paced technological developments, including internet search features and digital archiving of police databases, are making it easier for anyone to find out if

The Crimes of Others. Katerina Hadjimatheou, Oxford University Press. © Katerina Hadjimatheou 2026.
DOI: 10.1093/9780198925149.003.0001

someone has a criminal past. At the same time, lawmakers in many countries view sharing criminal records as a solution to a range of issues, amongst which increasing transparency in criminal justice, allowing employers to make better hiring decisions, and enabling citizens to protect themselves and their children from dangerous offenders. Governments around the world are relaxing legal and regulatory constraints on the disclosure of criminal records, giving more people more access to more information. As a result, someone who acquires a criminal record today can expect that information to be more publicly accessible, and enduringly so, than at any point in modern history. At the same time, more people are acquiring criminal records today than ever before.[1] In the United Kingdom and the United States, about 20% of the population have a criminal conviction, and many more have police records detailing any history of accusation, arrest, charge, and investigation.

These trends are changing the stakes of a criminal record both for individuals and for the public, but it is unclear how we should interpret and evaluate them. Is greater publicity around criminal records good for transparency in criminal justice, the just punishment of the guilty and the protection of the vulnerable? Does it serve an important purpose in fulfilling the public's right to know about who amongst their fellow citizens is dangerous or has been breaking the rules? Or does it undermine opportunities to move on and reform, stigmatizing people as dangerous or untrustworthy for life, with the result that those who have made mistakes in the past are still paying for them long after they have served their time? And how should we reconcile or balance these apparently competing demands of (criminal) justice?

Inconsistent practices

Looking to current practices for guidance can take us part of the way, but regimes of publicity and disclosure vary wildly between jurisdictions, even those which are similar in many other ways. Some countries treat criminal records as public records and so make them available online, while others treat them as confidential and subject to strict data protection. Differences are pronounced both within and between political and legal systems, regions, and cultures. In Spain and other European countries, for example, court records are anonymized and individual conviction records can be released only to criminal

[1] See, for example, UN Office of Drugs and Crime's 2024 report on the global prison population and trends (UNODC, 2024).

justice professionals and the person the record is about. In contrast, in the United States many states publish all police and court records online, complete with names and photographs of suspects, even if charges have been dropped or cases resulted in an acquittal (Myrick, 2013; Jacobs and Larrauri, 2012). African countries too diverge in their approaches to criminal records. Some, like South Africa, have made criminal record checks compulsory for a very broad range of jobs (Mujuzi, 2014), while neighbouring Botswana is only just beginning to digitize court records (Mosweu, 2021). In many other countries in Africa, police records are not maintained at all, let alone made publicly available, and the only criminal records that exist relate to convictions and sentencing (Mosweu, 2021).

Asia is, like Europe, a region of extremes. In Japan, criminal records are strictly confidential and criminal record background checks are not legal even for employers. But in South Korea, the Ministry of Justice runs a publicly searchable criminal justice portal through which citizens can trace all kinds of 'crime history data' through the justice system, from charge to prosecution, prison, and release. Meanwhile, China allows criminal record reports to be purchased by anyone online. China is also unique in operating a 'social credit' system, a kind of official trust rating for individuals. Social credit combines criminal record information with financial credit data and other supposed markers of trustworthiness to create a complex profile used by governments, business, and individuals to discriminate amongst people (Li, 2023).

Even *within* jurisdictions, the management of criminal records is often piecemeal and inconsistent, as different parts of the law and the justice system pursue diverging and sometimes competing aims. In the United Kingdom, those parts of the system that try to promote the rehabilitation and reintegration of offenders pull in opposite directions from those seeking to deter criminality or to protect potential victims through naming and shaming. For example, legislators have made moves to promote rehabilitation by removing legal requirements on people to disclose minor historic crimes to potential employers. Yet at the same time, they have encouraged police to post names and mugshots of local offenders on the internet, as a way of warning would-be criminals and reassuring the public that criminal justice is being delivered. On close inspection, the criminal records management 'regime' in the United Kingdom is just a hodge-podge of inconsistent and sometimes directly contradictory laws and regulations.

Looking beyond the law, it is also evident that foundational notions and principles of criminal justice, like 'public record' and 'open justice', have been silently transformed by the combination of the digitization of government records, the emergence of social media, and access to the internet itself. While classifying a record of a crime or arrest as 'public' previously meant giving access to any member of the public who had the time and inclination to visit the relevant archive, it now might mean 'available on your mobile phone'. Similarly, where the principle of 'open justice' used to mean that members of the public could attend court proceedings in person, it can now mean that those proceedings are broadcast on television or online, exponentially magnifying exposure of those involved. Meanwhile, the general practice of retaining press reports indefinitely online means that a simple Google search can reveal more about a person's criminal history than an official check ever would. All of this makes the efforts of those concerned about rehabilitation to restrict official disclosure through, for example, constraints on criminal record checks, seem pointless.

The limits of existing approaches

Existing research on criminal records has not been of much help in resolving these tensions and contradictions. This is partly because scholarly attention has been focussed almost entirely on articulating and demonstrating the human and social *costs* of sharing records with employers and the public, while overlooking the claimed benefits.[2] Those costs and harms are undoubtedly significant, as I discuss in depth in Chapter 2. They include indefinite stigmatization (Lageson, 2020; Hadjimatheou, 2016), disproportionate or otherwise unjust punishment (Corda, 2016), unfair disadvantage (Jacobs, 2015; Henley, 2019; Austin, 2004), and obstructing rehabilitation (Maruna, 2001). Some have also argued that disclosing criminal records to the public infringes the human right to privacy (Tunick, 2015; Larrauri, 2014) and the right to be presumed innocent (Larrauri, 2014a; Campbell, 2013; Purshouse, 2018). Others have sought to expose as fallacious the assumption that a public criminal record is a somehow inevitable or 'natural' consequence of having a free press or an open and transparent judicial system, by drawing attention to the practices of countries like Spain and the Netherlands which treat criminality information as confidential by default (Corda, 2016; Jacobs and Larrauri, 2012). Many scholars have put forward specific proposals for reform. All argue for

[2] For a useful summary of this body of work, see Hoskins, 2019.

much greater restrictions on public and employer access to criminal records as a means of addressing these problems.

That important body of work tells a powerful story about the reasons we should worry about policies and practices of disclosing or publicizing criminal records. It has helped inspire and provide evidence in support of new movements, notably in the United States and United Kingdom, to reverse policies of radical publicity around criminal records that have harmed many.[3] But it is only one side of the story. The fact remains that both legal practice and social norms in many countries imply that citizens have some kind of *right* to know about the criminality of others. Criminal proceedings and decisions that follow are generally treated as a matter of public record, and citizens' rights to access and disseminate that information are protected to some degree or another in all jurisdictions. And it is likely that many individual citizens would share the conviction or intuition that people who commit crimes and are convicted of them should not be helped by the law to conceal, deny, or as some would have it, 'lie'[4] about that. But the moral basis underpinning this pro-publicity position has never been clearly articulated or defended.

Some legal theorists have gestured at the existence of a right to know, by asserting considerations such as the overriding priority of freedom of expression (Husak, 2008); the value of public censure (Duff and Marshall, 2010) or public shaming (Hart, 1958: 409), as a form of punishment and deterrence; the importance of 'open justice' and transparency in the criminal justice system as a whole; or the rights of people to find out about the 'character' of those they associate with (Jacobs, 2015) and to protect themselves or those in their care from the risks of harm posed by people with criminal histories. Each of these arguments identifies a distinctive and important political or moral grounding for public access to criminal records (and all are considered in depth in what follows). But all fall short of the kind of systematic account we need if we are to be able to assess whether the purposes served by granting such access are weighty enough to justify the growing costs. As evidence of those costs mounts and the case for restricting public access becomes more persuasive, it is time to hear the other side of the story.

[3] See the #FairChecks campaign in the UK and the campaign for a Clean Slate Act in the USA.

[4] Colgate Love, 2011: 777. For an earlier expression of this view, see also Franklin and Johnsen, 1980. Lawmakers in the South African parliament similarly objected to a proposal to introduce processes for expungement of criminal records as authorizing 'a statutory lie by trying to rewrite history and pretending that an offence never took place' (cited in Mujuzi, 2014: 280).

The value of an interdisciplinary approach to examining a right to know

One reason for framing this project as an investigation into the basis for a *right* to know about the criminality of others is that assertions in favour of public access to criminal records often include some appeal to rights. Another is that persuasive reasons in support of such a right would make the presumption in favour of publicity relatively strong. Rights are generally held to be resistant to efforts to limit their exercise unless these promise demonstrably significant increases in benefits (or decreases in harms) for others, or unless they conflict with the exercise of other rights. If there is a general right to know about the criminality of others, then only certain arguments in favour of restricting publicity will be persuasive. It is therefore important that those scholars and campaigners whose work is devoted to demonstrating and reducing the harms and injustices of publicity and disclosure in criminal records understand what they are up against, morally speaking. Only then will they be able to develop the kind of positions and counterarguments that can engage coherently and persuasively with the strong intuitions and firmly held positions of those who assert such rights. Too often, those who have seen and documented the damage done by criminal records dismiss these intuitions and assertions as grounded in simplistic but politically convenient fictions about 'criminals', moral panics, and cynical populism on the part of political decision-makers (Naylor, 2011; Rovira, 2023). While this is understandable, it risks building a body of literature that speaks primarily to the initiated. Instead, this book takes as its point of departure a conviction that we need to take seriously the claim that people have rights to know about the criminality of others.

The approach taken to addressing these issues in this book is interdisciplinary. First, it draws on the conceptual and analytical tools of legal, political, and philosophical theory to articulate and examine positions and arguments critically. This involves identifying and drawing out rights-claims that are explicit or (more frequently) implicit in relevant literature, articulating them in their most compelling form, and then stress-testing their resilience under analytical pressure. This latter step involves subjecting those claims to systematic critical examination and pitting them against each other to see which is left standing, so to speak. It is a discursive process that will be familiar to philosophical and political theorists and is essentially 'epistemic' in the sense that, by allowing us to switch and change perspectives and play both sides in a debate, it helps us to reach a better understanding of the concepts and considerations at play. Ultimately, this enables us to settle on the most defensible set of relevant beliefs, in the confidence that we have considered the full range of alternatives and done justice to those who disagree with us. The aim is not to assemble an indefeasible arsenal of arguments to push a specific agenda, but to learn from evidence and rigorous thinking, and develop a well-informed and philosophically coherent position.

But to learn from the evidence we need the methods and findings developed by the social sciences, and criminology in particular. In doing so, we can meet Jesper Ryberg's recent challenge to penal ethicists that 'if there is no interaction between ethical theorists and those who conduct the requisite criminological research, then translating important theoretical considerations into genuine action guidance may well not be possible' (2025: 11). Criminological scholars have done more than any others to draw attention to the practical and human implications of current regimes of publicity and disclosure around criminal records. This book draws heavily on that body of literature to support its arguments, privileging the voices of those who have criminal records and those who have shared or accessed them. Chapter 2 surveys this literature through a philosophical lens to draw out its as-yet-unexplored moral implications. And Chapter 7 presents findings from my own research and that of others with people, vulnerable to crimes of sexual and domestic violence and abuse, about their experiences of schemes that allow the sharing of criminal records to prevent crimes of abuse. As well as putting forward concrete proposals for how to design regimes of disclosure and publicity of criminal records to make them more coherent and more just, the discussion provides an in-depth analysis of the role and value of labelling, publicity, and openness in criminal justice more broadly.

The main argument of the book is that citizens have no general or presumptive right to know about others' criminal convictions, nor to access other kinds of criminal records. Instead, *some* kinds of people have *limited* rights to know about *some* kinds of records. Who has a right to know about what depends on a) the status or role of the agent claiming such a right and b) the nature of the crime in question. I argue that special rights to know can be legitimately claimed by those who act as gatekeepers to vulnerability or have special duties of care to the vulnerable, as well as those who are themselves directly at risk of criminal harm from predatory and abusive offenders. I argue that the distinctive features of abuse and predatory crimes—namely their serial nature, widespread impunity, and the special role of secrecy, lies, and silencing in their perpetration—make criminal record disclosures for prevention more appropriate than they would be for other crime types.

As this latter argument implies, my approach in this book is not to appeal to ideal principles but to facts about our societies, social behaviour, and justice systems as they are today—that is, ad-hoc, inconsistent, flawed, and dysfunctional. In asking neither 'what would an ideal system of criminal justice and criminal records management look like?' nor 'how could we change society to remove the contingent injustices caused by the criminal justice system today?', but rather 'what is justified given the entrenched realities of actual criminal justice systems?', my approach continues a longstanding trend in what is known as 'non-ideal' theorizing about crime and justice.[5] For example, my arguments in favour of disclosing non-conviction records to prevent crimes of abuse only hold weight because the criminal justice system has failed systematically to hold serial perpetrators of such crimes accountable.

Some might consider that non-ideal penal theorizing of the kind this book engages in is both uninspiring and unambitious, aiming as it does merely to mitigate the shortcomings and harms of the criminal justice system, rather than to address their causes by changing the way society views criminality in the first place. I deal with that criticism in the closing chapter of this book. For the moment, I accept that scope of my ambition reaches only, in the words of Michael Tonry, to 'help people who make laws and apply them to think more clearly and consistently and modestly on what they do, and at what costs to other human beings' (2011: 24).

At this point some readers may be ready to get straight into the debate about the right to know. But others may have methodological and conceptual questions they would like answered before they read further. I encourage the first kind of reader to read the next paragraph in which I define criminal records and then skip the remainder of this chapter, which constitutes a detailed defence of the scope and focus of my inquiry.

Part II: The Scope of Inquiry: What Are Criminal Records?

Criminal records: an expansive category

The subject of analysis in this book is 'criminal records', but what exactly is included in this category? A criminal record is understood here as any official

[5] Recent examples include Jake Monaghan's (2023) *Just Policing* and influential and formative examples include Matt Matravers' (2017) article 'Legitimate Expectations in Theory, Practice, and Punishment'.

record of criminality, or associations of criminality, attributed to a named person by the criminal justice system. In practice, criminal records are made by police, courts, probation, or prisons and typically record an individual's status as dangerous, suspect, accused, convicted, or other such category. While different jurisdictions have different ways of classifying criminal records, I follow criminologists such as Lageson and Stewart (2024) in interpreting the term broadly to encompass official records relating not only to proven criminality but also to suspected and alleged criminality and records of official assessments of criminal risk.[6] The discussion in this book is therefore interested in records of reported crimes, convictions, cautions, anti-social behaviour orders, restraining orders, non-molestation orders and other prevention orders, records of fines, community service penalties, arrest, charge, prosecution and sentencing data, parole and probation records, and inclusion on registers for domestic violence, terrorism, or sex offences, amongst other things.

Why maintain this broad focus rather than, for example, restricting the discussion to records of criminal *convictions*, which has been the main concern of both empirical and philosophical work on criminal records in recent years?[7] At least one good reason is that there is today a global trend towards collecting, keeping, and sharing all kinds of criminal records, rather than just records of convictions. In particular, there is much more sharing than ever before of police records, especially those that relate to reported acts that have not been proven in court but still indicate a propensity towards a certain kind of criminal behaviour. For example, England and Wales operates an 'enhanced' criminal record check system, for occupations involving national security or contact with vulnerable people. These checks search for and then disclose non-conviction criminal history information, such as reported and alleged crimes, to prospective employers who then may choose to reject the candidate.[8] At the same time, new 'disclosure schemes', introduced in the United Kingdom, Australia, Canada, New Zealand, Malta, and Spain, share police records of reported crimes with potential victims and those who have a duty of care towards them, in order to inform them about ongoing risks to their safety. It is true that

[6] In the UK, these are sometimes called 'criminality information' (as in the government-commissioned Review of Criminality Information by Magee, 2008) but government and police still use the term 'criminal records'. It has been suggested to me that a more accurate term would be 'record of criminal justice contact' (thanks to Alessandro Corda for this). I do not disagree. However, for the purposes of convenience, linguistic simplicity, and general coherence with existing convention, I prefer to use 'criminal records'.

[7] For example, see Fitzgerald O'Reilly, 2018.

[8] Enhanced disclosure is enabled in the United Kingdom for people applying for positions involving working directly with children or vulnerable adults. It includes any relevant information held on local police files (Police Act 1997 s.115).

most of these relatively novel recording and sharing practices take place in economically and technologically developed countries. But as digitization spreads to criminal justice systems around the world, more will surely follow.

Another reason for drawing the boundary of criminal records broadly is that some of the reasons for and against making criminal convictions public apply equally to information relating to behaviour or to suspicion that never results in a conviction. For example, research in the United States shows that publicly available records of a person's arrests and reported crimes, known as 'rap sheets', are used amongst as a basis to reject job candidates (Jacobs, 2015). If making rap sheets publicly available enables the same kind of job discrimination that has been shown to unfairly disadvantage people with convictions, then concerns about unfair discrimination arise similarly with both kinds of records.

Similarly, the reasons that count in favour of disclosing conviction records for public safety purposes also extend to the disclosure of records of alleged crimes. For example, people who engage in certain kinds of criminal behaviour for which prosecution rates remain persistently low, such as domestic and sexual abuse, often have substantial police records detailing allegations that are strikingly similar but come from many different victims. These non-conviction criminal records can be far more reliable indicators of actual dangerousness than records of convictions alone, because the vast majority of people with police records for domestic and sexual abuse are never convicted.[9] If disclosing or sharing records of reported crimes is just as effective in protecting vulnerable people from serial abusers as sharing or disclosing records of convictions, then arguments that appeal to public safety as a basis for a right to know about people's criminal histories apply to both kinds of record. In other words, the same set of normative considerations apply both to records of convictions and to records of other kinds of involvement in the criminal justice system. For these reasons at least, it makes sense to include non-conviction records in the present inquiry.[10]

[9] Less than 4% of reported domestic abuse crimes ever result in a conviction in the United Kingdom. See the UK National Policing Statement for Violence Against Women and Girls (VAWG) 2024: 27. For rape, the figure is even lower.

[10] Of course, some will argue that there is a bright and important line separating records of convictions and other records, and that is the fact that the former relate to proven criminality while the latter are mere speculation. For those who hold this opinion, the criminal justice system is only justified in interfering with people who have been proven guilty of a crime. I disagree with this position. It rests on an excessively idealistic view of the criminal justice system—one that is tellingly held exclusively by academics and certainly not shared by anyone working in criminal justice, including those who work in the rehabilitation of offenders. I engage in depth with that position in Chapter 6 when defending the limited public disclosure of police records relating to suspects of domestic abuse.

Criminal records versus 'reputationally damaging information'

Though I have only just proposed a broad categorization of criminal records, I now want to resist attempts to expand it further. Some of the literature in this and adjacent fields treats criminal records as merely one amongst many kinds of unflattering and demeaning information about individuals that, if shared with others, is likely to result in negative consequences such as shaming, disadvantage, or unfair exclusion of various kinds. According to these accounts, it is this broader category of what we might call 'reputationally damaging information' that is morally and legally salient, so we should take that as our main focus of analysis.

For example, in a 2013 paper philosopher Mark Tunick argues that people have a legitimate moral claim to restrict dissemination of information about themselves even when that information is accurate, if leaving it in the public domain degrades their reputation. This moral claim is grounded in a 'legitimate privacy interest in avoiding unjust punishment', which Tunick argues is infringed when people suffer informal disadvantages and harms because information about them has been shared. He claims that the interests the public may have in freedom of expression with respect to such information should be balanced against this legitimate privacy interest and describes a range of cases in which the latter outweighs the former.

Tunick's argument applies both to information about behaviour that is criminal and to information about behaviour that is not illegal but is nonetheless embarrassing or humiliating, such as indiscretions or rude, insulting, and offensive speech or acts. It applies both to information published by criminal justice systems and to information shared informally by individuals on social media or other public channels. All these kinds of information should, according to Tunick, be subject to a single legal 'privacy regime'. His argument excludes the possibility that people with criminal records might claim any *default* or *presumptive* rights against that information entering the public domain. But it does support a moral and legal right to remove or conceal that information after it has been shared if doing so prevents unfair punishment. In this respect, his argument is similar to those put forward in support of a 'right to be forgotten' (which is recognized in European law but not in many other countries). Like Tunick's proposal, the right to be forgotten allows individuals to apply to have 'irrelevant' and damaging information about them removed from the internet but not to prevent its initial publication.

There are at least two reasons why it might seem to make sense to go with Tunick's approach and subsume criminal records under a broader category of accurate but reputation-degrading information (though I will ultimately argue that neither should convince us). First, doing so recognizes that the blame, censure, and social exclusion inflicted on people whose non-criminal misdeeds or transgressions are widely publicized online can be as disadvantageous and damaging as those prompted by a formal criminal record. In other words, Tunick's account acknowledges that the informal harms to an individual of (over)exposure of such information can be similar both in type and severity across the criminal/non-criminal and official/unofficial divides. Similarly, his position recognizes that some of the reasons why individuals would want to share and receive information about criminal records—for example, to enable them to better choose between candidates for a job—apply also to information about some kinds of objectionable or undesirable behaviour that do not involve crime, or which may involve crime that has never been officially recorded. These, it might reasonably be argued, are at least a couple of good reasons to treat the two categories of information together.[11] What's more, one might point out, these reasons are not dissimilar in kind to the reasons I just gave a second ago for wanting to focus on records of convictions and of police contact together. So I can't just dismiss them without also inviting scepticism about my own reasoning.

Second, and more importantly, it could be argued that focussing only on criminal records risks opening the door to unjust inconsistencies in the allocation of rights and entitlements between those whose behaviour is criminal and those whose behaviour is not. It would not be fair, this argument goes, to create rules about which aspects of one's personal history can be treated as confidential or otherwise concealed that privilege the interests of people convicted or accused of crimes over those whose misdeeds or missteps broke no laws; therefore, whatever privacy protections are provided to the former should, at a minimum, be extendable to the latter. It follows, one might argue, that whatever privacy protections are denied to the latter, must also be denied to the former. In other words, the rights and protections enjoyed by people with respect to their criminal acts should never be greater than those provided to those whose acts fall short of crimes. If this is correct, and the rights of people with criminal records are always normatively

[11] As a brief aside, it is worth noting that this line of argument would also likely resonate with 'zemiologists', a group of breakaway criminologists who became sceptical about the value of using an inherently limited and socially constructed category like 'crime' as an organizing concept, when the behaviours it includes have much in common with a much broader range of social harms. Differently, see philosophical arguments by Flanders (2017) questioning the institutionalization of the asserted link between character and crime.

tethered in this way to those of people without, then it makes sense to analyse the two together.

Analysing criminal records as a matter of criminal justice

I don't think either of these arguments justify conflating criminal and non-criminal information, and I'll explain why in a moment. First, it's important to say that my responses to both are going to begin from a core assertion, namely that it makes sense—both philosophically and criminologically—to analyse laws and practices governing criminal records as part of a *criminal justice system* that itself serves a specific function in a broader political order. Taking this position means defending a distinction between the duties of the state or legislatures to regulate access to and sharing of criminal records and its duties to regulate access to and sharing of other kinds of information that are not generated by the criminal justice system but nevertheless may resemble criminal records in arguably relevant ways. This distinction appeals to the state's monopoly on the delivery of formal criminal justice, and its *de facto* position as the unique producer and (to borrow a phrase from data protection terminology) the 'controller' of criminal record data, both of which positions imply special duties in relation to criminal records.

As philosophers of criminal justice have argued convincingly in recent years,[12] institutions and agencies of criminal justice—the police, courts, probation, and so on—and the regulations that govern their activities, require as much political justification as the laws they exist to enforce. Understanding criminal justice and penal practices as requiring *political* justification immediately invites us to think about what can be legitimately and justifiably done in the name of citizens, about the rights and responsibilities of citizens as such, and about what is required to satisfy principles of representative democratic government, such as accountability and transparency. It invites us, in other words, to engage in political theorizing of criminal justice.

Thinking about criminal records through the lens of political theory also allows us to recognize that criminal justice systems are in all societies designed with distinctive purposes and objectives in mind, including the detection, prevention, censure, and punishment of a specific category of 'public' wrongs, as well as the rehabilitation of those who commit them and the deterrence of those

[12] See the work of Antony Duff and Sandra Marshall, Chad Flanders, Vincent Chiao, Jake Monaghan, Brandon del Pozo, Luke William Hunt and others.

who might.[13] Some of the reasons for and against making criminal records publicly accessible are internal to these logics of criminal justice. Some of them make appeal to the special nature of crime as essentially 'public'. Neither can therefore be extended coherently to issues outside that sphere.[14] If I am correct, it follows that decisions about the routine or default exposure or concealment of criminal records must be justified *at least* in terms of those kinds of reasons.

In contrast, decisions about the proper balance between privacy and freedom of expression with respect to non-criminal but nevertheless reputation-degrading information need not be justified with respect to those purposes and objectives. Rather, they may appeal to considerations such as the overall costs and benefits, or the need to balance competing rights claims of individuals. These are considerations that have no recourse to the norms and values that govern political and government institutions in general and criminal justice in particular.[15] As I'll now argue, treating criminal records and reputation-degrading information as an undifferentiated category risks confusing any subsequent debate, for instance by misapplying considerations to both when they are in fact only relevant to one, or failing to recognize considerations that apply to one just because they do not apply to both. To see how, let's look more closely at each of the arguments that could be made in favour of Tunick's broader categorization.

As mentioned above, Tunick argues that unfettered public access to information about criminal and non-criminal reputation-degrading acts results in disproportionate and therefore unjust punishment ('disproportionate'

[13] See Duff who also takes distinct normative spheres as frameworks for analysis: 'we are responsible for particular matters, to specifiable people or bodies, in virtue of our satisfaction of relevant normatively significant descriptions. Such descriptions locate us within the normative structures of particular institutions and practices, within which and in terms of whose constitutive values and responsibilities - both prospective and retrospective - are recognised and attributed' 2007: 37.

[14] Certainly there are rationales that pervade and connect criminal justice and, for example, civil law, such as harm prevention. In the United Kingdom, for instance, civil law is used by police to impose measures which, like restraining and non-molestation orders, are designed to prevent a person harming another person by restricting their freedom of movement and association amongst other things. Breach of such orders constitutes a criminal offence, so the prevention of harm and the criminalization of those who commit it run together here as a thread between the civil and criminal sphere, as theorists of preventive justice have long argued (see the work of Andrew Ashworth and Lucia Zedner).

[15] The point being made here about criminal records being analysed with respect to the norms of criminal justice is relevant to other spheres of social life in which reputations can be ruined and livelihoods destroyed. When I first discussed the idea for this book with colleagues, someone asked me why one should analyse the harms or wrongs of publicity with respect to criminal records as apart from, for example, the harms of poor or even malicious restaurant reviews (thanks to Keith Hyams for this challenge). My response is that the hospitality industry as a whole benefits from a competitive public market where customers share and rate their experiences, and where restaurateurs can respond to public comments. The ability to post public reviews promotes the values of this business by increasing quality and value and exposing poor hygiene and standards, which overall promotes everyone's interests, even though in some cases poor reviews might be harmful. In contrast, it is not clear that practices of exposure in criminal justice benefit anyone at all.

meaning more than is deserved or conducive to the aims of punishment). This observation is not wrong. But neither is it particularly illuminating. For example, it does not help us address the argument that, unlike people whose social missteps are posted online, people with criminal convictions have already been punished formally; any publicity with respect to their record that persists after their sentence is served is therefore *by definition* 'extra' in some sense, and therefore harder to justify (even in principle) than that which results from publicising non-criminal behaviour. Alternatively, it might be argued that insisting that the state should intervene to correct disproportionate punishment of the latter just begs the question of whether the state's responsibility for preventing disproportionate punishment extends to all realms in which 'punishment' might occur, or only to the realm of punishment in the context of formal criminal justice.

In response to this latter question, we can point out that the question of whether the state has a duty to intervene to prevent informal punishment arising from the legitimate exercise of freedom of speech is a matter of ongoing debate. In contrast, it is hardly contentious to claim that states do have duties to design the criminal justice system in such a way as to tend towards the achievement of legitimate criminal justice aims, primary among which are the just punishment of offenders, their rehabilitation, and a reduction in the rate of reoffending. When publicity or disclosure of criminal records by criminal justice systems undermines these aims, that is one strong (though not indefeasible) reason to restrict it. But it is a reason that has little bearing on information that is *not* produced by and in the name of criminal justice systems. These arguments and considerations are elided by treating 'reputation-degrading information' as a unified category.

Along similar lines, we may also argue that conflating information about criminal records and information about other kinds of reputation-degrading information fails to acknowledge that disclosing or publicizing criminal records can interfere with the distinct set of civil liberties that is generated by the existence of a criminal justice system with coercive powers, namely those of 'due process' and particular among those the 'presumption of innocence'. The same risk does not arise with informal records or information about reputation-degrading behaviour, because there is no analogous set of liberties external to a system that wields the power to use force, censure, and punish. Here is another reason to focus on criminal records alone, at the very least as one step in a broader analysis.

A further reason to focus more narrowly on criminal records is that conflating them with all or any kind of reputation-degrading information begs the question of whether citizens should have the kind of access to criminal record information that would enable them to share it in the first place. Unlike with other kinds of reputation-degrading information, the publicizing or disclosure of criminal records is not typically something that occurs through the ordinary activities of individual members of the public exercising basic freedoms of expression with respect to information they have naturally come to possess. Rather, it necessarily involves an intentional decision on the part of government and agencies such as the courts or police to place (or not) information about criminal justice in the public domain. State agencies are the creators and publishers of criminal records. It is the state's 'slate' on which a criminal record is marked and which only the state can 'wipe clean'. States therefore can, and indeed routinely do, decide what the default position is with respect to their publicity and disclosure.

That states everywhere *already* consider the consequences of such publicity and disclosure carefully is evidenced by the wide variety of nuanced customs and rules of confidentiality, privacy, and disclosure within all countries' criminal justice systems. These include well-established practices of shielding criminal justice processes and their records from public view, such as through use of secret terrorism courts, protection of juvenile offenders' identities, restriction of journalistic reporting in certain cases, official 'expungement' or 'sealing' of convictions, and so on.[16] It makes sense for citizens to expect the reasons and rationales informing such decisions to be both transparent and justifiable in terms they can recognize as valid.[17] A person who shares a recording of another person acting in an unpleasant, humiliating, or embarrassing manner on social media has no analogous obligation to provide *public* justification for that act.

Conflating criminal records with other true but reputation-degrading information also has the distorting effect of concealing the special reasons or permissions a society might have *for* making such information public. These special reasons are precisely those that would support and justify a right to know about other people's criminality, and which form the basic subject of analysis in this book. For example, some argue that the foreseeable consequences of intentional publicity of criminal records should be counted as

[16] Many countries include provisions for the erasure of a criminal record for certain crimes after the elapse of a set period of time. Some allow records to be 'sealed' meaning they do not need to be declared, for example, to employers, but can be reopened by permission of a court order in specific circumstances. And there are many variations of these kinds of measures.

[17] This is the notion of public justification defended by thinkers including Rawls (1993), Larmore (2008), and Quong (2011).

part of the formal punishment meted out by the state and justified explicitly in those terms (as has been argued in relation to the 'collateral consequences' attending criminalization [Colgate Love, 2011]). Others say or imply that the public has a right to access public records of criminal justice processes, because such publicity is necessary for justice 'to be seen to be done'—on any reading of that dictum (Nicholls, 2018). Alternatively, it has been argued that crimes are not only wrongs but also breaches of the social contract and that, just as parties to a contract have a right to know about any breaches thereof, so the public has a right to know who amongst them has violated the criminal law. Further, we could adopt the kind of perspective that says that crimes are misdeeds against the public or 'the community' as such, and that all members of the public have a right to know who it was that wronged them in virtue of their status as (even indirect) victims. Differently still, publicizing or disclosing criminal records might be justified on non-punitive grounds, such as public safety or risk-reduction. Any or all of these arguments are relevant to deciding who should be able to find out what about people's criminal records and all are worth exploring (and all will be considered in what follows). None can easily be extended to justify continued publicity of 'accurate but reputation-degrading' information that is not produced by criminal justice systems.

The 'principle of less eligibility'

Let us turn to the second source of potential scepticism towards my decision to focus on criminal records only. This argument, first canvassed above, asserts that focussing on criminal records alone may lead us to support a position that defends special privacy protections for people with such records, while potentially leaving unprotected those who do not. To do so, the argument goes, would be unjust because people with criminal records should not be protected from being informally punished for their criminal acts when people are routinely punished in similar ways for lesser wrongs.

It's important to note that this latter line of argument implies the existence of a relevant moral distinction between crime and other kinds of wrongdoing. Distinctions of these kinds have been a long-running theme of political and academic debate about the treatment and rights of people with criminal convictions. As far back as the 1830s, Jeremy Bentham's principle of 'less eligibility' stated that 'in principle, the prisoner's standard of life should not be superior to that of the poorest citizen, as it would be contrary to the spirit of justice if the free and honest, but unemployed citizen should be able to enjoy, at least, the same standard of life as the prisoner' (Bentham, 1790: 7). Bentham's sentiment has proved enduring: 50 years later it was repeated by an indignant citizen who—writing to *The Times* newspaper in 1938 to protest against proposals to assist probationers in finding employment—declared 'wrongdoing cannot be a passport to preferential treatment'.[18] Opinions such as these continue to be voiced today, in relation not only to prison conditions but also to the entitlements of offenders after their sentence is served.[19]

Support for these sentiments is also sometimes expressed by those who argue (as Bentham did, amongst others) in a two-pronged manner that penal systems must provide effective *deterrents* through material deprivation or they fail in their core aim of preventing crime *and* that the deprivation must be comparatively worse than that suffered by the lower classes or these will choose crime over honest work. Other times such sentiments are grounded in moralistic and retributive penal rationales, which state that crime as a category is worse morally than other kinds of wrongdoing and so people who commit it *deserve* to be worse off than those who do not.[20]

Neither the deterrence nor the desert-based justifications stand up. Deterrence-based arguments for less eligibility discount what should be obvious, namely that loss of liberty and criminal stigmatization that tend to follow a conviction constitute distinct disadvantages beyond the threat of material deprivations, which any rational person would actively avoid. They also evince a simplistic—even insulting—estimation of the motivations of the 'lower classes' for refraining from crime.

At the same time, moralistic arguments deploring unfair privileges for offenders mistakenly locate the reason for what our *Times* reader calls 'preferential treatment' as lying *in the crime itself*—the 'wrongdoing'—rather than in the criminalization and attendant stigma that follows a conviction and subsequent punishment. But this must be contested. It is not *because someone is guilty* that we might think they deserve a clean slate. Rather, it is because a public record

[18] Quoted (on p. 95) in Mannheim's (2021) study of the dilemmas of penal reform. According to Mannheim, the principle of non-eligibility was later replaced in British penal rationales by a tempered 'principle of non-superiority' which stipulated 'a requirement that the condition of the criminal when he has paid the penalty for his crime should be at least not superior to that of the lowest classes of the non-criminal population' (Mannheim, 2021: 57). The latter marked a raising of the threshold from 'the poorest citizen' to 'the lowest classes' but both rest on a similar assumption, namely that effective deterrence and public support for penal systems can only be achieved by ensuring the standard of living of the criminalized never supersedes that of the least advantaged.

[19] In 1972 John P. Reed and Dale Nance referred to these arguments as subscribing to a morality that 'demands continued status degradation' of those who have broken the rules.

[20] Many US collateral consequences do explicitly say people who have criminal records are less 'deserving' of public benefits than others, or have demonstrated 'bad character' (Mayson, 2015: 312). All I'm arguing is that the existence of a criminal record is not sufficient to draw such a conclusion.

of their guilt predictably triggers reactions that lead to enduring stigmatization, social exclusion, and disadvantage, precisely at the time the person is expected to begin to rehabilitate and reintegrate. These reactions and impacts are explored in detail in Chapter 2 which discusses the harms of a public criminal record.

Even so, one might argue, endorsing greater confidentiality with respect to criminal records must entail endorsing it for records of non-criminal wrongdoing, because it would be unfair on those guilty of lesser wrongs to be exposed to greater disadvantage. But that general moralistic account of crime is simplistic and unconvincing, as many have argued before me. It is true that the most serious of interpersonal harms, such as murder, torture, or rape are nearly everywhere also crimes. But it is also true that nearly everywhere 'crime' includes fairly unobjectionable behaviours, such as shoplifting food when hungry, littering, drug taking, swearing at people in public and driving offences. Meanwhile, many behaviours that are despicable by the lights of any moral compass remain widely un-criminalized, such as bullying or environmental destruction. The point is that a person's having committed a crime does not by itself imply an impaired moral standing relative to someone who has not.[21] So it should not trouble us that my approach is open to the possibility that justice could require privacy protections for people with criminal records, without also pronouncing on the rights of those without.

It bears mentioning that even if we were to concede that crime is as a general category of wrongs worse than other categories of wrongs, this would still not be sufficient to justify a principle of less eligibility as a basis on which to either design penal policy or retrospectively test its fairness. Most people have committed at least one crime in their lives and most will never be caught, giving the lie to the often-repeated political flummery of 'the law-abiding majority'. Some of those convicted of crimes are in reality innocent of them.[22] This fact collapses a supposed moral distinction between actual people with criminal records and actual people without. So it is difficult to see on what principled grounds one might justify insisting that people without records should always be privileged over those who have them. And even if criminal wrongs were worse than other wrongs, it is neither inconsistent nor unfair to try to form

[21] Earle (2016: 94) has cautioned against the introduction of policies that persuade people that criminal records have a power far beyond their actual potential to tell us about the state of a person's conscience.

[22] Selbin et al.'s (2018) fascinating research discusses how in in some US states (e.g. Florida) two-thirds of criminal defendants plead guilty or no contest after only 3 minutes of contact with a lawyer—a statistic that should make anyone worry about the reliability of those convictions.

arguments about what people with criminal convictions or other kinds of criminal records deserve or are entitled to, or about how their records should be managed and maintained to achieve certain legitimate social aims, without in the same breath making claims about what should happen to those without.

So far, I have been trying to defend the decision to focus this inquiry on criminal records alone. Along the way I have distanced my position from accounts of criminality that assert the moral worseness of crime, yet I have also insisted on criminality's normative distinctness. Is there an inconsistency here? I hope not. To say that criminal records are normatively distinctive is to say that decisions about how and when to impose, publicize, conceal, or erase them involve considerations of a *specific* set of values, norms, and principles. The normative distinctness of crime comes from its role and status in a political and legal order, and we can analyse it in that context without committing ourselves to any deeper position on the moral standing or status of those who engage in it, relative to those who do not.

Of course, there will inevitably be analogies and continuities between formal practices of publicity and disclosure with respect to criminal records and informal practices with respect to behaviour that is reputationally degrading. And certainly, it is undesirable for the rules and regulations of criminal justice systems to conflict in fundamental ways with the principles underpinning legal regimes around individual rights to privacy and freedom of expression. But when inconsistencies do arise, we should consider whether these are legitimate results of the proper consideration of the norms and reasons at play in the relevant domain, rather than reflexively attempting to resolve and eliminate them. Doing so is more likely to suggest appropriate and sensible avenues for addressing those inconsistencies.

Figuring out how we should think about and regulate access to criminal records is a worthwhile project. The process is likely to yield arguments and conclusions that contribute usefully to broader questions around publicity and disclosure in a range of spheres of public and private life. As we develop our thinking on this issue, it will be helpful to reflect on our intuitions and accepted practices around other kinds of information, including for example information shared in court, information about civil cases, information about what happens to people after they are sentenced, and information about informal allegations of criminal and other harmful, abusive, and dangerous behaviour when these are made publicly. I have not intended in this section to imply that considerations around the publicity and disclosure of these related kinds of information are irrelevant to the concerns of this book. Only to justify its focus on criminal records in particular.

Conclusion and outline of the book

The current chapter has explained what criminal records are and why we should care about public access to them. It has also defended the interdisciplinary approach taken in the book compared to legalistic alternatives. Chapter 2 examines the harms and wrongs that result from unfettered public access to criminal records and conceptualizes these morally in terms of human flourishing. Chapters 3–7 examine critically distinct lines of justification for a public right to know, concluding in each case that public access to criminal records is justified in a much smaller range of cases than proponents of those lines of reasoning typically recognize. Chapter 3 examines the idea that people should have a right to access criminal records because crime is an inherently public matter. Chapter 4 considers whether making criminal records public is necessary for democratic accountability and open justice. Chapter 5 explores punitive justifications for making people's criminal records public. Chapter 6 proposes a limited public right to know, grounded in the need to prevent criminal harm and protect the vulnerable. Chapter 7 draws on empirical evidence to look in more depth at the ways in which criminal records might be shared to prevent predatory crimes and crimes of abuse. Taken together, these chapters weigh in favour of a significant reduction in public access to criminal records in most contexts in which they are currently shared, but for a radical expansion of criminal record disclosures to protect people from predatory crimes and crimes of abuse. With respect to the latter, it also advocates, controversially, for disclosures of information about behaviour that has not resulted in a conviction such as police records of reported crimes. Chapter 8 draws together the conclusions reached in each chapter and considers some lingering objections.

2

The Harms and Wrongs of Public Criminal Records

A Matter of Human Flourishing

Introduction	23
Part I: The Consequences of Visible Criminal Records	25
Disadvantage and exclusion from work, public goods, and opportunities	26
Persecution by the public	31
The process of criminal stigmatization	33
Chilling effects, social withdrawal, and system avoidance	35
Cascading costs to communities and society	40
Conclusion of Part I	41
Part II: The Moral Harms of a Public Criminal Record	42
Diminishing a person, stunting a life, and writing people off	42
Flourishing as a unifying concept	44
Dignity as part of flourishing	45
Conclusion	47

Introduction

Should criminal records be publicly accessible? The question is not new, but it is worth revisiting because the stakes of the debate have changed. This book re-examines the arguments for and against the publicity of criminal records by posing the question: Do we have a right to know about each other's criminal histories? The current chapter examines what the available evidence tells us about the impacts of a publicly accessible criminal record on individuals and society more broadly. It first surveys and synthesizes that evidence and then articulates its implications in moral terms. The main claim advanced is that imposing a visible or otherwise publicly accessible criminal record on a person harms and wrongs[1] them by *undermining their flourishing and violating their*

[1] These effects are understood as harms in the sense developed by philosopher Joel Feinberg when he asserted that: 'harm is conceived as the thwarting, setting back, or defeating of an interest' where to 'have an interest' is to 'have a kind of stake' (Feinberg, 1984: 33). The effects are understood as wrongs when they violate a person's moral or political rights.

The Crimes of Others. Katerina Hadjimatheou, Oxford University Press. © Katerina Hadjimatheou 2026.
DOI: 10.1093/9780198925149.003.0002

dignity. Any assertions of a right to know about criminal histories must, therefore, be assessed against countervailing entitlements grounded in these fundamental human values. In later chapters, I argue that some of these harms can be justified in the name of a right to know, but only in limited circumstances and to the limited extent required to protect the vulnerable from predatory crimes and to ensure fairness and transparency in criminal proceedings.

The current chapter begins by examining what we know from empirical research about the impacts on people, families, communities, and society of a visible criminal record. The process of synthesizing and surveying this previously broad and disparate body of literature has not yet been attempted elsewhere. But as this chapter shows, doing so allows common patterns and themes across the various studies to emerge. This inductive approach (drawing generalizations from a set of specific observations) allows us to tell a coherent story about what happens when a person's criminal record is made publicly accessible. The story goes like this: When a person's criminal record is accessible by employers, insurers, education and housing providers, and others, it results both in their exclusion and in their withdrawal from those social and economic goods and opportunities; when their record is visible to the public at large, this can prompt persecution, violence, and other kinds of abuse from members of the public.

Sociological and other socio-psychological theorizations of stigmatization help us explain the processes driving these reactions. They show us that it is primarily the fact of being labelled as (potentially) criminal, rather than that of being implicated in criminal behaviour, that prompts the negative social reactions to a criminal record. Because it is the label itself, rather than a person's choices and behaviour, that leads to their stigmatization, it is very difficult for a person to counteract or mitigate the stigma they receive by demonstrating good or otherwise redeeming behaviour. The result is that people whose criminal records are shared with employers or otherwise made public are thereby diminished and written off. Their identity is reduced to their criminal record, their life prospects, and their ability to realize their potential stunted.

Previous studies have shed light on the ways in which these effects undermine or infringe the exercise of discrete human and political rights, such as the right to freedom from discrimination, the right to work, the right to rehabilitation, and the right to citizenship. While insightful and useful, none of these analyses alone tells the full story of what these effects mean in the context of a human life. This chapter takes that overarching perspective as its viewpoint, observing how these discrete effects co-occur, generating an impact that is both deeper and broader than any fragmented analysis can capture. That impact is articulated through the moral concept of flourishing.

Part I: The Consequences of Visible Criminal Records

Philosophers of argumentation tell us that in a debate, the burden of proof should rest with whoever is making the more outlandish or less well-evidenced claim.[2] Burdens of proof can shift over time with changes in the accepted wisdom and the availability and weight of evidence. Part of what I want to do in this section is to show readers that we now have convincing evidence that making criminal records publicly accessible leads to serious harms for individuals and their families and has negative consequences for society as a whole. If this is correct, then it means the ball is back in the court of those who think criminal records should be public. In other words, it is they who should now acknowledge the evidence and re-examine their position, or else find a way to justify the considerable harms it imposes. Let's look at that evidence.

In the United Kingdom, about a quarter of working-age adults has a criminal record (Ministry of Justice, 2024). In the United States, it is about a quarter of the adult population. In all countries in which they are kept, criminal records affect many more people than prison or any other criminal justice sanction. Indeed, research shows that people with criminal convictions outnumber those who have experienced incarceration or community sanctions by at least ten to one (Corda et al., 2023). These figures are dwarfed by the number of people with non-conviction records such as police reports, 'rap sheets', and so on, though reliable statistics on those are harder to find. In the United States, evidence suggests that by the age of 23, almost 50% of all African American and Latino men, more than a third of White men, and almost one in eight women have been arrested (Selbin et al., 2018: 3).

Legislative trends around the world have removed barriers to access and disclosure of criminal records, and as a result, rates of criminal record checks are rising globally both for conviction data (Rovira, 2023) and non-conviction data (Maurutto et al., 2023). In the United Kingdom, 2,657,121 of the lowest-level criminal records checks were carried out by employers in 2022. This represented a 60% increase from three years previously, indicating a sharp trend upwards (Unlock, 2023a). People everywhere appear to have developed a

[2] See for example Hahn and Oakesford (2007: 49).

sense of entitlement to know about other people's pasts.[3] So the question of whether and how public criminal records harm or wrong people is anything but niche or marginal. Whatever those harms and wrongs turn out to be, they are suffered widely.[4]

Disadvantage and exclusion from work, public goods, and opportunities

In 2009, Lord Neuberger, once president of the UK's Supreme Court of Justice, admitted that the disclosure of even old and trivial criminal records would represent a 'killer blow' to a person's job application.[5] Today, that remains an accurate description of the situation facing people with criminal records around the world. The overwhelmingly negative impact of a public or accessible criminal record on employment prospects has been demonstrated extensively, with dozens of studies on the topic published since the late 1990s. From experimental approaches that involve sending fictitious resumes to employers and seeing how they respond, to large-scale surveys, analyses of national population data, longitudinal studies, and qualitative interviews with applicants and HR departments, the findings are conclusive. Employers everywhere seek access to criminal history information now more than ever; and when they have it, they use it to discriminate against candidates, whatever the nature of their criminal record, in ways that often appear arbitrary.[6]

Unlock, a UK-based charity campaigning and advocating for the rights of people with criminal records, shares case studies on their website. Among these is the story of Ian who lost his job with a professional services firm after

[3] Writing about the United States, Roberts (2015) calls this a 'national obsession'. A recent study estimates that about 15% of Americans had searched online for records of criminal convictions over the space of 2019 alone (Lageson, 2020).

[4] To be sure, there will be many exceptions. Plausibly having a visible criminal record provides no new knowledge to anyone in communities that are so small that everyone already knows what happened. In others, a person criminalized may be part of a subculture in which having a criminal record is a mark of pride or achievement. Some people enjoy a social status so privileged that a visible criminal record would do little to disadvantage them. The negative impacts on specific individuals differ depending on many factors. Still, the negative impacts discussed in this chapter are inevitable for most people in most circumstances in most societies today. That's a good enough reason to take them seriously.

[5] The case he was concluding is *R v. Chief Constable of Greater Manchester Police*, 2016.

[6] The body of work is far too extensive to list here, but some influential studies include Holzer, Raphael, and Stoll (2006), Pager (2003), Stoll and Bushway (2008), and Uggen et al. (2014). The UK research from 2022 found that 27% of employers surveyed would not consider hiring a person with a conviction in any circumstances, and over 60% would not consider hiring people with one of a list of common convictions (Working Chance, 2022).

a historic criminal record came to light at his workplace. Due to changes in human resources policy, Ian's company became aware of his conviction 25 years after he started working there. The conviction related to a robbery he was involved in 31 years earlier. But despite his many years of service and his excellent record, the company fired him, stating that they could not take the reputational risk of clients finding out they employed people with convictions.[7]

The apparent arbitrariness of this and much other current practice and decision-making around the employment of people with criminal records has been confirmed in empirical studies. Research shows that employers tend to request or otherwise seek access to criminal record data even when they are not required to by law or policy. In some cases, they do so even where their organization has explicitly adopted a policy of inclusion with respect to candidates with criminal records.[8] In most countries where employers have access to criminal records, that access is broad and not limited to records that have been assessed as being relevant to the kind of employment offered. Employers also tend to adopt a blanket approach to ruling out candidates with any kind of criminal record even if the record is minor, long-past, or has no bearing on their ability to perform the job at hand.[9] Non-conviction records such as arrests or charges are also used to disadvantage applicants where disclosed or otherwise accessed (Uggen et al., 2014). A quantitative study from the United States found that people with arrest records were significantly less likely to find employment than those without (Fields and Emshwiller, 2014).[10]

Similar results have been found in studies of the use of criminal records by other providers of social goods and opportunities including education, health, housing, and financial services. For example, even though requirements for university applicants to disclose unspent convictions were dropped in the United Kingdom in 2018, research found that 103 universities were still requiring such disclosure 5 years later (Brooks, 2023: 83). Experimental studies in the United States have found that the rejection rate for prospective students with convictions for serious crimes was nearly 2.5 times that of those without (Stewart and Uggen, 2020). In China, the United Kingdom, and parts of the United States, criminal records are also used as a basis to reject prospective

[7] See Unlock Charity Case Studies, at: https://unlock.org.uk/casestudy/case-ian/.

[8] The discretionary uses of criminal records as a basis for denying people access to goods and opportunities discussed here should be distinguished from formal disqualifications, for example, from taking employment in certain professions. Those disqualifications do not rely on making criminal records public or accessible to employers.

[9] See for example analyses by Furst and Evans (2017) and Lageson et al. (2015).

[10] Interestingly, the practice of posting arrest records on the Internet was opposed by 88% of respondents in a 2018 public opinion poll from the United States, where the practice is widespread (Lageson et al., 2018).

rental tenants and to deprioritize people for welfare benefits (Thacher, 2008; House of Commons, 2017; Pager, 2003; Vallas and Dietrich, 2014). In some parts of the United States, housing providers evict or deny leases even in response to criminal allegations that have not resulted in a charge or a conviction (157). In the United Kingdom, some women's refuges and safe houses for victims of domestic violence will not host anyone with a criminal record (Unlock, 2021: 21), even though a recent study shows that almost 60% of women with criminal records have been victims of domestic abuse (Unlock, 2024: 1).[11] A 2016 study of the management of elderly sex offenders in England found that those who required hospital care for prolonged periods sometimes found themselves denied treatment from nurses who refused to care for them, despite them being graded very low risk by police (Bows and Westmarland, 2016). Insurance of all kinds is also routinely denied to people with criminal records in the United Kingdom and elsewhere (Unlock, 2023) as are mortgages (Henley, 2018). Similar findings are reported for non-conviction records. Maurutto et al. studied the negative impacts of police record disclosures in Canada and found that these are, in many respects, indistinguishable from those of conviction records, with people experiencing 'disadvantage, exclusion, stigmatisation . . . marginalization [and] insecurity' (2023: 1378).

The exclusions just described come at a serious cost to those affected. Denial of employment opportunities at crucial ages of career or skills development can significantly set back a person's ability to get on in life. As British MP David Lammy wrote in his report on racial disparities in the criminal justice system:

> People can change quickly but their criminal record does not. For example, an 18 year-old serving a seven month sentence will wait until their mid-20s before their conviction is spent – and even then, only for some jobs. Selling drugs as a teenager could prevent you becoming a plumber or licensed taxi driver in your thirties. Often young adults can find a criminal record holding them back in the key period in their working lives. (Lammy Review, 2017: 64)

Lageson and Maruna's qualitative research with people negotiating their own online records echoes this, showing how young men's efforts to reconstruct a new identity for themselves as they move through the stages of life—for

[11] Women working in refuges and with victims of domestic abuse are subject to 'enhanced' criminal record checks in the United Kingdom, meaning reported crimes, cautions, and spent convictions can be disclosed where relevant. The exclusion of women from such roles on the basis of a criminal history probably ends up denying victims the invaluable insights and peer support of people who have been through similar trauma themselves.

example, 'by settling down in a relationship and assuming the identity of the "angry kid" that has become a "family man"'—are undermined by an enduringly public criminal record (Lageson and Maruna, 2018: 125).

For those whose criminal records are only accessible for a fixed number of months or years until they are 'spent' or can be 'expunged', there is at least a limit, or an end date, to the disadvantage and exclusion,[12] and to the emotional or psychological impacts. For example, research from the United States suggests that people who've had their records cleared through expungement processes express increased confidence and self-esteem, and a sense of hope and agency (Reiter et al., 2014). Another found that on average, people whose convictions were expunged saw their wages rise by over 22% a year versus their pre-expungement earning trajectory, an effect 'mostly driven by unemployed people finding jobs and minimally employed people finding steadier or higher-paying work' (Prescott and Starr, 2020: 2460). But for those whose convictions are never spent, or who reside in jurisdictions in which criminal records are accessible indefinitely online, the impacts can last a lifetime. Exclusion from employment opportunities has been shown to have a negative knock-on effect on the reintegration of people with records and, notably, on desistance (the process of abstaining from crime after an incident or pattern of offending), which is strongly correlated with being in work, as multiple international studies have shown.[13]

A whole other set of issues arise in post-authoritarian jurisdictions with a legacy of unjustly criminalizing people who were exercising their legitimate freedoms. In some such countries, processes of transitional justice have neglected to address the issue of what to do about people who have records for convictions that should never have been imposed. For example, in South Africa, current debates around expungement have been prompted by campaigns to clear people convicted 'in terms of oppressive and discriminatory laws under the apartheid regime' such as laws against sex or marriage between different racial groups (Mujuzi, 2014: 286). Many are still being excluded from employment on the basis of records relating to unjust criminalization, long after the laws themselves have been repealed. Certainly, the principal injustice

[12] Selbin et al. (2018) observed longitudinally the effect on earning power of people with criminal records before and after successful application for records to be sealed through clean slate legislation in the United States. Unsurprisingly, earnings rose significantly.

[13] The literature is too substantial to list fully here, but some notable examples from the early to most recent studies include Laub and Sampson (2003), Winnick and Bodkin (2008), Van der Geest et al. (2011), and LeBel (2012). The research remains inconclusive as to the source of the correlation. It could be because employment offers a 'hook for change' that motivates people to refrain from offending, or because people naturally mature as they get older and become less likely to engage in crime anyway (Skardhamar and Savolainen, 2014).

faced by individuals who find themselves in such a situation is the undeserved conviction, rather than the record. But it is the accessibility of the record of that conviction that results in the person's loss of access to important goods and opportunities of the kind considered here. Both wrongs contribute to what is a double injustice. The lack of established mechanisms for people to contest or challenge a criminal record in many such countries enables these kinds of injustices to persist.

Even in jurisdictions in which constitutional commitments to human rights preclude the kinds of unjust criminalization just mentioned, it is often impossible for people to correct errors in their criminal records, leaving them bearing the burdens of a history that is not their own. In their 2023 study, Lageson and Stewart reveal how records available online in the United States, sometimes by private records check companies who bear no liability for the accuracy of the content they collate and reproduce from official sources, frequently include information that is entirely false. It is difficult for a person to correct or contest these records through legal routes, for at least a couple of reasons. The default publicity of the information makes it hard to identify a company or agency responsible for the error, and at the same time people affected by the error have to prove in court that it has caused them direct and demonstrable harm in order to force its deletion (Lageson and Stewart, 2023).[14]

Legal anthropologist Amy Myrick spoke to and observed people who had come to a US legal clinic set up to help them correct and seal or expunge their criminal records. Her study explores what she calls the 'wrongful representation of the self' that arises from a record that is perceived as erroneous but cannot be corrected. Her participants expressed feelings of helplessness and powerlessness in response to their inability to negotiate the content or existence of the record with the state. The lack of reciprocity between citizen and state was shown to impede the ability of those with police records to manage or repair their relationship as a citizen with the authorities (Myrick, 2013). In the United Kingdom, an independent monitor appointed by the government can receive and examine public complaints about mistakes in police records,[15] but proving error is difficult even then, and in most countries there is no such mechanism at all.

[14] Similar points are made in relation to 'fuzzy laws' that regulate criminal record access somewhere between the criminal and administrative. Their ambiguity ends up denying people the protections and redresses afforded to those sanctioned by the criminal law, while enabling the expansion of what are essentially criminal justice penalties (Zand Kurtovic, 2017: 42).

[15] The role of the independent monitor is set out in detail online, see the Bibliography for 'Independent Monitor for the Disclosure and Barring Service'.

Persecution by the public

Alongside exclusion from social goods and opportunities, people with visible criminal records can and do experience direct persecution by members of the public. Unlock charity shares the story of Kieran, an autistic boy who was 17 when he received his criminal record. Keiran's conviction was for 'outraging public decency' on a train after a 'lewd, obscene or disgusting act in the presence of at least two members of the public'. He was given a 12-month youth referral order and lost his place at university as a result. Despite this, he worked with supportive youth offending officers to change his behaviour and rehabilitate, and eventually found a job, in which he was quickly promoted. Then his neighbours found out about his conviction, and suddenly everything changed. Apparently unsatisfied with the leniency of the sentence, his neighbours began to persecute him, falsely reporting him to the police multiple times for indecent behaviour. Because Keiran had a relevant criminal history, police took these reports seriously and arrested him each time. They also arrested him at his place of work. But each time they investigated, they quickly realized there was no evidence, and released him without charge. The allegations stopped as soon as he moved to a different area, but by that time he had lost his job, ended up in £5,000 of debt, attempted suicide, and been committed to a psychiatric hospital.

Public abuse and exclusion of people with visible criminal records or convictions is well documented, though systematic empirical studies across offense types are lacking. Persecution appears to be directed particularly towards people with convictions for sexual offences. In the United Kingdom, people have been murdered by neighbours after being accused or convicted of child sexual offences.[16] In certain US states, sex offender notification practices involve the collation of information about convicted sex offenders, including names, addresses, and photographs, which is then made publicly available via media releases, mailed or posted flyers, dedicated websites, door-to-door contacts, and community meetings.

A quantitative review of the research literature on the impact of community notification for sex offenders in the United States found that 8% of participants reported being 'physically assaulted or injured', 14% having their 'property

[16] In 2013, a Bristol man was murdered by neighbours after being falsely rumoured to be a child sex offender, https://www.theguardian.com/uk-news/2013/oct/29/vigilante-murder-paedophile-bristol-bijan-ebrahimi. In 2014, a convicted sex offender was similarly attacked and killed by neighbours, https://www.independent.co.uk/news/uk/crime/convicted-paedophile-killed-after-broom-handle-sex-assault-court-hears-a6693216.html.

damaged', 44% receiving threats or harassment by neighbours, 16% having family members or cohabitants experience harassment, assault, or property damage, 19% losing their housing, and 30% losing their job.[17] Between roughly 40% and 60% of participants reported negative psychological consequences such as loss of friends, feeling lonely and isolated, embarrassment, and loss of hope, and 60% of participants reported that community notification interfered with their recovery. Overall, the more intrusive and exposing the community notification strategies used, the worse the social impact on the person and their close associates.

Of course, some will argue that these negative consequences are deserved or in any case outweighed by the protective effects of notification laws (or both). We will address questions of desert, deterrence, and just punishment in detail in Chapter 5 and the prevention of harm in Chapter 6. For the moment, it is worth pointing out that with respect to protective effects, multiple empirical studies have shown that notification measures neither deter offending nor prevent reoffending, nor correlate with a reduction in the incidence of reported sexual offences (Logan, 2009: ch. 5). On the contrary, two studies from the United States found a positive relationship between community notification and reoffending, supporting the conclusion that 'the punitive aspects of notification laws may create perverse effects' (Prescott and Rockoff, 2008) and that, 'as one's status as a registrant is made known to the public, resulting hostile attitudes can predict an individual's likelihood to reoffend' (Hamilton and Fairfaz-Columbo, 2023). Here again, we see that even those who would defend public stigmatization and shaming as just punishment for offenders must acknowledge that the measures they support are not cost-free for communities.

Sexual offences are paradigmatic of abuse following public stigmatization, but abuse of people with criminal records can occur irrespective of the type of conviction they have. In the United Kingdom in the mid-2000s, political efforts to reassure the public that 'something is being done' about crime led to measures compelling offenders to wear high-visibility 'community payback' vests while serving community service sentences for minor crimes. In this case, the criminal stigma was conveyed not through a written record but by the imposition of a conspicuous physical label, materially visible to everyone in the local vicinity. Police reports from the time chronicle offenders being verbally abused, beaten, and even shot (Travis, 2008). In the end, public abuse

[17] Effects differed across locations and in some the impact was much more severe, with one study from 2000 stating that 'employment and housing have become nearly impossible' for sex offenders subject to notification in Wisconsin (Zevitz and Farkas, 2000, cited in Logan 2009: 125).

of offenders was so bad that the union of probation officers staged a protest against the high-visibility clothing, and some organizations offering offender work placements started refusing to use the vests (Fletcher, 2009).

It is worth highlighting that as with employers, public reaction to offenders in these cases was not responsive to differences in the nature or severity of the crime. People passing by did not stop to ask what the offender had done before deciding whether or how to react towards them. Rather, the mere identification of a person as 'criminal' was sufficient to prompt serious abuse. In the United Kingdom, this risk has been explicitly acknowledged by the courts. In 2014, a court deciding the conditions of release for a convicted murderer obliged him to change his name before leaving prison and re-entering the community. The court's concern was that members of the public would become aware of his residence in state-funded halfway house accommodation and would subject him and others living there to violent attacks as they sought to drive him out (*R v. Secretary of State for Justice*, 2014). The continued practice of public pillorizing, where it occurs, illustrates the enduring power of criminal stigmatization as a means of facilitating social condemnation, rejection, and exclusion.

The process of criminal stigmatization

The research and cases discussed so far illustrate the power of the mark or 'stigma' of a criminal record. To see why and how this power is exercised, it's worth pausing our empirical investigation for a moment to set out briefly how stigmatization has been theorized and how it occurs in the context of criminalization. In the 1960s, the pioneering sociologist Erving Goffman defined stigmatization as process of marking someone out in some visible and identifiable way as having a characteristic that is 'deeply discrediting' (Goffman, 1963: 3). The more discrediting the characteristic, the more stigmatizing the marking out; the more visible and identifying the mark, the more it dominates and overrides other (potentially redeeming) characteristics.[18]

In their fascinating 2011 interdisciplinary theorization of stigma, Oaten et al. observe that humans respond consistently across a range of undesirable or discrediting properties, from disease to personal characteristics to moral standing. In particular, humans react as if the stigmatizing attribute can be

[18] See Braithwaite (1989) for a criminological justification of the criterion of dominance over other features of a person.

transferred by contact, and therefore people consistently avoid those who are stigmatized others even when the evidence linking the label to the negative property (e.g. bad character) is evidently poor or unreliable. This 'stigma by association' process means in practice that people avoid proximity with a labelled individual, fearing that it will prompt others to evaluate them negatively by association (Oaten et al., 2011). This whole process can occur without anyone actually being worried that a person with a criminal record might harm them and without anyone judging the person's character negatively. That's because it is the fact of being labelled, rather than the thing the label apparently signifies, that makes the criminalized person 'contagious' or undesirable.

There is scant research exploring why people so often exclude or reject people with criminal records in these ways, so we can only speculate on the beliefs and intentions motivating such actions. Could it be that the association of 'crime' with serious moral wrongdoing means that a criminal record of any kind is taken as conclusive evidence of 'bad character', signifying untrustworthiness or even dangerousness?[19] If so, this would certainly be irrational. Most crimes concern arguably minor wrongs such as theft, public order offences, driving or drug offences. Many if not most people have done at least one of these things at some point in their lives. And, as we saw in the case of Ian above, even very strong evidence of good character may not be sufficient to mitigate criminal stigma. Perhaps then, it is not the fact of having committed a criminal act, but rather of having been caught and, more importantly, *criminalized* that is the stronger trigger for rejection and exclusion. Perhaps Ian's employers were not worried about his trustworthiness or credibility. Perhaps they merely feared that his record might taint them by association and so felt justified in protecting themselves by firing him. But the evidence suggests such fears are unfounded. Research shows that lawsuits against companies that knowingly hire people with criminal records who then go on to cause harm or commit crimes at work are rare. Most people with convictions or police records do stop offending, especially if they manage to gain steady employment.[20]

[19] This was certainly the case historically. In an 1898 legal case between a doctor called Hawker and the city of New York, the court found in favour of the city's decision to disqualify convicted felons from the practice of medicine to protect its citizens. The law took conviction to demonstrate that a person was 'a man of such bad character as to render it unsafe to trust the lives and health of citizens to his care' and the court found the city right 'to protect its citizens from physicians of bad character'. *Hawker v. New York*, 171, 1898.

[20] Survey research from the United Kingdom shows that as many as 56% of public and 81% of private sector employers had 'anxieties' about employing someone with a criminal record (Fletcher, 2001, in Weaver, 2018). Rovira's (2022) study found that employers request more detailed or intrusive checks than is necessary for the position in question. And McElhattan (2022) contributes a valuable analysis of the incongruence between employer concerns about liability and the reality of cases in the courts.

But anxieties about liability and a risk-averse culture make employers impervious to this evidence, as appears to have been the case for Ian's company.

Seen this way, avoidance, exclusion, and rejection of those with criminal records may be explained at least in part as a hangover from a time when criminality was understood as congenital or a pathology that could be transmitted like a disease, and in which the criminal label acted as a health warning as much as an alert to potential danger. If this is correct, it would help explain why a criminal record attaches to a person rather than their acts, and in turn why its stigmatizing effects are so difficult to counteract through evidence of good character. It also has a couple of important implications for the current discussion. First, as will be argued in more detail later, it suggests that there are reasons to believe that some of the proposals to reduce the negative effects of a criminal record we will consider in future chapters—notably those seeking to change public responses to criminal labels through public education campaigns or 'redemption certificates'—are unlikely to succeed. Second, and more importantly for the current discussion, it suggests that a visible criminal record has a negative effect not only on a person's interests and opportunities but also on their agency and autonomy. If Ian's extensive track record of trustworthy and competent work over a quarter of a century was not sufficient to neutralize the stigma of his criminal record in the eyes of his employers, there was nothing he could do, ever, to redeem himself. In other words, he is not only disadvantaged but also rendered powerless to address or improve his situation. This is the reality facing many people with visible or disclosable criminal records in workplaces around the world. In Part II of this chapter, we will consider the moral implications of these claims. First, we must consider a further way in which stigma can undermine a person's aspirations and efforts to author their own lives, better themselves, and regain social standing.

Chilling effects, social withdrawal, and system avoidance

The research presented so far in this chapter has examined the impacts on people with criminal records of being stigmatized as criminal and thereby 'discredited' in the eyes of others. In other words, it has focussed on the impacts of other people's reactions to criminality. But the very prospect of discreditation can also influence the behaviour of people with criminal records in ways that are ultimately harmful to them. In the 1960s, Goffman observed that people carrying stigma could avoid becoming discredited by taking steps to conceal it or by avoiding situations in which it might be revealed. He also noted that, even when concealment works in some contexts, people remain vulnerable to exposure in others, especially in the light of rapid changes in technology and regulations. Stigmatized people therefore always remain, in the words of Goffman, 'discredit*able*' (emphasis in original) even when they have not actually been exposed and thereby discredited (yet). Managing this risk is one of the burdens with which they must live.

Since Goffman, much has been written on the 'chilling effects' of a criminal record on people's engagement in social activity that carries a risk of exposure.[21] Sociological and criminological theorists in particular have shown how people abnegate participation in social, economic, and political activities (referred to by sociologists as 'pro-social' behaviour) as a way of avoiding becoming 'discredited' (Pager, 2003). This self-protective behaviour has been conceptualized in the sociological literature as 'social withdrawal'. Psychological research with people with convictions has also shown that social withdrawal is a response to anticipated stigmatization related to potential criminal record exposure (Moore and Tangney, 2017) and that social withdrawal is directly related to decreased quality of life (McWilliams and Hunter, 2021).

This section examines the harms of chilling effects and social withdrawal. It argues there are good reasons to believe that the psychological burden—or in sociological terms the 'pains'[22]—of anticipating, avoiding, and experiencing criminal stigmatization are harms in themselves and not only in virtue of their expression in contrived economic quantifiers such as 'quality of life'. Chapter 2 conceptualizes these harms morally in terms of their effects on human dignity and human flourishing.

To see how a criminal record chills or inhibits social behaviour in ways that damage a human life, let's consider Monica's story, another case study shared by the charity Unlock. Monica had a difficult start in life, growing up in care from the age of 2. She lived in a poor area and went to a local school with a bad reputation, where she learned to use violence to settle disagreements. She left school young, without qualifications. At 18, she received a conviction for 'threats to kill', for which she received a conditional discharge. But over time she matured and learned to manage her anger and communicate effectively. As an adult, she found employment as a professional in the public sector and managed to build a successful career lasting 30 years.

[21] Unlock charity, in their report on the impact of criminal records, explains that 'general and specific examples of discrimination and social stigma contribute to a sense that having a criminal record is an insurmountable barrier' (Unlock, 2023: 4).

[22] Gresham Sykes's classic 1958 analysis of the 'pains of imprisonment' appears in ch. 4 of his *The Society of Captives*.

During the first part of her working life, her professional body was not informed of her conviction and she was not asked about it. But then the rules around background checks changed and people in her sector were required to undergo regular criminal record checks. Monica handed in her notice. She felt she couldn't run the risk of being found out. Luckily, she later managed to find work in the same sector as a freelance contractor, as being self-employed allowed her to circumvent criminal record disclosures. She continued to work for another 7 years. Then the rules changed again. Now, she could no longer tender for contracts without undergoing a criminal record check. She considered whether she would be able to manage having to tell prospective clients about the record. But eventually she decided that she could not face the inevitability of having to disclose her conviction. Reluctantly, she made the decision to retire early. She told Unlock: 'I felt cornered. The decision was made for me. I left the world of work, a move I would never have made on my own. I would have worked until I dropped. Work defined me. But I'm just not brave enough to put myself in a position where I have to be judged again' (Unlock Charity).

Monica was lucky to have 37 years in work. Changes in UK regulation (and mirrored around the world) mean someone starting out today would never be able to 'pass' in the same way she did. Aside from changes in regulation, the advent of the information age also reduces the possibilities of avoiding stigma. For example, in jurisdictions like the United States and China where public records previously housed in courthouses are now posted online, the ability to remain discreditable rather than discredited has been 'whittled away' (Jefferson-Jones, 2014: 507, fn.47). Comparative European research suggests that anticipated rejection in the labour market discourages people with criminal records from even applying for positions for fear of being stigmatized (Kurtovic and Rovira, 2017).

Note that Monica's reason for withdrawing from the labour market was not related to anticipation of disadvantage or exclusion through losing potential clients. Rather, it was fear of being 'judged again'. Research internationally with people leaving prison or dealing with potential exposure bears out this overriding concern with shame, humiliation, and having to revisit a painful and mortifying time in one's life.[23] It highlights the emotional burdens of criminal stigma that accompany the loss of opportunity, in particular a sense

[23] Harding (2003) provides a powerful qualitative analysis of the dilemma faced by those seeking to avoid discreditation but also striving for self-improvement. Lageson and Maruna reveal the 'humiliation compounded by uncertainty as to exactly what information the internet might reveal' for people with online records (2018: 125). See Zhang (2024) for a qualitative analysis of Chinese women's re-entry to the labour market after white-collar convictions.

of hopelessness about the possibility of personal reinvention and being able to move on from the past (Maruna, 2011). The uncertainty as to whether and when the judgement will occur is a further source of psychological and emotional destabilization. Monica dealt with this by withdrawing entirely and so regaining some certainty and control (though it is important not to overlook her assertion that 'the decision was made for me', a denial of autonomy we will return to later). Research shows that others become stuck in an agonizing cycle of applying for jobs and then losing heart and pulling out before more questions can be asked, swinging between hope and despondency, aspiration and resignation (e.g. Zhang, 2024). In Chapter 2, we'll consider the ways in which a system that exposes a person to such judgment indefinitely—as an enduringly public criminal record does—might wrong them or violate their dignity. For the moment though, let us focus on the harms and losses.

Recent empirical research examines how people's desire to avoid the stigmatization of a criminal record inhibits their activity in a range of social and economic spheres. We have just considered work and employment, but Sarah Lageson's and Sarah Brayne's respective analyses provide important insights into similar dynamics at play in other areas of life. Whereas Lageson's work focuses on private and family life, Brayne's examines interactions with social and political institutions. Taken together their work suggests that the chilling effects of a visible criminal record can permeate all aspects of life, even those we might normally assume would be protected from the impacts of a criminal conviction.

Developing a strand of research on social withdrawal that began in the 1980s but has since been neglected, Sarah Brayne (2014) introduced the concept of "system avoidance" to describe how individuals with a criminal history avoid contact with social and state institutions that keep formal records. Her quantitative analysis of health and other statistics from the United States found that individuals who have been stopped by police, arrested, convicted, or incarcerated are less likely to interact with (as opposed to being excluded from) medical, financial, and educational institutions, than their counterparts who have not had criminal justice contact (Brayne, 2014: 367). For example, after controlling for other variables, Brayne found that 30% of respondents, who had a history of criminalization, did not seek medical care when they needed it compared to 22% of relevantly similar respondents with no criminal history (Brayne, 2014). Her analysis found no significant difference between people with records of serious convictions and those with records of low-level criminal justice involvement, confirming the observations made above that criminal stigmatization follows from any kind of formal labelling.[24]

Sarah Lageson's work in this area is complementary, showing how people with online criminal records avoid contact with organizations important to the development of a flourishing personal and family life and exploring their motivations for doing so (Lageson, 2016). Lageson's research, which involves in-depth qualitative interviews with people seeking to expunge their criminal records, is particularly important in revealing the damaging effects for parents of the uncertainty and fear around what might appear online. Specifically, it shows how they feel constrained to retreat[25] from family and community institutions in order to avoid exposure, in ways that conflict with their own views of good parenting (Lageson, 2016: 138). For example, her participants report amongst other things making excuses to their children to avoid activities which carry a risk of record exposure, like attending school trips and events, accompanying them to sports competitions that might involve border crossings, or volunteering. Participants also report refraining from providing for their families as they would like and are able to. Some did not look for housing in a safer neighbourhood, despite having the means to do so and despite wanting to move their families to a better area. And some did not apply for a higher-paying job to improve their family's standard of living, even though they had spent years successfully developing the skills and qualifications to do so. These findings are also reported in testimonies of people with convictions collected by the charity Unlock, one of which is given by a woman who says: 'I am too embarrassed and scared to apply for jobs. I'm resigned to the fact that now, though in my 40's, I will be one of those people that just stays in their job until such time that they can retire, because the thought of having to bare my soul each time I apply for a job, well, it's soul destroying'.[26] Unlock found similar feelings of pointlessness discouraged people from exploring further education

[24] This is not to deny that people judge those with criminal records differently depending on the crimes they commit, support longer sentences for more serious crimes, and so on. It is just to say that the chilling and stigmatizing effects of criminality manifest in ways that are far less sensitive to these differences and far more consistent across crime types than one might expect.

[25] Lageson herself conceptualizes the responses she describes as 'opting out' or 'self-selecting out' of family activities, and therefore as an active choice. This risks misrepresenting her participants' behaviour as fully autonomous (at least, it is a misrepresentation according to my reading of that behaviour), so I prefer to use avoidance or inhibition when discussing her findings.

[26] Vicki's story 'Soul Destroying Fear'. Unlock. Personal Stories. At: https://unlock.org.uk/personal_story/soul-destroying-fear/.

'long before the point of application', internalizing an expectation of rejection and failure.[27]

Notably, none of Lageson's participants felt there was any point being upfront with schools or other organizations about their records, or in trying to pre-empt stigmatization and exclusion by explaining their history and providing evidence to reassure or convince the relevant authorities of their trustworthiness (an approach Goffman called 'stigma management', 1961). Rather, they were resigned to the fact that they would remain powerless to demonstrate redemption. They knew that their record would inevitably continue to dominate other aspects of their lives, overshadowing and ultimately undermining efforts to assert a different narrative or self-identity and thereby to neutralize or even just attenuate the stigma. As James Jacobs wrote in his seminal work on criminal records, 'it is not an exaggeration to say that the criminal record is, for many, the most important marker of their public identity' (2015: 303).

Cascading costs to communities and society

The negative impacts on individuals just described also have ripple effects for communities and society more broadly. Jacobs points out that '[t]he criminal justice system feeds on itself. The more people who are arrested, prosecuted, convicted and especially incarcerated, the larger is the criminally stigmatized underclass screened out of legitimate opportunities' (387). Recall that about a third of the working-age population in the United Kingdom and about a quarter of US adults have a criminal conviction. Even if only a relatively small proportion of these people have records that are accessible to employers and others, the negative impact of their arrested social mobility on both economy and communities will be significant.

Because these impacts are unevenly imposed between different social groups, the class of the criminally stigmatized includes a disproportionately high number of people from deprived and minority backgrounds. In the United Kingdom, for example, people from Black, Asian, and "Chinese or other" backgrounds are more likely than others to be sent to prison. Notably, Black women are 25% more likely to receive a custodial sentence than White women convicted of similar offences. Because convictions carrying custodial

[27] Unlock. Fair Study: A toolkit to help universities develop fair practice for students with criminal records. 2.2 The Chilling Effect. At: https://unlock.org.uk/toolkit/fair-study/understanding-awcrs/the-chilling-effect/.

sentences take longer to be 'spent' under UK law, the visibility of the criminal records and all the attendant disadvantage that it brings is experienced for longer by ethnic minorities. Women with criminal records also suffer greater disadvantage, stigmatization, and chilling effects than men, according to a UK study by the charity Unlock, in part because the kinds of jobs they apply for involve caring roles, which require an 'enhanced' criminal record check disclosing even historic and 'spent' convictions (Unlock, 2021: 16). In other words, unjust inequalities are also worsened by making criminal records accessible.

Other societal costs of public criminal records include higher rates of reoffending. Empirical studies show that the mere fact of having a publicly accessible criminal record is positively correlated with reoffending. In 2007, researchers Chiricos et al. analysed reconviction data for 95,919 men and women in the United States to examine the relative impact on reoffending of serious or 'felony' convictions that are accompanied by a publicly accessible criminal record compared to those in which the judge restricts the publicity of the record so that it need not be declared on employment applications and elsewhere. Their analysis found that those formally labelled are significantly more likely to reoffend in two years than those who are not (Chiricos et al., 2007). Longitudinal studies have produced similar findings (Bernburg et al., 2006). For example, a 2018 empirical study in certain US states found that the existence of websites making criminal records public led to an increase of approximately 11% in reincarceration amongst those leaving prison with at least one prior record for a serious offence (Luca, 2018).[28] Society also bears the cost of these higher rates in crime.

Conclusion of Part I

The work surveyed so far in this chapter is chiefly sociological and as such asks variants of the question 'how do visible criminal records affect people's access to and involvement in social life, and what are the broader social implications?' It responds by demonstrating empirically the disadvantage, social exclusion, racial and ethnic inequalities, and negative impact on 'prosocial behaviours' such as desistance from crime and involvement in aspects of family life that

[28] It is not addressed in the paper whether some of this phenomenon could be explained by jurors looking defendants up online and therefore becoming aware of their previous records, which could increase willingness to convict.

follows a visible criminal record, as well as the measurable social impacts.[29] Theories of stigmatization supplement these findings by providing us with a unifying explanation of how and why these specific effects occur. Taken together, these bodies of work paint a detailed picture of the chain of events and effects that follow the imposition of public or visible criminal records.

But the stories these studies tell are essentially descriptive. In order to understand how these impacts might constitute moral harms[30] and how their imposition might be morally justified or not, we need to go beyond description to evaluation. In other words, we need to conceptualize the impacts of visible criminal records in moral terms—that is in terms of human values, interests and entitlements—and then evaluate them against the background of a philosophical account of a worthwhile or dignified life and a just political community. Only then will we be able to assess claims (discussed in Chapters 3–7) that the negative impacts of a visible criminal record are justified because they are deserved, or because they are outweighed by our democratic interests in transparency in criminal justice, or because they are an unavoidable cost of legitimate efforts to protect the public from crime. And only then will we be able to assess the relative merits of diverse proposals to protect against these harms, including those that assert moral and legal entitlements to restrict access to criminal records, through rights to privacy (Tunick, 2015), 'rebiography' (Jefferson-Jones, 2014a) or 'to be forgotten' discussed in Chapter 1. Part II of this chapter takes a first step towards this normative task, by articulating the moral foundations of any such rights in terms of flourishing and dignity.

Part II: The Moral Harms of a Public Criminal Record

Diminishing a person, stunting a life, and writing people off

How do criminal records harm people morally? The research presented above suggests, I want to argue, that making criminal records public has *reductive* or *diminishing* effects upon the people who have them. Reductive effects occur when a record prompts someone to treat another person as if there was little

[29] Lageson argues that these cycles of stigmatization and avoidance work in concert to amplify and fortify disparities already endemic to the criminal legal system, 'reproduc[ing] inequity at the speed of the internet' (2020: 11). Brayne claims that efforts to avoid the stigmatizing gaze involve a trade-off between creditability and 'full participation in society' (2014: 386).

[30] Harms can be anything negative that happens to a person. I am harmed by falling over and breaking my leg. A moral harm is a harm to my moral standing or a violation of my agency, autonomy or other moral right.

more to them, or at least little that is more telling or salient about them, than that criminal record. We saw this in the case of Ian who was fired after years of exemplary conduct because his criminal record eclipsed all his other qualities, skills, and achievements in the eyes of his employers. We also saw it in the example of offenders in high-visibility clothing on community service being subject to physical and verbal abuse. Diminishing effects occur when a criminal record limits a person's ability to chart and pursue a life that reflects their own values, aspirations, efforts, merits and achievements, thus stunting their development and constraining their horizons. Diminishment can occur directly when a person is excluded or denied goods or opportunities and/or indirectly, through chilling effects that cause people to shrink back from claiming those goods and opportunities, and from developing valuable connections and relationships. In Part I argued that these constitute ways of undermining a person's autonomy and agency. I now want to argue that thinking about these effects on autonomy and agency in terms of the core moral values of human flourishing and dignity can help us to get to the heart of the moral harms that result from public criminal records.

Human flourishing is a metaphor used to describe a philosophical notion of human good that originated in Aristotle's thinking but has since inspired and informed moral and political theory of all stripes, from liberalism to Marxism, feminism and more recently medical and public health ethics.[31] Its attractiveness lies partly in its intuitive recognition that, like all living entities, humans and their collectives seek to thrive and prosper but can languish and struggle when things go badly. As a concept, flourishing has been criticized as being a poor basis on which to construct an entire moral philosophy, not least because its metaphorical character invites moral codes that are excessively relativistic (Harman, 1983). But we can draw on the metaphor of flourishing here without committing ourselves to the view that it is the only human value; as we will see, flourishing is expansive and encompassing enough to accommodate other foundational human values from virtue and wellbeing to dignity.

Flourishing is a useful way of thinking about human goodness, both because of its natural analogies with other living things, and, as philosophers Kleinig and Evans point out, because it 'gets us to focus on humans as developmental,

[31] Most famously Sen and Nussbaum's capabilities approach to justice (2011) but also Marx's ideas of human flourishing involving self-realization through work, and more recently environmental feminism, for example, in Chris Cuomo's work (1998). Moral theorist Michal Masny has drawn on the concept recently to claim that 'the goodness of a life also depends on what could have happened, but didn't, that is the degree to which [a person] realize[s] their potential' (2022: 7); for an autobiographical account of wasted potential due to criminal records, see Collett (2023: 'Martin'). Prah Ruger's (2020) work applies flourishing in the context of public health.

natural objects' that 'progress over their life cycle' (2013: 541). This dynamic aspect of the concept of flourishing captures the intuition that human value and interests lie as much in the *pursuit* of meaningful and 'good' activities and relationships, and in the *development* of personal qualities and 'virtues', as in the achievement of specific outcomes. A person who does not progress over their life cycle or who changes for the worse does not flourish but stagnates, withers, suffers, or weakens. John Stuart Mill utilized this observation in his liberal theory when he conceptualized moral value as lying in 'the permanent interests of man as a *progressive* being' (1859: I, 11). Flourishing's dynamic perspective focuses our attention usefully on the person and their life as a whole, in ways that help us appreciate the range and diversity of the impacts of a visible criminal record.

Flourishing as a unifying concept

A person's flourishing is undermined when their criminal record stigmatizes them in ways that thwart their journey through life, holding them back and impeding their development and self-realization. Nowhere is this easier to see than in the thoroughly documented effects of a criminal record on access to employment, and on access to the type of employment that might contribute to flourishing. The importance of work to self-realization has long been recognized as a vital component of human flourishing (Nussbaum, 2011; Prah Ruger, 2020). Work is for most people an essential source of self-respect and dignity as well as being a means of obtaining of vital resources, and rights to work have accordingly been recognized as fundamental human rights in canonical legal documents around the world.

Some of the personal stories shared in Part I also illustrate the importance of work in people's efforts to redeem and redefine themselves following a conviction, as we saw in the case of the young men seeking to progress from a phase in their life in which they were an 'angry kid' to being a 'family man'. When a criminal record prevents a person improving themselves and their circumstances through work, it shrinks their horizons and aspirations and inhibits their flourishing at a vital level. Similar claims can be made about the effects of a criminal record on access to education.

Flourishing also involves self-realization through one's development as a moral or normative agent, and that is also undermined by a public criminal record. Arpaly (2002) argues that a morally good agent is one who responds to the right sorts of reasons. If this is correct, then we can see that it is vital to my own flourishing that I am free to recognize the reasons I take to be the right ones as authoritative for me. In other words, flourishing presupposes the exercise of autonomy and agency. To flourish, we must be able to exercise our autonomy and agency materially and not only cognitively. What this means is that, alongside the freedom to adopt reasons as my own, I must be able to be guided by and conform to those reasons through my actions and behaviour. In other words, being free to both *decide* what is right and to *try to do* what is right are important.

While what constitutes self-realization as a normative agent is to a great extent subjective, there are some areas of personal life in which most of us tend to hold ourselves to high standards of duty as self-imposed moral requirements. One such area is parenting. Being a 'good' parent in the sense of fulfilling one's duties towards one's children is for most people fundamental to moral self-realization, as well as being a crucial source of a sense of achievement and self-respect over a lifetime. In Part I we saw that people with visible criminal records report being inhibited from doing the things they believe makes a person a good parent and therefore from meeting their own self-imposed normative standards in that role. For example, they described holding back from participating in their child's school and extra-curricular life for fear that their criminal record would be exposed and, in turn, lead to humiliating judgement or exclusion, or indeed the stigmatization of their child by association. When an accessible criminal record stymies a person's good faith efforts to determine and live by their own moral values and moral commitments, it undermines their flourishing in ways that harms them morally. Plausibly, self-realization as a moral agent might also be impacted when people withdraw from roles volunteering or fostering children, or are excluded from caring roles in nursing, social care, or medicine, or even politics or activism through the legal profession. Current studies do not provide much insight into these aspects of self-realization, but it would be worthwhile to explore them.

Dignity as part of flourishing

More philosophically inclined readers will note that the way of talking about flourishing here is reminiscent of the ways in which human dignity—the value that animates 'duty-based' theories of morality such as that of Kant—is often discussed. That is neither coincidence nor contradiction. Realizing our status as normative beings who are free to articulate and conform to our own moral 'laws', that is our status as self-determining moral agents, is just what it means to have dignity . Dignity is widely considered a human value that is foundational in the sense that it grounds many of our claims to moral and human rights, those fundamental entitlements of all human beings, whose infringement or violation can only be justified in exceptional circumstances and with very good reason.

The importance of recognizing and taking into account the enduring potential for rehabilitation of offenders has been recently recognized by European Courts as a positive obligation of states that is 'grounded in human dignity' (Meijer, 2017: 161). That legal position has been supported philosophically by Zach Hoskins, who has argued convincingly that punitive or preventive state restrictions that 'fail to take seriously the prospect of offenders' reform' (Hoskins, 2019: 168) or communicate to individuals and the community 'that the state does not really regard their redemption as a genuine prospect, or at least not a prospect that is worthy of its concern' (p. 116) expresses contempt for those individuals, and are therefore incompatible with respect for their dignity.

Living with dignity and being treated in a way that respects our dignity are vital elements of human flourishing. The reductive effects of a visible criminal record undermine both dignity and flourishing. When a person's criminal record is treated as their most representative attribute and when the possibility of their moral redemption is discounted or foreclosed, their capacity as normative or moral agents (i.e. their capacity to choose and act well, morally speaking) is subverted and impaired. We saw above how this happens when a visible criminal record leads people to be denied opportunities for redemptive potential such as volunteering or education indefinitely, or to be judged, rejected, or even persecuted by members of the public. To say this is not to claim that human flourishing requires others to enable our ambitions in each and every encounter. No one has an entitlement to an entirely obstacle-free journey through life, and most of us can flourish even in the face of some struggle and adversity along the way. But it does entail that governments should refrain from introducing laws and policies that result inevitably in people being stunted, and we have seen in this chapter that (other things being equal) a policy that makes criminal records accessible to employers and others in an unfettered way does just that.

So far, I have focussed on flourishing in its metaphorical aspects, but the concept has a more literal or naturalistic dimension too. This is why the fields of public and mental health have been drawn towards it in recent years as a way of articulating the goals of their policy and practice. This more organic aspect of flourishing allows it to accommodate comfortably the diminishing impacts of a visible criminal record on a person's health, such as reduced access to medical insurance and decent housing, a reluctance to seek even much-needed medical attention, the psychological burdens of hopelessness and shame, and of course the direct harassment and physical attacks that research shows can follow criminal stigmatization. Encompassing both the material and the political in this way, the notion of flourishing articulates, unifies, and gives moral meaning to the full range of negative impacts of a visible criminal record. To this extent at least it is superior to other approaches to characterize normatively the negative impacts of criminal records.

The extent to which a visible record actually undermines flourishing in any particular life inevitably varies. The impacts will differ according to how visible the record is, to whom, and for how long. They also differ according to the practices and prejudices of the state and community in which a person lives.[32] Further variations will arise from the particular aspirations and intentions of the individual to whom the record applies. Someone who does not intend to gain employment, to access social benefits like education, housing or insurance, to engage in voluntary activities or travel abroad, may carry a criminal record without suffering any of the indignities and setbacks described above. But this description would only apply to a small minority of the very privileged, very elderly, or those who live a non-conformist lifestyle of some kind (including but not limited to those that revolve around crime). For the vast majority of people with a record, at least some of what has been described here will be their story too.

Conclusion

The discussion in this chapter suggests that even those criminal justice systems that only make records visible to employers, insurers, and educational institutions seriously undermine the flourishing of those people who hold them. Radical visibility of criminal records, as is practiced in some US states, and conspicuous public labelling of people with criminal records, violates rights and sets back lives in ways that may be difficult to justify. Being clear about these consequences now will equip us better to assess the merits of the arguments in favour of a right to know later. Even if readers eventually conclude that the harms of publicity are justified or even deserved, it is still

[32] For example, some businesses in the United Kingdom explicitly commit to offering employment to people with convictions, but these opportunities are not available in every town or village.

useful to be clear about the nature, gravity, and scope of the risks publicity brings, if only to ensure that proper consideration of these is factored into decisions about policy and regulation in this field. This chapter has sought to articulate those risks in a conceptually systematic and empirically grounded way.

3

Are Criminal Records an Intrinsically Public Matter? Political Theory and The Publicness of Crime

Introduction	49
Does the Idea of the Social Contract Imply a Right to Know?	50
The right to know who we are contracting with	52
The right to know as necessary for the stability of the social contract	54
Does the Idea of Crime as a 'public wrong' Imply a Right to Know?	57
The right to know and the rights of victims: does crime always victimize the public?	58
Does crime wrong the public by threatening the civic order?	60
Does crime harm the public like professional misconduct harms a profession?	63
Do we have a right to know about crimes that directly or 'causally' wrong the public?	66
Does crime wrong the public by violating public values?	69
Conclusion	70

Introduction

Are criminal acts intrinsically 'public'? And if so, does this imply that citizens have a right to know who commits them? One way of defending a general right of citizens to know about each other's criminal history is by arguing that criminal acts are by their very nature a public matter. In this chapter, we examine such arguments. Doing so takes us away from the field of empirical criminology and towards the more abstract world of political theory. In this world it is generally accepted as given that crime should be understood as in some essential or defining way 'public'. But few of those who assert the publicness of crime have considered what this might or should mean for how we manage public access to criminal records. The aim of this chapter is to explore those implications, posing the question: in what way might crime be understood as

The Crimes of Others. Katerina Hadjimatheou, Oxford University Press. © Katerina Hadjimatheou 2026.
DOI: 10.1093/9780198925149.003.0003

intrinsically public, and to what extent do those accounts entail a public right to know?

Two approaches to accounting for the publicness of crime are considered. The first draws from a key notion in political theory—the social contract—and explores the extent to which publicity about compliance is necessary for its validity or stability. The second focuses instead on the ways in which crimes might be understood as wrongs against the public, and therefore objects of legitimate public concern. Like arguments from the social contract, claims that crimes are distinctively public wrongs rest on assertions about the role of the criminal law in establishing civil order and maintaining social stability. But they also draw on basic norms and intuitions from interpersonal morality, about the rights we all have to know who has wronged us.

Other theorists working in this area have not paid much attention to what their positions imply for the public accessibility of criminal records; so there are few ready-cooked arguments in favour of publicity for us to consider in this chapter. In their absence, I will try to reconstruct such arguments in their most convincing form and then consider how well they stand up to critical scrutiny. By giving arguments in favour of publicity the fairest possible hearing, we can be more confident in the soundness of the conclusions we reach. Ultimately, I will conclude that neither the social contract-based account nor the argument from the publicness of crime provides a sound grounding for a general right of citizens to know about the crimes of others, of the kind that would provide a default or prima facie entitlement to access criminal records. But I also hope to show that engaging with these accounts is still worth doing, because it helps us make progress in thinking about who should have a right to access different kinds of criminal records. In particular, it draws attention to the special entitlements to information that should be accorded to certain categories of people, especially victims of crime.

Does the Idea of the Social Contract Imply a Right to Know?

Our inquiry starts with one of the most iconic concepts in political theory: the social contract. The metaphor of the social contract has been deployed throughout the history of Western political thought to help us think about what citizens owe one another in a just society and which political arrangements we should accept as legitimate or authoritative. The social contract has been core to the thinking of Locke, Hobbes, Beccaria, and Rawls—and it continues to animate contemporary 'contractualist' philosophy, an important subfield of political theory. Beyond the rarified world of academia, the idea of the social contract remains a powerful rhetorical device for public debate too. Political actors invoke it frequently in their declarations and speeches to remind us of the nature of the common bonds and civic duties that we should aspire to in our political arrangements with each other. A quick search on the UK parliament database reveals that British legislators mention the social contract on average once a day in their speeches and debates[1]. Declarations of a 'breakdown in the social contract' have been made by many of the key social justice movements of our times including climate activism, Black Lives Matter, and the Occupy campaign amongst others.

The enduring power of the metaphor of the social contract, in both political theory and public life, lies in the intuitive way it represents citizens' relationship to one another as grounded in the values of fair play and reciprocity, cooperation, and the peaceful pursuit of mutual interests. The question we are interested in, of course, is whether these values also imply that citizens' criminality should be a public matter. Does social contract theory provide the conceptual tools and arguments to settle the question of who has a right to access criminal records? Let's consider some potential ways in which one might argue that it does.

Social contract-based arguments for a public right to know about criminal records are about the fair terms of social cooperation rather than the requirements of criminal justice as such.[2] In other words, they are about what citizens owe each other *as citizens*, rather than what people who commit crimes deserve, or where the limits of punishment should lie. (Those kinds of arguments are dealt with in Chapter 5.) But social contract theory still has something important to say about crime, because criminal laws help define the mutual bounds of personal liberties in a society. Social contracts are interpersonal agreements between citizens by which all sacrifice some personal liberty to secure much weightier mutual benefits, typically benefits of security and prosperity. Criminal laws are therefore generally understood as constituting an important element of the rules of the contract: to commit a crime is to breach the rules of the contract.[3] Because the parties to the social contract are citizens

[1] See 2019–2024 debates as transcribed in UK Parliament search engine Hansard: https://hansard.parliament.uk.

[2] And therefore should be distinguished from social contract-based justifications for criminal punishment, for example, the Beccarian idea that breaches of the social contract incur a debt to society which must be repaid through punishment of some kind.

[3] Of course, to claim that a crime is by definition a breach of the social contract is not to imply that that is *all* it is. Certain kinds of crimes such as murder or rape are serious moral wrongs inflicted on an individual victim and would remain so even in the absence of a social contract. The fact that they are also breaches of the social contract may therefore not be the most important or salient of their features. But it is the feature that a social contract account would consider sufficient to ground a general right of

who stand in horizontal relation to each other, the person who offends is ultimately accountable to every other citizen for their violation of the rules. It is this aspect of the social contract that intuitively suggests a right to know.

The right to know who we are contracting with

The most straightforward and probably most obvious way of making a case for a right to know is to draw a simple analogy between actual and social contracts. An argument that takes this approach would appeal directly to the basic features of actual legal contracts—in particular the entitlements of contracting parties—and then apply these to metaphorical social contracts of the kind that we invoke rhetorically in political debate.[4] The reasoning would take something like the following form: In normal contractual practice, the parties have a right to know who is upholding or breaching the terms of the contract; the criminal law is a fundamental part of the social contract; therefore, members of society have a right to know who amongst them has broken which criminal law. Note that this argument does not say anything about the reasons or interests grounding the principle that parties have a right to know the identity of breaching parties; rather, the fact that publicity around identities and breaches is a basic norm of contracts as such is taken as sufficient to demonstrate that it applies also to the social contract. Note also that the focus on breaches means this argument could only justify public access to information about criminal convictions; it cannot be used to defend public access to police records, arrests, and charges, or other activities that fall short of 'proven' crime.

The argument from analogy is simple and intuitive, but it is also simplistic. In treating all contracts as fundamentally the same, it elides some important differences in contracts between individuals and the contract between citizens as such. One relevant difference is that most actual contracts are bilateral agreements between individuals or corporations whose identities are

citizens to know about each other's breaches. The rights of victims are important and are considered below. Our immediate concern is to answer the question whether citizens as such (and not only direct victims) can claim a legitimate entitlement to know about the criminal histories of their fellow citizens.

[4] The social contract tradition attempts to derive the content of public morality from the notion of an agreement between all those in the political community. Metaphorical contracts are thought experiments used by moral philosophers to model how we can rationally and fairly justify certain political relations between individuals. Perhaps most famous amongst such constructs is John Rawls' Veil of Ignorance. This asks what principles rational people would select as the fundamental organizing norms of society, if they had no knowledge of factors about themselves that would likely skew their decisions in ways that would unfairly benefit people like them over others (such as social position, gender etc.).

easily knowable to each other, whereas parties to a social contract are all citizens of a particular state. Clearly, it would be impossible for any single citizen to know the identity of every other citizen. So making access to knowledge of identities a requirement of contractual validity undermines the very idea of a social contract. Arguably, a right to know who one stands in contractual relations with would also imply a derivative right to *verify* the citizenship of every person physically present within a state's jurisdiction, so as to be able to distinguish accurately between contracting and non-contracting parties.[5] But that is even more impossible than knowing the identities of those we contract with. Impossibility aside, knowledge of who one is contracting with also seems superfluous and even irrelevant to the validity of a social contract. Surely it is enough for us to know that 'we' as 'citizens' stand in certain relations to each other, to assent to, and be bound by a social contract. The concrete and legalistic nature of actual contracts generates requirements that cannot be coherently extended to the political and metaphorical realm of the social contract.

One might argue in response that the right to know need not extend to the identities of all parties to the contract, but only to those of parties who have broken the contract. In other words, it is only in the breach that a right to know is activated, because a breach calls for a response.[6] This seems closer to being correct, but only to the extent that it shows that *someone* has a right to know who broke the rules. It does not by itself answer the question of *who* can legitimately claim the right to respond. To those who would argue that we need to know who has broken the rules of the social contract if we are to be able to enforce them, the appropriate response is to ask: who does 'we' refer to in this context? And the answer, in most modern societies, would not be citizens but the state. More specifically, it is the police and the courts that have responsibility for enforcing the criminal law, rather than 'we' as such. This is because, in political theorizing about a social contract, part of what individuals are understood as agreeing to is to authorize a body—typically a state—to resolve conflicts and prosecute breaches. Indeed, many have argued that the very purpose of a social contract is precisely to avoid the insecurity and brutality of a vigilante society by delegating our right to self-defence to a neutral authority.

[5] As helpfully pointed out by Duff, this of course also raises the question of the status of non-citizens who are within the state's jurisdiction. That is a question that goes beyond the scope of this study, but does arise in the application of the law and policy. In practice, convictions acquired in origin countries are not routinely shared with host authorities.

[6] This claim should not be confused with the argument that a person who breaches the social contract by committing a crime thereby forfeits their right to privacy. That is an argument that would ground a right to know in the broader justification for punishment, rather than in the norms and principles of contract.

If this is right, then it is only the state that can claim a presumptive or prima facie right to know—and indeed a duty to investigate—who has broken the rules of the contract and to respond to breaches. Here again, the differences between actual and social contracts make it difficult to build a case for a public right to know by analogizing between the two.

To argue all this is not to claim that individuals consign their freedom to respond to a breach of the contract entirely to the state, in a way that then prevents them from responding in some way, when and if they do find out about criminality. It is just to say that citizens have neither civic rights nor civic duties to respond under the social contract, and neither does the social contract oblige anyone to furnish citizens with information necessary or conducive to facilitating any such response. Any responses to crime that citizens do end up making are constrained by morality and the law in specific ways that state responses are not. For example, individual citizen responses to crime lack legal standing, typically represent only individual or partial interests and not those of the political community as a whole, and most importantly, must only involve actions that are compatible with respect for the legal rights and freedoms of others. In other words, they are incidental to, rather than a constitutive element of, what we call 'criminal justice'. So we should stick with the conclusion that, as long as we live in a society where the right to inflict official punishments is claimed exclusively by the state,[7] it is the state that has the presumptive right to know. The question of whether such a right can *also* be claimed by individuals on whose behalf the state acts when it enforces the criminal law remains open.[8] But it cannot be settled by appeal to some equivalence between actual contracts and social contracts.

The right to know as necessary for the stability of the social contract

Let's turn to a different way of grounding a right to know in the notion of the social contract. Rather than analogizing from interpersonal agreements, this approach draws on more sophisticated debates in contractualist political

[7] There is a live debate about whether there is a convincing philosophical case for the state's supposedly exclusive right to punish (see Mendlow, 2022 in debate with Husak, 2008). But in practice it is only the state that has the legal and political authority to impose certain kinds of hard treatment such as imprisonment, community service, electronic tagging, and so on. What we can say for now is that if anyone has a duty to punish on behalf of the public, the state does.

[8] For example, rights to know and arguably even to respond may be claimed by citizens who have been directly victimized by a criminal act. But such entitlements derive from the rights of individuals as victims rather than from their status as injured parties to a social contract.

philosophy. These focus on the importance of public knowledge in securing the 'stability' of the social contract. The specific argument we will consider involves the key claim that citizens need to have access to knowledge about others' compliance with the rules of the contract in order to be able to make an informed decision about whether they too remain obliged to uphold them. The intuitive basis for this line of argument lies in the moral and political value of reciprocity, and the idea that what we owe our fellow citizens depends in part on how we are treated by them. Let's see how it plays out in relation to access to criminal records.

In order to sustain cooperation over time, a social contract must continuously provide citizens with good enough reasons to accept it as authoritative and abide with its terms. In other words, it must provide the conditions for its own stability. 'Stability' in this sense is not an empirical description of society, as it would be if it were used to mean the opposite of 'social unrest'. Rather, it means sound grounding in good reasons, such that citizens make a voluntary and informed decision to commit themselves to be bound by the contract. We should understand stability as the coordination of collective commitments that can only be achieved if we can have well-founded confidence in our own and other people's knowledge of and assent to the common rules. The relevant question for our purposes then becomes: how much knowledge of each other's commitments and compliance (with the criminal law) is necessary for stability?

Political theorist John Rawls (1971) argued famously that stability requires 'publicity'. By this he meant that citizens should be able to know not only what the rules of the contract are, but also that other citizens know what the rules are and that they agree to be bound by them too. To see Rawls's point, imagine a situation in which people are not sure what the rules of the social contract are. Or imagine a situation in which they cannot find out whether other people understand those rules or agree to adopt them as a guide to action. It is not hard to see how either of these kinds of uncertainty would be enough to undermine people's commitment to upholding the rules themselves. So publicity in Rawls's sense seems important to the achievement of both the 'social' and the 'contract' elements of the social contract. Rawls himself did not spell out how what became known as his 'publicity condition' would translate into actual rights to information in practice, but others have extended his arguments in ways that do.

Building on Rawls to develop his own interpretation of the publicity condition, Andrew Williams argued that stability can only be achieved if people are 'able to attain common knowledge of the rules' (i) general applicability,

(ii) their particular requirements, and (iii) the extent to which individuals conform with those requirements' (Williams, 1998: 233). It is the last of these three conditions that is relevant to the question of whether we should have a right to know about each other's criminal acts.[9] Williams defends condition (iii) by arguing that we should all be capable of 'mutually verifying the status of' each other's conduct if we are to meet our 'basic concern for the achievement of well-ordered social cooperation' as well as to 'harmonise the pursuit of equality and social unity' (1998: 246).[10] But Williams is vague about how granular the knowledge must be. Does stability require access to information about compliance at the level of the individual, or only in general or statistical terms? It is a significant jump from saying we should have access to knowledge about the general extent to which others comply, to saying that we should have access to information about the *identities* of those who have breached or are breaching specific rules. But the latter is what would need to be demonstrated if the publicity condition is going to yield a right to know about people's criminal records.

It is helpful at this point to think about the kinds of situations in which it seems plainly evident that we *would* need access to knowledge of others' compliance with the rules of the social contract to be able to decide whether we are obliged to abide by them. Driving seems an obvious example. In all countries, the laws governing driving include the obligation to stick to a specific side of the road. Disordered driving is at worst a threat to life and at best a serious hindrance to getting anywhere in a car (which is after all the whole purpose of driving). If enough people were to stop driving on the same side of the road, the fact that there is a law obliging people to drive on the left would not by itself provide anyone with much of a reason to do so. So in this case it does seem reasonable to claim that we need to be able to know the extent to which people are following this rule to decide whether we are bound to follow it. The same conclusion can be drawn with respect to many other crimes which enforce rules designed to prevent harms arising from social discoordination. It also follows with respect to legal rules of fair play in collective action, like those prohibiting tax evasion or littering.

What does not follow, however, is that we also need to be able to know *who* is driving on which side of the road, not paying their taxes, or throwing rubbish on the street. As others have also argued, the identities of those breaching

[9] Though neither Rawls nor Williams were themselves interested in this question. Rather, they were discussing publicity in relation to the principles of justice establishing social institutions, as opposed to the far narrower and more applied domain of the criminal law.

[10] I am grateful to Chris Nathan for pointing out to me the relevance of Williams's arguments about publicity to the wider concerns of this book.

the rules are largely irrelevant to my reasons for maintaining my own commitments.[11] Interpreted as a requirement to know who is breaching the rules, William's condition (iii) seems to demand far more than is necessary for stability. And the irrelevance of identity to the fulfilment of the publicity condition seems even more obvious when we think about rules which correspond to *moral* prohibitions, such as rules against attacking or abusing other people. My reasons for abiding by rules against attacking or abusing those around me are moral reasons, which exist to a significant extent independently of both their codification in law and others' behaviour. In other words, even if I could never know the identities of those who break rules against attacking or abusing others, I would still have strong reasons to refrain from such behaviour myself. Those reasons relate to the simple fact that human beings are valuable in themselves and so it is wrong to hurt them or cause them to suffer. My commitment to not intentionally attack or abuse other people just isn't dependent in any significant way on other people's commitments to refrain from doing so.[12]

Let us set aside then claims that the integrity or stability of the social contract requires or indeed even implies a right to know about each other's criminal convictions. At best, it could be argued that stability is well served by public access to knowledge about the *general extent* of compliance with some kinds of criminal prohibitions. But we cannot say the same for knowledge of who has breached what rule. If there is a sound grounding in political theory for a general right of citizens to know about each other's crimes, we will not find it in thinking or theorizing about the social contract.

Does the Idea of Crime as a 'public wrong' Imply a Right to Know?

We'll now turn to a quite different way in which political theorists have conceptualized the publicness of crimes, one that is concerned less with the extent to which publicity is necessary for other goods like enforcement and stability, and more with the normative status of criminal wrongs. It is often remarked by theorists of the criminal law that legal systems around the world treat criminal

[11] See G.A. Cohen's (2008) response to Williams.

[12] Here I only recognize two kinds of crime: those that concern the kinds of coordination issue, when all we need to know is whether others are generally conforming; and those which criminalize conduct from which we ought anyway to refrain, even if we do not know who else is or is not refraining. Do all crimes that are wrongs fall within one or both of these two categories such that my arguments apply to the full range of acts typically criminalized? I struggle to think of one which does not, which at least implies that my arguments apply widely, even if I cannot demonstrate that they apply comprehensively.

acts as distinct from other kinds of illegality insofar as they are investigated and prosecuted in the name of the state, rather than that of their specific victim/s. In most countries it is the sovereign, (in republics 'The People' and in monarchies 'The Crown') that brings proceedings against a criminally accused, and those proceedings can be brought without the participation or even the consent of the victim.

As a strategy for both explaining and justifying this descriptive fact, legal theorists have sought to conceptualize crime as such as a distinctively 'public wrong'.[13] The idea of crime as a public wrong is not uncontroversial, and thinkers continue to disagree on the correct account of a public wrong and indeed about whether such a concept is needed at all. But the notion has garnered significant support and enduring attention amongst legal theorists. For that reason at least it is worth thinking about what different conceptualizations of crime as a public wrong imply or entail about the public's right to know. We'll consider two kinds of accounts of crime as a public wrong. The first understands crime as always involving a wrong *done to* or *against* the public as well as against any specific victim. On this account, crime concerns the public because it harms or wrongs them directly or 'causally'. The second approach claims that crime is a public wrong because it violates the shared values of the public, or the values that constitute the civic order.

The right to know and the rights of victims: does crime always victimize the public?

If we were to construe the public as a victim of crime, this could plausibly yield a presumptive right of all citizens to access criminal records as well as information about sentencing, parole, risk assessments, and so on. An argument based on such a construal would take the following form: victims of crime have a right to know who has harmed or wronged them; crimes always wrong the public alongside any direct victims; therefore the public has a right to know who commits crime. The argument is supported partly by the fact that in our normal dealings with each other as individuals we would expect not only that

[13] For an overview of the competing positions see Kennedy, 2021. Fortunately, the main points of contention in that debate centre on issues that fall outside the scope of our current inquiry. These are broadly speaking the extent to which the status of some wrong as public is a ground on which to criminalize or punish it (Lamond, 2007; Duff and Marshall, 2010; Lee, 2015; Edwards and Simester, 2017) and the question of whether conceptualizing crime as a public wrong supports the claim that the state has an exclusive right to punish (Mendlow, 2022; Husak, 2008).

people who wrong us should own up to it, but also that others who witness or learn about the wronging should answer truthfully when asked who did it (or at the very least not obstruct us in our efforts to find out). And it is supported partly by the fact that victims of crime in many countries already enjoy well-established legal rights to information about the person who has harmed or wronged them, including about any criminal proceedings against them and information about sentencing and parole in cases of serious crime in which a victim may remain at risk. While the institutionalization of such rights has not been entirely uncontroversial over the years, there is undoubtedly a strong precedent across countries for victims, especially those who have suffered serious, targeted attacks or abuse, to be given such information (alongside related rights to provide a victim statement or to be involved in proceedings in some way). And we have no reason here to contest the assertion of such rights. If anyone has a legitimate moral right to know about a person's criminal record, then their victims do. If crime is a public wrong in the sense that it always victimizes the public, then it would seem that the public should be able to claim the same, or at least some of the same, entitlements to information as victims.

This line of thinking is attractive, but there are two problems with it. These should give us pause for thought before accepting it. The first problem is that not all wronging amounts to victimization; the second is that asserting some normative equivalence between victims and 'the public' leads to questionable conclusions. What makes someone a victim of violence, fraud, or abuse? Surely it is being wronged or harmed directly and personally. It is *the victim's* wellbeing, health, safety, and so on, that has been attacked via the criminal act, and it is *they* who will have to struggle to regain these, if they can. In other words, it is precisely the personal nature of victimization that grounds victims' special rights to information, where they exist. That is why victim contact services and information provision tend to address questions like: What happened to me and why did it happen *to me*? How will I know that justice has been done in relation to my experience? How can I be confident that the person who did this to me won't go on to do it again, to others like me? Will I and my family will be safe in the future?[14] The special rights of victims spring from the harm they personally suffer and their corresponding needs for recovery and restitution.

[14] An illustrative example of victims' claims to a right to know is provided by the UK's Undercover Policing Inquiry. Over decades, undercover officers infiltrating peaceful social justice and environmental movements had long-term relationships with female activists, in some cases even marrying and fathering children with them. Despite admitting gross abuses of power, the police sought to deny the victims the right to know the real identity of their abusers, citing security concerns. The testimonies of those victims illustrate powerfully the harm and re-victimization inflicted by such denial.

These may be shared to some extent by their close family, but not by members of the public as such. Arguments that conflate the wrong to the public with individual victimization are therefore conceptually problematic. But they are morally questionable too, because they would have us diminish unjustifiably the experience of victims, which is both qualitatively and morally different from any affront that may arguably be suffered by 'the public'.[15]

Does crime wrong the public by threatening the civic order?

If what has just been argued is correct, then crime as such does not wrong the public by victimizing them. But not all assertions that crime is always a wrong *against* the public imply public victimization or displace the personal and direct wrongs done to victims. There is a long tradition of political theory that understands crimes as threats to civil order, public harmony, or social stability. This tradition originates with political thinkers in ancient Greece and Rome and has been given modern articulations in the work of philosopher Robert Nozick and others. It also resonates beyond legal theory, for instance in Durkheimian sociological understandings of crime as an act that violates the 'collective consciousness' and undermines 'social solidarity'.[16]

Some political theorists have developed this line of thinking to argue that crime by its nature always threatens or harms our collective interests and wrongs us for that reason. For example, in 1974 Becker argued that crimes are public wrongs because their commission causes 'social volatility', by which he means 'the potential for destructive disturbance of fundamental social structures'.[17] On Becker's account, social harmony is something each of us has a strong interest in preserving, just in virtue of living together in a political community. If crime threatens social harmony by prompting citizens to abandon their own stable behaviour in favour of a self-defensive or hostile stance, then it damages those interests directly. Others have put forward arguments that take

[15] The same kind of points have been made in relation to the claim that something's being a 'public wrong' (rather than a violation of the victim) is a ground to criminalize it (see Marshall and Duff, 2010: 12 and Edwards and Simester, 2017: 8).

[16] For a discussion of the historical conceptualization of crime as a threat to the collective order, see Tripkovic (2019:20). For an overview of Nozick's fear-based argument for the publicness of crimes, see Lamond (2007).

[17] 'Social volatility is to be regarded as a disvalue in itself, the creation of which, by acts produced by an individual's socially unstable character traits, is a social harm. It is this sort of social harm, I want to argue, which justifies the public law response we make by defining the acts involved as criminal' (Becker, 1974: 274).

a similar structural form to Becker's but substitute 'causing social volatility' with for example, 'undermining social trust' (Dimock, 1997).

Becker's argument and those related to it focus primarily on exploring the social harms of crime rather than the extent to which the public have a right to know about it. The question of public access to criminal records is not addressed even indirectly in their work. Still, if we are interested in exploring the extent to which the notion of crime as a public wrong could ground such rights or entitlements, then it is worth considering whether this kind of account of public wrongs can get us there. It seems unlikely that it can. There is little evidence for the causal relationship this line of argument asserts between crime and social volatility or other societal ills. It might be easy to *imagine* a society in which crime is rife and volatility, instability, and unrest are the norm. Countless dystopian films and novels have provided vivid examples of how such a society might be. But many of the actual societies in which we live today do tolerate serious, pervasive, and intractable violations of the criminal law on many fronts, yet also enjoy relative peace and harmony. Let's consider some examples.

Crimes involving violence against women and girls (or 'gender-based violence' as it is referred to in some countries) constitute, it is no exaggeration to say, a global epidemic. Even the most apparently safe and stable countries around the world report very high rates of femicide, domestic abuse, and sexual violence. Readers can verify this by looking at any United Nations or World Health Organization report on the subject, not to mention the constant headlines in countries around the world. Take Canada and New Zealand, places equally known for being prosperous, tolerant, and stable. In both these countries 35% of women have experienced sexual or physical violence in an intimate relationship, a figure which rises to over 50% if psychological and emotional abuse are included (Government of Canada, 2024; Fanslow and McIntosh, 2023). Yet even in comparatively well-funded and uncorrupted criminal justice systems, rates of conviction for these crimes are invariably and persistently low. In the United Kingdom, where this book is being written, about 20% of calls to police are about domestic abuse. Yet conviction rates are well under 5%. Those for rape are even worse at less than 1%, a figure one can only describe as vanishing (Hohl, 2022). This kind of criminality does untold harm to individuals, families, and communities. And it clearly violates moral norms against harming others. But allowing people to perpetrate it with impunity does not tend to result in anything one could accurately describe as 'social volatility' (unless we stretch the concept of social volatility beyond recognition). Volatility implies being subject to rapid, unpredictable, and destabilizing changes; it brings to mind social unrest, riots, looting, and short-lived and violent political rule. Statistically predictable, widespread, and unaccountable violence that follows well-worn patterns and is carried out against a defined group in largely private settings is compatible with social stability.

Similar points can be made about other kinds of crimes, such as the illegal supply of toxic drugs like Fentanyl. Fentanyl is a highly addictive and dangerous opioid. Its illegal production and sale has fuelled an epidemic of addiction and death in the United States in recent years. Individual lives and entire communities have been destroyed in its wake. The illegal Fentanyl market harms society, but not by causing its members to adopt a hostile and defensive stance towards each other, as Becker would have it. Rather, its harms lie in the terrifying efficiency with which it turns previously autonomous, healthy, responsible, and productive people into addicts, ruining lives and destroying families. The harms of the illegal Fentanyl market are serious and can be measured in terms of social as well as individual effects. But again, one would have to perform some impressive intellectual contortions to be able to conceptualize this as 'social volatility'.

To say that crime cannot be defined in terms of its tendency to cause social volatility is not to deny that some types of crime could erupt into social volatility if left unpunished. Neither is it to deny that if *all* crime went unpunished social volatility could ensue. Vincent Chiao has argued quite reasonably that one of the reasons we need a system that imposes criminal sanctions on individual defections from shared rules is to maintain political and social stability, and most would agree with that claim. But to agree with this does not commit us to accepting the claim that *acts of crime* cause social volatility. Nor does it commit us to accepting that crime's tendency to cause social volatility is what makes it a wrong against the public. And if threatening social volatility can't ground a unifying concept of crime as a public wrong, then neither will it give us the kind of argument we need to support a public right to know.[18] The weakness of the social volatility account for our purposes is further revealed if we look at what it might imply when applied in the personal, rather than the

[18] There are of course other reasons to reject this way of thinking about public wrongs. Mendlow, for example, has pointed out that the fact that an act causes social volatility is not normally considered grounds for criminalizing it. Rather, only those acts of intentional or culpable interpersonal wrongdoing tend to be criminalized. In his own words: 'When alleged murderers appear in court, the accusation to which they must answer is that they killed another human being without justification or excuse – not that they deprived the state of a member, sowed public mischief, increased social volatility, or aroused fear in other members of the community' (2022: 247). But we should keep in mind that Mendlow's is an argument about whether causing social volatility is a ground for criminalization, whereas we are interested more narrowly in the question of whether crime causes social volatility and thereby wrongs the public.

social, domain. We don't generally behave as if we each have moral rights to know about every act that threatens our personal wellbeing or security in some way, so it is hard so see why we would acquire such rights as a collective.

Does crime harm the public like professional misconduct harms a profession?

In a moment, we will move away from arguments which, like Becker's, claim that crime is public in the sense that it directly or 'causally' violates the public. But before we do, it is worth considering one last potential argument in this vein. The argument invites us to take professional associations and the codes of ethics that regulate their members' behaviour as a model for thinking about political communities and their criminal laws. More precisely, it invites to accept the following claim: that an act of crime is to citizens as an act of professional misconduct is to members of a profession. This claim was originally made by Duff and Marshall to defend their distinctive account of public wrongs as acts that violate the defining values of a political community or 'polity'.[19] It is important to be clear that Duff and Marshall's argument does not, like Becker's, rely on the empirically shaky claim that crime wrongs the public causally by leading to social harms like unrest or volatility. On the contrary, they position their argument for crime-as-public-wrong as an alternative to those kinds of accounts. However, I want to argue here that taking their analogy with professional ethics seriously *does also* commit us to claiming that crime wrongs the public causally (even though Duff and Marshall themselves do not acknowledge this). What I want to argue now, is that the analogy fails to show that crime wrongs the public causally. Ruling out this line of argument makes it even harder to claim that crimes are public wrongs because they are acts *against the public* rather than (merely) *against public values.*

To see how a violation of professional ethics[20] wrongs all members of the political community causally, we need to look a bit more closely at some of the features of professional wrongdoing that Duff and Marshall leave out. First, let's call to mind some examples of professional misconduct that are likely to be familiar to anyone who reads the news. A police officer brutally beats an unarmed civilian stopped for a suspected traffic offence. A doctor takes kickbacks

[19] This is paraphrased from Marshall and Duff (1998:20); and Duff and Marshall (2010: 71).

[20] My understanding of professional ethics in this chapter aligns strongly to Michael Davis's account in his excellent and timeless 1991 paper 'Thinking Like an Engineer'.

from a pharmaceutical company in return for prescribing painkillers they know to be highly addictive and harmful. A defence lawyer acting for a rapist seeks to undermine the credibility of their client's victim by bringing up irrelevant details about their clothing and sex life in court to smear them.

Who is harmed or wronged by these breaches of professional conduct, and in what way(s)? I would argue that first and primary amongst the wronged are those individuals personally affected: the casualty of police brutality, the patient whose life is ruined by addiction, the victim of abuse who is shamed and silenced, knowing there will be others after her. Theirs is a personal wrong. But second come all the individual members of the profession, whose shared identity has been tainted or sullied by the act of misconduct that was done in their name. And third amongst the wronged comes the profession itself, which has through the act of misconduct been 'brought into disrepute'.[21] Let's take a minute to see how the second kind of collective wrong, which I will argue *is* a causal wrong, occurs.

Professionals share a common identity in the sense that they each act in the name of and with the special privileges and responsibilities of their specific profession. The power to use force, the authority to prescribe, and the privilege to ask questions in court are powers bestowed on individuals only in virtue of their status as a professional. The privileges of professionals have a moral grounding. Their exercise is only legitimate when done in the service of a clearly articulated and commonly affirmed public mission (in our three examples these are public safety, health, and justice, respectively). The standards of conduct for professionals pursuing their public mission are significantly *higher* than would be expected of any citizen seeking to achieve the same ends. For instance, police are expected to run towards danger rather than away from it. Similarly, they are permitted to use force only as a last resort, that is, only when de-escalation and incapacitation techniques have failed, even when they are being physically attacked. The same is not demanded of the public. A profession's ability and effectiveness in achieving their mission is dependent on the public trusting them to uphold these high standards. Police need the public to report crime to them if they are to solve it and maintain public safety. Doctors need the public to consent to procedures and take the medicine they prescribe if they are to prevent, cure, and heal us. And lawyers need the public to trust them in interpreting and applying the law in good faith, for justice to be done.

[21] This ordering tracks the moral priority that should be given to correcting the wrong in question.

When a professional abuses their privilege and power to oppress, exploit, or otherwise violate the rights of others, and even when they merely fall short of the high standards expected of that profession, they undermine the public trust needed for the effective pursuit of the profession's public mission. They do this by sullying the name of the profession and by extension the reputation of all its members, past, present, or future. This is why the notion of 'bringing into disrepute' is so closely tied to the field of professional ethics: because the strong sense in which identity is shared means the bad behaviour of one damages the reputation and standing of all. It is also why codes of professional ethics tend to include an explicit duty on all professionals to call out and report breaches by others, and why a failure to uphold that duty itself constitutes a serious breach of the code.

Can the same be argued for crime and the political community? It seems unlikely. Consider that we do not usually accuse people who commit crime of bringing 'the public' or 'the polity' into disrepute by their actions. Indeed, the notion of bringing into disrepute is alien to the world of criminal justice and would jar if applied in that context. And most criminal codes do not criminalize a failure to report a crime by another citizen. There are good reasons for this. Unlike a breach of a code of professional ethics, a crime does not sully the 'good name' of citizens. That's because it's understood that a person who commits a crime acts in their own name and their own name alone, rather than that of the collective. Crime might violate the values of the collective, in the sense of breaching prohibitions imposed by legitimate public processes. But then, if expressions of condemnation or censure in professional ethics take the form 'not in our name!', for criminality the appropriate sentiment is likely to be something closer to 'not on our watch!'.[22] Of course, there will always be some people who do *claim* to be acting in the name or interests of the collective when they commit crimes. Take the fascist who attacks ethnic minorities in the name of protecting 'the people' or 'the nation'. But this is a particular kind of case, rather than typical of the way most people think about what they are doing when they commit a crime. Nor is it in any other way a general feature of crime as such.

The point of drawing attention to these disanalogies between professions and polities is to show that crime does not in some essential way wrong the public causally or directly and so cannot be considered the public's business

[22] In contrast, criminal justice processes and procedures undertaken by the police and courts *are* carried out in 'our' name. As I will argue later on in this chapter, this grounds a right to know about, and even to some extent to participate, in them.

on that ground. And the point of asserting *that* conclusion is just to show that attempts to ground a public right to know about the crimes of fellow citizens in some claim about the way crimes causally wrong the public are unlikely to be successful. But this does prompt the further question of whether causal wronging might be a basis for a right to know about some kinds of crimes. In particular, some readers may well be wondering what these arguments about causal wronging imply about a public right to know about those who commit crimes that *do* threaten or wrong the public directly. We now consider this possibility.

Do we have a right to know about crimes that directly or 'causally' wrong the public?

Crimes like terrorism seem to wrong the public causally by seeking to subvert the democratic political order that protects collective rights, though violence, fear, and intimidation. Political crimes such as vote-rigging, illegal funding of political parties, and bribery of public officials for personal or corporate advantage all wrong or harm the public causally by corrupting political processes. Tax evasion and benefit fraud cheat the public and certain kinds of environmental crimes harm current and future generations of publics. And crimes like rioting—and even potentially the use of certain kinds of malware to target public services—directly threaten the public with social volatility.[23] We might not be able to argue for a general right to access *all* kinds of criminal records on the basis that crime as such wrongs the public causally. But if causal wronging turns out to be a sound grounding for a presumptive right to know, then we might be able to argue for general access to information about who commits these particular kinds of crimes.

In order to examine this question, we need to turn away from political and social theory and look for a moment to the rules and principles of interpersonal morality. In other words, we need to think about what we owe and can demand of each other as persons (rather than as citizens). For if causal wronging can ground a right to know at the level of the individual, we will need to explain why it should not do so at the level of the collective.

When I am wronged by another person, do I have a right to know who it is that wronged me? It seems evident that I do. We might disagree about whether

[23] For a discussion of these kinds of wrongs, see Zimmerman (2019) on the concept of political wrongdoing.

that right yields an entitlement to compel others to reveal the identity of the wrongdoer, or merely an entitlement not to be obstructed in one's efforts to identify them. And in some cases there might be overriding reasons to deny a wronged person that information, for example, if doing so would facilitate their causing serious retaliatory harm to the wrongdoer. But it seems fair to claim that, if *any* rights accrue to a person just in virtue of being wronged, one of them must be to know who the wrongdoer is. As there is no reason to deny this right to collectives of individuals, it seems fair also to assert a general right of the public to know who has wronged them as a political and civic body. This right does not reduce to a right to respond to wrongdoing or 'address the breach', because it can legitimately be claimed even by those who for other reasons have no such right. And while it overlaps with the rights of victims, neither is it identical to them. Not all causal wronging victimizes. And the rights of victims as generally practiced today have been defined in the context of a (state) criminal justice process and are fundamentally conditioned by that process.

So if we as 'the public' have a right to know who has wronged us 'causally', as I have just said it does, does that mean we must always be informed about the identities of people who commit crimes directly against us? Not necessarily. Asserting such a right does imply that there is always *a* reason to make information about public wrongdoers available to the public. But that reason might be weightier in some circumstances than others, depending on the nature and importance of the interests it promotes or protects. It may also be overridden by countervailing considerations, for example, the rights of the wrongdoer not to be attacked or otherwise seriously harmed. In other words, our right to know who has wronged us is not an absolute right that must be respected at any cost. Looking carefully at how varying circumstances affect the scope and weight of the right—in other words, the extent to which it can be claimed in different situations—can help us to understand what it might actually entail in practice.

One thing to notice about the crimes against the public just listed above is that assertions of a right to know seem much stronger with respect to some of them than others. For example, people are more likely to insist on the public's right to know which politicians and other public figures have acted corruptly, than on their right to know who has participated in a riot or committed benefit fraud. This is plausibly explained by reference to the fact that the right to know about political crimes acts as a kind of gateway entitlement: in the sense that its fulfilment is necessary for the exercise of other, arguably more vital political rights. These include the right to make informed choices about which party or individual to vote for (or not) and which cause to protest or campaign against. Without a right to know which political actors wrong us in these ways, we cannot exercise these important political rights. The same cannot be argued for the right to know about who has committed benefit fraud, participated in looting or rioting, and so on. In these cases, the right to know does not facilitate the exercise of other rights or the promotion of other interests.

We might assume that our right to know who has wronged us becomes stronger in proportion to the severity of the wrong they have committed. But on reflection severity seems less determinative than what we might call the 'facilitatory aspect' of the right to know who has wronged us, which I have just described above. For example, terrorism is a very serious crime against the public. But knowing the identity of a terrorist seems less vital to the exercise of democratic rights or important public interests than knowing other information about them. Specifically, information like the kind of person they are, what their motivations and influences were, and which the circumstances and triggers drove them to take such action. This kind of knowledge is far more important for understanding the threat and for a citizen's ability to hold state agencies and services accountable for addressing terrorism effectively. Knowing the identity of a terrorist does little to facilitate the exercise of any such rights.

To point this out is not to deny what has already been established above, namely that the public has a prima facie right to know who the terrorist is because they are causally wronged by their acts. Rather, it is to suggest that the interests protected by this entitlement are not as vital as one might assume. What does this mean for our inquiry? Just that being causally wronged is one reason to claim an entitlement to know the identity of the wrongdoer. But that it may not be sufficiently weighty a reason to override the rights of wrongdoers, unless it also facilitates the exercise of other more important rights or the protection of other more important interests. And as we saw in Chapter 2, the rights of wrongdoers include the right to rehabilitation. This conclusion has practical implications. It implies that policies around publication of identities of criminals, and public access to their criminal records, should be informed by specific considerations. These are: whether the crime is a wrong against the public; what other civic rights are facilitated by publicizing the identities of the offenders; and how these can be balanced against countervailing rights, including those of people with criminal records and their families.

Does crime wrong the public by violating public values?

There is one final account of public wrongs we must consider before wrapping up our inquiry into the publicness of crime and what it means for a right to know. In 2008, Douglas Husak argued that 'criminal conduct must be regarded as a *public* wrong – not in the sense that it is a wrong done *to* the public but rather that it is a wrong that is the *proper concern* of the public [emphasis in the original]' (Husak, 2008: 135). According to Husak, crimes are public wrongs because they 'violate the values that define and structure the civic enterprise . . . to ignore such wrongs would be to betray the values that are violated, to which the polity is supposedly committed' (Husak, 2008: 111). In arguing this, Husak was articulating a conceptualization of crime as a public wrong first developed by Antony Duff and Sandra Marshall, who together have done more than anyone to advance and refine thinking and debate in this field. Duff and Marshall argue that crime is a public wrong in the sense that it 'violates the polity's defining values' (Duff, 2011: 128, 142). According to Duff and Marshall, the values violated by crime are public not only in the sense that they are shared by the public, but also, and more profoundly, in the sense that they constitute the public realm. This latter claim could potentially allow them to carve out a space in which crime might be conceptualized as a wrong *against* the public without necessarily also being understood as wronging the public *causally*.

Duff and Marshall use the analogy between crime and professional misconduct (discussed above) to drive this argument home. The analogy is important to their case because it helps them to argue for a substantive or weighty sense of identification, belonging, and connection between citizens, which is violated by crime. For example, Duff argues that citizens 'see themselves as belonging to a particular political community, and as connected through the practices and values of that community to their fellow citizens. . . in particular, in the context of discussions of the criminal law, in their relationships with each other as members of a political community' (Duff, 2010: 5, 27). But, as I have already argued above, the shared identity and shared moral purpose that connect members of professions go significantly beyond those that characterize membership of a polity. The problems with the analogy between professional misconduct and crime weaken the extent to which Duff and Marshall (and the many others who have adopted their account of public wrongs) can claim that public wrongs are also wrongs to all citizens. And they undermine the extent to which crime can be considered an attack on our 'shared enterprise . . . on us as a collective' or as a wrong done 'to the community at large' (Lernested, 2014: 192; Husak, 2008: 136). Of course, one could try to argue that people have a right to know whenever others violate values they happen to share, but this just begs the question of what is meant by 'shared' and why the fact that values are 'shared' should be seen as so normatively important, which is precisely the question we have already been exploring in this chapter.

Conclusion

The upshot of this is just that the fact that crime might violate public values (if we accept for the sake of argument that this is one of the things that criminal acts do) does not mean it violates or wrongs the public as such. And if crime as such does not wrong the public, then we can't justify a general right to know about it by appeal to the moral entitlements of the wronged. So far, neither the concept of the social contract nor the idea of public wrongs has provided us with good enough reasons to accept that the public should have a presumptive or default entitlement to access information about people's criminal records.

Our inquiry has, however, revealed strong grounds for limited rights to know, claimable by those directly wronged or victimized by crime. But, unlike arguments from the social contract or from public wrongs, these grounds do not make any claims about the intrinsic publicity of crime. Indeed, the discussion in this chapter suggests that looking to the essential properties of crime to provide us with answers to these questions does not take us very far. They suggest, further, that assertions of a right to know are more likely to be justified by appeal to the interests of those who claim an entitlement to it, than by appeal to the nature, features, or even consequences of crime. In other words, the question we should be asking is not 'in what sense is crime properly understood as "public"?' but rather 'what public interest, if any, is served by giving citizens access to information about who has been involved or implicated in crime?'

There is, however, another sense in which criminality might be considered normatively 'public', a sense that is far less controversial than that of a public wrong. Criminality is, as a matter of fact and convention (irrespective of morality or justice), met with a public response in the form of what we call *criminal justice*. It seems more obviously correct to say that criminal justice is an intrinsically public matter than to say crime is, because unlike crime, criminal justice is always done in the name of the public and on the public's behalf (at least in a democracy). The idea that criminal justice is the public's business is also compatible with all accounts of the intrinsic publicness of crime, and indeed all theories of crime. And it is the basic principle behind important norms such as transparency, openness, and participation of the public in criminal justice. Might the publicness of criminal justice be a better principle from which to derive a public right to know about crime and criminality than the publicness of crime? That is the question we turn to in the next chapter.

4

Transparency, Accountability, Open Justice, and Public Facts

Introduction	73
Democratic Accountability: The Public's Right to Scrutinize Actions Done in Its Name	75
Sunlight Is the Best Disinfectant: Publicity to Reduce Corruption and the Abuse of Power	80
Open Justice and the Criminal Court As the Ultimate Public Forum	82
Contesting the doctrine of public fact	85
Criminal records and naming parties during criminal proceedings	90
Openness in Courts but Confidentiality in Policing	94
Conclusion	96

Introduction

Some values are so entrenched in contemporary democratic identity that their importance is beyond debate. Transparency, accountability, open justice, and the notion that justice must be 'seen to be done' are such examples. All imply a strong presumption in favour of openness when it comes to courts, legal processes, and official records. In this chapter, we consider the extent to which this presumption implies a public right to know about criminal records. Would justice still be open if the names of people involved in trials were redacted from court records? Or if journalists in court were not always permitted to report those names to the public? Would democratic accountability still be meaningful if the public could not readily find out who had been investigated for, accused, or convicted of a crime? We now ask whether and how far the public's right to know about criminal justice extends to criminal records.

One of the reasons for asking these questions today is that the conflict between promoting transparency and openness and protecting the rights and interests of those with criminal records has intensified. Until the advent of digitization and the internet, criminal procedures were relatively easy to access in real time, but difficult to access once those procedures were over. Court

The Crimes of Others. Katerina Hadjimatheou, Oxford University Press. © Katerina Hadjimatheou 2026.
DOI: 10.1093/9780198925149.003.0004

records tended to be stored in paper form or microfiche in clerks' offices, courthouses, and archives that took hours and even days to search through. News reports of criminal proceedings could only be accessed through a trip to the library.[1] Today, the preservation of the media online means that articles written about criminal proceedings remain available indefinitely, forever associating a person publicly with their criminal record. At the same time, a combination of widespread access to the internet, the digitization of criminal justice data, and an explicit political drive towards greater transparency of official records has led governments to routinely publish far more criminal record data than ever before. Because this kind of publicity allows a person's criminal record to be visible to anyone at the click of a button, it poses a serious problem for rehabilitation and reintegration. The question addressed in this chapter is whether this problem is an inevitable cost of a democratic commitment to open justice, transparency, and accountability, or whether we can address it without undermining that commitment.

In what follows, I aim to show that respect for democratic transparency, accountability, and open justice is compatible with respect for the rights and interests of people with criminal records. My arguments suggest that general presumptions in favour of publicity or, conversely, of confidentiality should differ between different areas of the criminal justice system, as conflicts between individual rights to privacy and the public right to know are resolved in different ways. I acknowledge that there are strong reasons for adopting a presumption in favour of openness and real-time publicity in criminal trials, and for giving the accused opportunities to draw attention to their case and invite scrutiny. But I also argue that the question of whether there are grounds to name defendants and those convicted beyond the forum of the court is contingent on the interests at play in the particular case. For this reason, it should always be a routine part of the judge's decision-making about the conditions under which any specific trial should be conducted. In contrast, policing should operate under a strong presumption of confidentiality with respect to the identities of suspects, but have wide discretion to publicize those identities when doing so serves an important public interest.

The arguments put forward here are supported by reference to a number of distinctions. The first is the distinction between transparency with respect to information pertaining to *the conduct of criminal justice agencies and officials*, and transparency with respect to the *identities of those implicated in or*

[1] For a discussion of how the 'practical obscurity' of court records protected the privacy of all parties to proceedings, see Bailey and Burkell (2016).

suspected of crimes. The second is the distinction between openness with respect to criminal justice *processes* and publicity with respect to the official *records of the outcomes* of such processes. The third is the distinction between rights to *receive* criminal record information and rights to *disseminate* that information to others in various ways. Failure to acknowledge these distinctions risks supporting a misguided assumption that arguments in favour of the importance of publicity or openness with respect to one kind of information extend to the other.

Democratic Accountability: The Public's Right to Scrutinize Actions Done in Its Name

Criminal cases are prosecuted in the name of 'the Public' or 'the State'. Those officials who 'do' criminal justice—judges, magistrates, lawyers, police, parole officers—perform their roles on behalf of the public. Criminal justice is, in other words, quite literally the public's business. In his 2016 essay entitled 'Accountability and Insolence', legal theorist Jeremy Waldron argues that the fact that officials act as agents of the public generates duties of transparency and openness on their part. In his words, 'ordinary members of the public, in all sorts of modes and combinations, are entitled to participate actively in supervising the conduct of government business because it is their business conducted in their name' (Waldron, 2016: 183). According to Waldron, this entitlement puts the onus of 'generating that transparency and the conveying of the information that accountability requires on the persons being held accountable' (p. 194). In other words, the public has a right to know about all aspects of public activity. For Waldron, it is the nature of the relationship between officials and the public that generates a right to know about official business, and that alone. This means that, while Waldron might recognize that a right to know can bring beneficial consequences, for example, by motivating officials to fulfil their roles more diligently, and warding against abuses of power, any such outcomes are incidental to his case for transparency. Waldron's focus on the duty of officials *as agents of the people* is what makes his a distinctively democratic theory of accountability.

Waldron's theory implies that all citizens have a very strong entitlement to information about activity done in the name of the public, an entitlement that is an integral element of the right to hold representatives to account. He himself does not consider how this entitlement would play out with respect to different kinds of state business in practice. But his position implies that it would apply equally to the business of the military, as to local government, as to criminal justice. Meanwhile, courts in the United States have adopted reasoning similar to Waldron's to defend the publication of criminal records explicitly. For example, in a case deciding the freedom of the press to publish details of an individual's encounter with the police, one US court insisted that 'no right to privacy is invaded when state officials allow or facilitate the publication of an official act such as an arrest' (*Holman v. Central Arkansas Broadcasting Company*, 1979). In the opinion of the court, the fact that an arrest is made in the name of the public means it is by definition the public's business. This, in turn, precludes anyone claiming a right to privacy with respect to records of it, even if those records are about them personally. In this way, the court asserted that the public's right to scrutinize acts done in their name creates an overriding presumption in favour of publicity.

At first glance, the US court's interpretation of the right to know may seem both unremarkable and uncontroversial. But its implications are actually radical and sweeping, supporting rights to information that go far beyond what any democratic country, including the United States itself, currently provides its citizens.[2] Around the world, freedom of information and transparency laws include standard categories of exemption specifying certain kinds of information governments are not obliged to disclose. These typically include information relating to matters of national security, intelligence, and evidence gathered by police in criminal investigations, which are treated as 'secret'.[3] They also include a wide array of personal or sensitive information about private individuals gathered by agencies of the state in their normal business but treated as 'confidential'. Examples include medical, social services, and welfare payments. The reasons for constraining publicity in these arenas differ, but they all appeal ultimately to the threat to the public interest that exposure would imply. The court's claim that there can be *no* right to privacy with respect to any official information flies in the face of widespread practices of confidentiality with respect to these examples. Indeed, it seems much closer to the radical transparency advocated by organizations such as Wikileaks. Ironically, that organization's efforts to expose secret government records have been met with aggressive attempts by the US state to prosecute them under criminal law.

Aside from representing an extreme deviation from established practice, the kind of radical publicity implied in the US court's judgement above would on

[2] Even the most publicity-friendly jurisdictions, including the United States, do not allow citizens access to records of all 'official acts'.

[3] See Mokrosinska (2018) for a comprehensive and insightful discussion of both conservative and radical accounts of the right to know.

the face of it endorse actions many of us would find distasteful or even dangerous. It would imply, for example, that the public should be given ready access to the records of psychiatric patients sectioned in state institutions, photos of victims taken at the scene of murders, the results of rape kit analyses, or the content of applications for disability support. It is hardly controversial to say that publishing that kind of information would be disrespectful. But doing so would also likely undermine the pursuit of important public goods, like public health, the welfare state, and crime prevention. Credible guarantees of confidentiality are essential to the ability of police officers, social workers, welfare caseworkers, doctors, psychologists, and lawyers to establish frank and trusting relationships with the people they support and, in turn, to carry out their work effectively. Publicity would destroy the strong norms of privacy and confidentiality on which the pursuit of these important public goods depends.

Let us look more carefully at Waldron's argument then. Does it really support unfettered public access to all information about official acts? His assertion of a public right to know is certainly strident. He even claims that it would be 'insolent' of public officials to refuse to provide the public with information 'on demand'. But his description of what kind of information the public has a right to is, on closer inspection, rather vague. In Waldron's own words: 'What the agent owes his principal(s) in the first instance is *an account of what he has been doing* [my italics]' (Waldron, 2015: 172).[4] The obvious question then is: just how much and what kind of information constitutes 'an account of what a public official has been doing'? More pertinently to our concerns in this book, to what extent is information about people's criminal records a vital or necessary element of an account of what criminal justice officials 'do' in the name of the public?

Looking to the declaration of the US court in the quote above does not help clarify things, even though at first glance it appears to provide a practical application of Waldron's principle. For when we examine the wording up close, it is also vague. The court states that 'no right to privacy is invaded when *state officials allow or facilitate the publication of an official act* such as an arrest [my italics]'. But this just begs the question of what kind of information state officials *should* be permitted to 'allow or facilitate publication' of. And to answer

[4] Similar wording focussing on the conduct of officials is used in legal contexts to support Freedom of Information and transparency legislation around the world. For example, in an overview of public records law in the United States, Daniel Solove (2002) cites a range of legal opinions defending public access. All are similarly formulated as ensuring that citizens have the right to examine 'the mode in which a public duty is performed', the 'working of public agencies' and 'the operation of government', and to enable 'free discussion of governmental affairs'.

that question we need an account of the just boundaries of state officials' legitimate discretion to disclose government information. Such an account is missing from the court's judgement.

The court does provide us with an example of the kind of information it holds that public officials would be justified in disclosing, namely records 'of arrest'. But it does not explain why the record of an arrest should be disclosable, beyond saying it is 'an official act', which as we have just seen is not sufficient to justify publicity. Neither does the court explain why officials should be permitted to disclose the identity of the individual arrested, rather than that of the official who carried it out, given that it is the conduct of officials that is the primary legitimate subject of scrutiny.

Something important is clearly missing from both the court's formulation and Waldron's account of the right to know. That something is a principle or set of principles that would guide us in determining which kinds of information constitute an account of what officials have been doing—and which should therefore be made available to the public on demand—and which kinds of information do not. What does it mean to provide an account of official conduct of public business? I propose that it means exposing to public scrutiny information that sheds light on the agency or agent's performance of their official duties, and other activities conducted in their capacity as public agent. Information which is gathered or generated by state agencies but which reveals little or nothing about the agency's own conduct can therefore be exempt from disclosure without undermining accountability.

Deciding in practice which information *should* fall within such an exemption may require the use of discretion and case-by-case judgements, as the rest of this chapter will argue. When a defendant is themselves a public official or when their crime involves public officials, there is a clear case for publicity—and not only transparency—around their identities.[5] But certain categories of information would on the face of it be obvious candidates for confidentiality. Personal and sensitive information about private individuals, that is, that which relates to a person's identifying characteristics and aspects of their life normally considered sensitive or intimate is one such category. Many kinds of information provided as examples above, like medical records and social services or public welfare records, would not be necessary to disclose under such considerations. And in case their disclosure *were* in some particular

[5] Elster distinguishes the two in this way: (emphasis in the original) 'one can perhaps define transparency as what is *not hidden* (but may be costly to find) and publicity as what is *revealed* (with low or zero costs) (Elster, 2013).

cases deemed necessary for meaningful scrutiny, this could be done while maintaining confidentiality with respect to the identity of the private citizens concerned, by redacting names and other identifying information. It is, after all, the activity of *the official* which is the proper object of a right to know, because it is they who act as agents of the public. So the identity of any private citizen involved in that activity could in principle be pseudonymized without either compromising democratic accountability or violating anyone's privacy.[6]

These considerations already have clear implications for the public right to access actual repositories of criminal records. Many countries maintain registers or databases of different kinds of offenders or suspects, with varying degrees of publicity. But knowing that someone has been subject to a judicial judgement or police investigation does not by itself help the public decide if that official act or decision was corrupt or fair, unreliable or robust. Sex offender registers in some countries publish the name, date of birth, address, and convictions of individuals with relevant offences, as well as their photographs and even their social security numbers. Similar registers for people convicted of domestic violence offences are maintained in Spain and Guam, while some US states do the same for all those who have had any contact with the criminal justice system, even if they were never charged or convicted of any crime. Lists of 'high-risk' suspects and offenders as are currently maintained in countries like the United Kingdom in relation to stalking, gang crime, and terrorism contain information about individuals' estimated dangerousness. US laws also permit companies to collect, collate, and commercialize criminal record information for sale to the public and other businesses, resulting in a large and thriving market in background checks.[7]

When published online, these registries and screening services do much to stigmatize those whose identities they expose, as discussed in Chapter 2. Yet they do nothing to inform the public about how officials are carrying out their duties to implement criminal justice. The rationale for public registries of offenders or suspects cannot therefore be convincingly grounded in the value of democratic transparency and accountability (though, as we see in Chapter 6, they may be grounded in other values such as public safety).[8] And there are no grounds in Waldron's theory of a right to know for making them public.

[6] This reasoning was given by the US Department of Justice to contest freedom of information demands by the media in the 1989 legal case DOJ v. Reporters Comm. for Free Press, 489 U.S. 749.

[7] Sarah Lageson has written interestingly about this market in her 2023 paper.

[8] It may of course be justified on other grounds, such as the value of shaming for deterrence, or the need to protect the public from people known to be dangerous, but these issues are discussed in Chapters 5 and 6 respectively.

But Waldron's is not the only accountability-related argument for a right to know. Others have put forward cases for publicity which, unlike Waldron's, do not rest on claims about the nature of the relationship between state officials and the public in whose name they act. They rest, instead, on claims about the positive effects of publicity on the behaviour of those who know they might be watched. According to this line of argument, publicity in criminal justice is necessary to motivate those who act on our behalf to uphold standards, abide by the rules, and resist temptations of corruption. Let's see then what these accounts have to say about the public's right to know about criminal records.

Sunlight Is the Best Disinfectant: Publicity to Reduce Corruption and the Abuse of Power

'Sunlight is said to be the best of disinfectants' wrote famously Louis Brandeis, one of the fathers of US privacy law and a Supreme Court Judge, in a 1913 article. Brandeis was echoing Jeremy Bentham, perhaps the strongest and most influential proponent of publicity in government and criminal justice. Bentham argued a century before Brandeis that exposing state activity to the public gaze was the only reliable means of disincentivizing corruption and abuses of power.[9] In his own words, 'Publicity is the very soul of justice. It is the keenest spur to exertion, and the surest of all guards against improbity' (Bentham, 1790). According to Bentham, agents of the state are inevitably subject to temptations to use their official power in self-serving ways rather than for the public good. This natural incentive to benefit oneself by doing wrong can, he argued, only be counteracted by more powerful incentives to do right. In Bentham's view, such positive incentives can be provided only by the glare of publicity. Bentham argued that knowing one's actions are open to scrutiny brings positive incentives in the form of 'respect for public opinion—dread of its judgments [and] desire of glory'. Meanwhile, the 'the dread of shame', and 'the fear of being removed' are so powerfully motivating that 'under the auspices of publicity, no evil can continue' (1999: 37).

Many have since followed Bentham in arguing that publicity with respect to official information is a corrective to the naturally corrupting effects of power and vital to deter poor conduct (O'Neill, 2002). Bentham's student John Stuart

[9] Kant before him also made publicity central to his moral and political philosophy. Luban (1998: 156) describes Kant's 'publicity principle' as posing the question 'could I still get away with this if my action and my reason for doing it were publicly known?'. In this way publicity acts as a test for the legitimacy of official acts, practices, and policies.

Mill was also a strong supporter of transparency in official information. Mill (1859) agreed with Bentham about sunlight's morally edifying effects on public officials. But whereas Bentham thought that the credible threat of disapproval was all that was needed to ward against abuses of power, Mill argued that transparency alone was insufficient for accountability. For Mill, transparency constitutes only the first step in a continuous process of accountability through active public participation. He argued that well-informed public scrutiny and debate is essential to genuine public accountability and that actual participation is what counts in making a thriving and well-administered public sphere.

Others have since developed Mill's efforts to highlight the limits of transparency without accountability and participation, pointing out that officials and political actors frequently engage in corrupt and unjust behaviour openly—and retain strong public support regardless. For example, Bauhr and Grimes's (2014) study of transparency in corrupt societies showed that openness about official acts is linked to public resignation about official wrongdoing and greater acceptance of the view that corruption is the only or the most efficient way to 'get things done'. Without strong and effective mechanisms of accountability, transparency can also fuel a sense of impunity and entitlement amongst those who break the rules in full view and get away with it. This body of work shows that access to information about the conduct of state agencies and officials *alone* may not be enough to secure effective public accountability and ultimately more efficient and fairer government.

Bentham and Mill give us multiple, important reasons to support publicity with respect to official information. But because the reasons relate to publicity's *instrumental* benefits, they only justify publicizing information when doing so actually delivers what it promises. In other words, the question remains whether releasing all kinds of 'official information' would have equally 'disinfecting' or 'informative' effects in practice. If publicizing some kinds of personal information about individuals normally has *no* such effects, then the very strong reasons in favour of doing so fade away. In which case, we need to look elsewhere to justify giving the public a presumptive entitlement to access it. And if there is no presumption in favour of publicity with respect to criminal record information, then policy and practice around disclosing it should be responsive to those considerations that do bear on them, such as the rights to privacy and rehabilitation of those it identifies.

Let's take a moment to reflect on what this implies for the public's right to access criminal records. I have already argued that considerations of transparency and accountability provide no grounds for a presumptive right to access repositories of such records. Neither do they provide reasons for the creation of such repositories in the first place. That remains the case whether we justify publicity in terms of its ability to shed light on official conduct, or its tendency to be morally edifying of public officials, or indeed in virtue of its role in informing and thereby improving public participation in the business and scrutiny of the state. In the next section, I consider how these points can be developed in relation to criminal record information that is shared or aired in the criminal courts, where norms around transparency, openness, and the public's right to know are far stronger than they are for registers and databases.

The accountability of officials and agencies to the wider public in whose name that power is exerted is not the same as the accountability of such actors to the specific individuals they exert power over. It is the former kind of accountability that Waldron, Bentham, and Mill emphasize in their theories, and which we have been considering until now. But the latter is just as central to debates about openness in criminal justice and seeing justice to be done. And the two kinds of accountability are mutually reinforcing. For it is often through the publicity given to individual cases of injustice and individual struggles to correct them that wider and systematic kinds of misconduct, corruption, and incompetence are exposed and, ultimately, addressed. As we will now see, this is especially important in the context of criminal trials.

Open Justice and the Criminal Court As the Ultimate Public Forum

Criminal records enter the public domain in a variety of different ways, including during criminal proceedings in a trial and as court records. Nowhere does the individual and the public right to accountability by the state intersect more evidently than in the legal entitlement of those accused of crimes to a 'public hearing' in 'open court'. That right is enshrined in individual constitutions and human rights instruments around the world, including the European Convention on Human Rights, and the Universal Declaration of Human Rights. At the same time, the principles of 'open justice', of justice needing to be 'seen to be done', and the notion that the criminal court is an essentially public forum are longstanding and entrenched in most democracies. Jurisdictions do differ significantly in the way they interpret these rights and principles in practice. But in many places, individual citizens and members of the press can attend and report from courts and, in some, proceedings are even streamed online for anyone to watch, record, and comment on. The public's right to know about and access criminal records is therefore closely entangled with strong norms and customs around the openness of criminal trials.

The publicity of criminal proceedings and of their records is strongly supported by principles of transparency and accountability put forward by Waldron, Bentham, and Mill above. I have just argued that those principles are not served by making repositories of criminal records publicly accessible, because even though those repositories might be created in the name of the public, the records themselves do not shed light on the conduct of state institutions and officials. The same cannot be argued for the proceedings of criminal trials. Trials involve close interaction between officials and individuals and therefore tell us much about the way our representatives treat individuals on our behalf. The conduct of police and prosecutors is itself often an object of explicit scrutiny during trials because errors, misconduct, corruption, or prejudice on their part can undermine the integrity of a case against a defendant. Both Bentham's and Waldron's theories therefore support publicity in criminal trials. But Waldron's theory is less helpful than Bentham's in explaining why the presumption in favour of publicity tends to be so particularly strong in this specific context. For Waldron, the public right to know arises in the same way with respect to any and all conduct performed in the public's name, irrespective of the context in or the purpose for which officials act. In contrast, Bentham's is sensitive to contextual differences in the risk of poor conduct by officials, and to the factors that might make publicity more protective against such risks in different arenas. As we will now see, the nature and the seriousness of the risks associated with secrecy in courts have long been held to provide special reasons to make publicity a fundamental feature of their practice.

Arguments for the publicity of criminal trials have been put forward throughout the history of liberal political and legal thought. They are repeated so often in so many writings on the topic that it would be artificial for us here to attempt to attribute them to any specific thinker or thinkers. It makes sense instead to provide a generic summary of this line of argument, highlighting its least contested and most important claims. That argument proceeds something like this: The state, and the criminal justice system in particular, wields exceptional freedom-infringing power over individuals on behalf of ordinary citizens. As we all know, 'power corrupts and absolute power corrupts absolutely'. So, the mere fact that trials concentrate power in state hands provides us with good reasons to institute strong mechanisms of transparency and accountability.

The argument I have just presented is abstract, but it is far from based merely in speculation and theory: history also provides us with strong evidence that such measures are necessary to prevent otherwise inevitable abuses of state power. Governments all over the world have used and still do use the judicial system to intimidate and silence opposition and to persecute those from oppressed ethnic, political, and religious communities. As I write this chapter, courts have supported a US President in pardoning his own son's criminal convictions, the jailing of dozens of pro-democracy activists in Hong Kong for 'conspiracy to subversion', and the arbitrary detention and reconviction for crimes already served of eighty-four Emirati human rights and other campaigners. Public scrutiny of criminal justice agencies, processes, and practices helps to identify these kinds of manipulation and unfairness. Ideally, it also helps to reduce it, through the application of public and international pressure. The particularly high stakes in a criminal trial justify particularly strong presumptions of publicity. Trials have the power to legitimately deprive people of their freedom for the rest of their lives, and in some jurisdictions also to deprive them of their lives. And governments everywhere have a strong track record of using secret trials to abuse that power and sentence people unjustly.

There are equally strong and related reasons to favour real-time scrutiny of trials through participation of the media. For one thing, contemporaneous review allows public pressure to bear in time to prevent an unjust punishment, rather than trying to contest or undo it after the fact.[10] But the courts are also often the last place of official recourse for people to challenge and appeal unfair criminalization by the state. If they are also turned against citizens, then the only place left to turn is the 'court of public opinion'. For this reason alone, it is vital that individuals can invite the media to report on their case or take other measures to draw public attention to it. Publicity is of course no guarantee of justice, but it is a necessary condition of it. It is because we all may one day find ourselves subjected to unjust criminal proceedings, as victim or suspect, that we all have an equal interest in being reassured that power will be exercised in ways that are fair and respectful of our rights. Justice must, for this reason, not only be done but be seen to be done. The openness of courts means the public can in principle be reassured that justice is being carried out impartially, or at least that departures from impartiality will be detected and exposed, and this helps to maintain public confidence in the criminal justice system.[11]

[10] 'Whatever other benefits the guarantee to an accused that his trial be conducted in public may confer upon our society, the guarantee has always been recognized as a safeguard against any attempt to employ our courts as instruments of persecution. The knowledge that every criminal trial is subject to contemporaneous review in the forum of public opinion is an effective restraint on possible abuse of judicial power' (Globe Newspaper Co. v. Superior Court, 1982).

[11] Public confidence is important, but its pursuit does not ground a right to know. And we should be wary of measures of publicity in criminal justice that are publicly justified in terms of 'maintaining public confidence'. Drakulich (2018) describes how in the United States, '"stagedperp walks" involve explicit coordination between the police and the press to provide the press with the opportunity to

But the media also has a deeper role to play in building public confidence, because without the active attendance and reporting of journalists at trials, the public would have no access to information about the proceedings that is comprehensible and accessible. Journalists attending court are often able to read information shared in the court but not publicly available, such as witness statements, without which they would not understand proceedings nor be able to report on them properly. Evidence and procedure in courts often involve huge amounts of information delivered over many days involving complex argument and counterargument, technical matters and legal jargon, all of which must be summarized and translated for the public. And good journalistic coverage can counteract the spread of misinformation or even just uninformed and inaccurate comment about criminal proceedings, which might otherwise undermine confidence or conceal injustice. All these considerations weigh heavily in favour of real-time public and media access to criminal trials, and freedom to report on what happens during proceedings.[12]

These reasons for making courts and court processes public are as relevant today as they were when they were first articulated. They remain powerful and convincing. But, as I will now argue, they do not address the question of what should happen to the records of those trials and, more specifically, to records that identify people as criminally suspect or convicted. To make that argument in its strongest form, it is worth considering the opposing view. In particular, it is worth considering a specific strand of legal thought which claims that open justice and public courts *always* require that court records too must be public.

Contesting the doctrine of public fact

In this section, we consider an influential strand of legal argument that is often relied on to justify what we might call total publicity of criminal records, and which I refer to as the doctrine of public fact.[13] The doctrine of public fact was developed in the United States, through case law concerning attempts to

photograph accused offenders as they are moved in public places'. The 'perp walk' of Harvey Weinstein is a familiar example. Here, transparency is being co-opted by the police to repair the (correct) public impression that the criminal justice system had persistently failed to hold known serial sexual offenders accountable for their crimes.

[12] It is an interesting question whether transparency should require the presence of a representative of the media. In some jurisdictions, local newspapers are legally obliged to print the outcome of cases relating to the area.

[13] For an in-depth legal and philosophical discussion of this notion, see Tunick, 2015, chapters 3 and 6. And for a detailed defence of it, see Anderson, 2012.

exercise a right to privacy with respect to information shared in courts. It claims that all court information must be freely available to the public, and that any less than untrammelled publicity would illegitimately undermine the openness of courts. The doctrine of public fact is categorical and may seem extreme to Europeans used to a public and legal culture that places much more value in privacy and rehabilitation. But it is not a straw man, for its total rejection of the notion of privacy in public has enduring power both in certain strands of popular opinion (Friedewald et al., 2015) and in certain academic circles.

The doctrine of public fact adopts the following reasoning. Criminal courts are public spaces, just like a town square or any other self-evidently open civic forum. Since people cannot reasonably expect to have privacy while in public spaces, there can be no right to privacy in courts. Similarly, any information shared in a court for the purpose of a criminal trial enters the public domain (i.e. the court) *legitimately* (i.e. without violating anyone's rights). Therefore, no one has any right to assert rights to privacy with respect to that information. And because the information has already been made public legitimately through its airing in court, no one may claim a right to prevent its further sharing or publication. The public has a right to speak about things that are already in the public domain. Therefore, were anyone to attempt to restrict access to or sharing of information shared in open court, that would constitute a violation of the right to freedom of speech. Indeed, to attempt to assert confidentiality with respect to court records would be equivalent to censorship. In this way, the doctrine of public fact supports a general public right to find out about and share any criminal record information shared or aired in court. Because it is the publicness of the court as an open forum that establishes the publicness of the information shared therein, it does not matter for what purpose the information is shared, nor what the consequences of sharing might be. The right to know is absolute.

Some of the US courts that have adopted this doctrine do recognize rights to hear elements of evidence in private, but not on grounds of privacy. If airing certain information in open court would undermine *the administration of justice* during the trial, then the court may be 'closed' while it is heard. For example, if a case concerned the alleged theft of trade secrets, and if airing the evidence in public would expose those very secrets, thereby undermining the entire case, and indeed its purpose, then US courts might accept a legitimate need for confidentiality. In such circumstances, no conflict with freedom of speech occurs with respect to those court records heard in private. That's because, in such cases, the closed court is no longer a public space, so information shared within it does not qualify as 'public fact'. For those who accept the doctrine of public fact, it is the nature of the space rather than the nature of the information that determines its status as public or private.

As I will now attempt to show, relying on the doctrine of public fact to determine the boundaries of the public's right to know is not only misguided but dangerous. It is misguided because the reasoning on which that doctrine rests—and which I have just set out above—sidesteps the real moral question at stake. That question concerns how we can reconcile respect for rights to privacy, dignity, and rehabilitation with the need for democratic accountability and openness in criminal justice. It is dangerous because, when applied in practice, it enforces rules that are arbitrary, and which senselessly harm some people without benefiting any others. To see why, we need to bring to the surface and expose the problematic assumptions and claims that underpin the core position of the doctrine of public facts. There are at least three. The first is the claim that the nature of the space in which some information about a person is aired *alone* determines whether that person could legitimately assert a right to privacy about that information. The second is the claim that the fact that some information is shared or recorded in *one kind of public space* with *one kind of audience* means there can be no legitimate claims of a right to privacy when it is shared in *other kinds of public spaces* with *other kinds of audiences*. The third is the claim that if some information is shared or recorded in a public space at *one moment in time*, no one may legitimately claim a right to privacy with respect to its further sharing *at any other time, ever*. Not only do these claims defy practice and intuition. They also support practices that are plainly unjust.

The problems with the doctrine of public fact are well illustrated by the real case of *Briscoe v. Reader's Digest Association Inc.* In 1956, Marvin Briscoe, an American man, was convicted of hijacking a truck. He was sentenced to time in prison and served it fully. After his release, Briscoe made efforts to clean up his act and turn a new leaf. He eventually built a successful life and career for himself, leaving his early involvement in crime far behind. Then, eleven years after the hijacking, the Reader's Digest magazine published an article titled *The Big Business of Hijacking.* Everything changed. The article exposed the world of truck thefts, detailing various incidents amongst which was that involving Briscoe, who they identified as a hijacker by name. It was published in thirteen languages and distributed in a hundred nations. In California alone, where Briscoe lived, its circulation reached almost two million copies. After reading the article, Briscoe's friends and daughter cut him off and would not speak to him. He also claimed to have been subjected to widespread social 'humiliation, contempt, and ridicule'. His case against the Reader's Digest concerned his claim to a right to privacy with respect to information about his criminal history which had entered the public domain through court reporting at the time of the trial.

At its first hearing, Briscoe's complaint was dismissed as ineligible, on the ground that information about his conviction was a 'public fact' and was therefore by definition excluded from any claim to privacy. In dismissing the case, the court did not consider the impact of the publication of his criminal history on Briscoe's life. It did not consider the amount of time that had passed between the conviction and the publication. Nor was it interested in whether identifying Briscoe as a hijacker served any public interest. Instead, it held that such considerations were simply irrelevant. The fact that the information was accurate and had been aired in open court was, in the court's view, sufficient to establish the public's right to know and the press's right to publish. This was the doctrine of public fact in action.

Briscoe appealed against the initial decision to disallow his suit against the Reader's Digest. This time round, he was successful. The court of appeal rejected the doctrine of public fact and upheld Briscoe's right to privacy. It accepted that the court in which Briscoe had been tried was a public forum to which the public had a presumptive right of access. But, unlike the first court hearing, it did not accept that this settled the question of the public's right to access or republish historic or non-recent court records. In fact, it rejected the idea that the fact that the criminal trial is designated a public space is sufficient reason to exclude such considerations from weighing on its judgement in any particular case.[14] This allowed it to put back on the table the real moral questions about how to resolve apparent conflicts between the values at stake. And so the court argued that judges had every right to consider whether the publication of court records undermines the ability of the criminal justice system to achieve its purposes, amongst which it explicitly included the rehabilitation of offenders. It also affirmed the judges' right to consider whether there was any countervailing public interest in the publication of Briscoe's name alongside his crimes. In other words, both the purposes and the impact of publication were relevant to determining the merits of Briscoe's claim.

The appeal court's reasoning in upholding Briscoe's right to privacy with respect to his criminal record rested on two key claims. The first was that the state had an important interest in enabling citizens to rehabilitate after criminal

[14] In his 2009 book on sex offender registration, Logan argues rightly that the mere fact that the information is public in a technical sense in no way resolves the deeper question of whether individuals have a legitimate privacy interest in preventing or limiting its publication (Logan, 2009: 143).

punishment and that, in the case of Briscoe, recognizing a right to privacy was necessary to protect this interest. As the judges said: 'where a person has ... rehabilitated himself, we, as right-thinking members of society, should permit him to continue in the path of rectitude rather than throw him back into a life of shame or crime'. The second was that the identification of the actor in reports of long past crimes usually serves little independent public purpose. In their words: 'Once legal proceedings have terminated, and a suspect or offender has been released, identification of the individual will not usually aid the administration of justice. Identification will no longer serve to bring forth witnesses or obtain succor for victims. Unless the individual has reattracted the public eye to himself in some independent fashion, the only public "interest" that would usually be served is that of curiosity'. The appeal court held that the satisfaction of public curiosity does not justify torpedoing Briscoe's rehabilitation.

The length of time that had passed between the conviction and its publication in Reader's Digest was an important factor in the court's decision and worth paying attention to here. The judgement implied that, the closer in time to the trial and conviction, the stronger the public interest in asserting a right to know about the records of those proceedings, but the weaker the individual case for a right to privacy, and vice versa. This makes sense. Rehabilitation is not typically something that happens immediately. Rather, it is a process that takes place over time, sometimes years, even decades. As Briscoe moved on from his crime, making new life plans and increasingly achieving them, his criminal history became less and less representative of who he was. Yet the informational trace of that history, immortalized in the records from his trial, did not change in step with him. For this reason, the potential harm done to his rehabilitation by publicly associating him with his record increased over time.

Briscoe's experience confirmed this. When his record resurfaced eleven years later, the effect on his life was immediately destructive, despite the evident dissonance between the person described in the criminal record and that which he had become. At the same time, few or none of the very strong reasons for facilitating contemporaneous public and media access to criminal trials—detailed in the previous section above—still applied to Briscoe's case eleven years later. No one, including Briscoe, doubted the fairness of his conviction. Nor had anyone, not even Briscoe, sought at any time to contest it. Restricting the reporting of Briscoe's name in relation to his crimes was no interference with open justice once that justice had been seen to be done.

Briscoe's case serves to show that the importance of openness, transparency, and accountability in criminal trials does not always justify making criminal records aired in court publicly available after the fact. In other words, the reasons for giving publicity to criminal proceedings do not by themselves justify publicity of criminal records once those proceedings have concluded. Practices in many jurisdictions reflect this conclusion. For example, the European Union recognizes a 'right to be forgotten' by which people can apply to have reports of their convictions and other records removed from media sites and search engines such as Google, once the information is no longer 'relevant' to their identity. Similar regulations are being introduced in India, Russia, Mexico, Japan, and Colombia (Nunziato, 2017). In many countries, including Germany, France, the Netherlands, Japan, and South Korea, court records and judgements are anonymized before being published, with exceptions for trials of particular public interest, for example, those concerning public figures or political corruption. And in common-law countries such as the United Kingdom and Australia, records of convictions become 'spent' after a specified amount of time, after which they cannot be disclosed by officials or published freely by the press. There is no evidence that these practices have eroded transparency or accountability in criminal justice, nor that they have increased the risk that criminal justice officials are less likely to act in the public interest.

Above, I argued that the creation and maintenance of repositories of criminal records cannot be justified by appeal to the values of democratic transparency and accountability. Now, I have also just rejected the doctrine of public fact's insistence that there can be no right to privacy with respect to records of criminal proceedings. I have argued that such a right can be asserted, in virtue of its promotion of the important value of rehabilitation. And I have argued, further, that recognizing a right to privacy need not involve any trade-off with open justice or public accountability, because the records it protects from public view would in most cases provide no insight into the conduct of criminal justice officials, or the fairness of the outcome. But I have also argued that timing is important, and that both acknowledgement of the status of the trial as a public forum and real-time public scrutiny of live criminal proceedings are necessary for justice to be seen to be done. The question arises then whether openness requires freedom to report the *identities* of the parties publicly, beyond the confines of the court. How and when is naming people important to seeing justice to be done? We now take up that question.

Criminal records and naming parties during criminal proceedings

Familiarity often leads us to assume that the way things are done in our own judicial system is the right or natural way to do them. Such assumptions often characterize reactions to proposals to change the status quo around public access to criminal records. Such reactions range from incredulity to dismissing the proposals as obviously impractical. In publicity-friendly countries such as the United States and the United Kingdom, where people are used to reading the names of people accused and convicted of crimes in the daily news, proposals to restrict public access to the identities of those accused and convicted have been decried as impossible and disruptive. For example, in 2009 one UK Judge, Lord Hope, argued that preventing the media from reporting the real names of defendants in trials would threaten the very existence of the free press. Stories about crime that omitted real names would, he argued, be 'devoid of human interest' and forcing the press to publish them would 'threaten the viability of newspapers and magazines, which can only inform the public if they attract enough readers and make enough money to survive' (Lord Hope of Craighead in In re British Broadcasting Corporation, 1999, para.25). Let us not get distracted by Lord Hope's morally questionable implication that it is acceptable to use those accused of crime as clickbait to keep the public reading the news. More important is his claim that the media would not survive the anonymization of trials, which is demonstrably preposterous.[15] In Germany and Spain, where identities of defendants and offenders may not be published subject to exceptions, but all the other details of criminal cases can be reported, there is a thriving independent media.[16] And, incidentally, reoffending rates in Germany are one third lower than those in the United States, where trials are routinely televised (Yukhnenko et al., 2023).

Around the world, both legislatures and judges are constantly grappling with and finding ways to resolve tensions between privacy and openness. In most jurisdictions, legislation and judicial discretion are used routinely by judges to place restrictions on what kind of information shared during any specific trial can be reported outside it. Concern for the privacy, dignity, and safety of those involved in trials are the reasons most often motivating such restrictions. For example, in the United Kingdom and many other European countries, restrictions on media reporting the names of people involved in a trial are often imposed to protect the privacy of children, witnesses, and certain kind of victims, in particular victims of sexual assault and rape. In many jurisdictions, the identities of those who appear before juvenile courts are concealed by law. Witnesses may be permitted to give evidence anonymously and from behind

[15] This has not stopped other Judges repeating it.

[16] For an excellent analysis of the contrasting approaches of the USA and Spain, see Jacobs and Larrauri (2012).

screens if their safety and security might otherwise be at stake.[17] Restrictions are also frequently placed on the republication of distressing or humiliating material shared in a trial, such as photographs or video of crimes or their aftermath, including in particular when sharing these would violate the dignity of a victim or witness.[18] Even the identities of those accused are sometimes subject to reporting restrictions, when there are concerns that publicizing their name might expose them to serious harm.

Do courts that impose such restrictions undermine open justice, transparency, or democratic accountability? To argue so would be absurd. In the United Kingdom, even when judges impose reporting restrictions, court proceedings remain public to the extent that private individuals and journalists can attend, view, and hear material and information shared during the trial, and report on all aspects of it that have not been barred from further dissemination. Judges also must be open about what they are restricting and why. In other words, the public has a right to know what is being excluded from its right to know and on what grounds.[19] We can of course have a reasonable debate about whether a specific law or judge is getting the balance right in any particular case. But the fact that concerns about potential violations of privacy, dignity, and safety may in some cases justify restrictions on court reporting seems already to be accepted even in places where there is a presumption in favour of a right to know. The question remains to what extent such concerns justify restrictions on the identification of defendants and offenders, given the countervailing requirements of openness.

Can public scrutiny and accountability in the courts really be effective if ordinary members of the public can't find out who is accused without personally attending the court or share information about them when they do attend? I think that it can, as long as defendants retain the right to draw public attention to their case, by speaking to the media about their criminal record, and inviting the media to report on their trial.[20] It is difficult to see how knowing the

[17] There are strong reasons not to allow defendants anonymity within court, to do with the importance of faces and expressions to support judgements of innocence or guilt, and of allowing actors in the proceedings to look people in the eye when questioning or referring to them.

[18] For a detailed discussion of the special intrusiveness of photo and video material, see Moreham, 2006, who cites Judge Lord Phillips M.R's statement in Douglas vs Hello! that: 'Nor is it right to treat a photograph simply as conveying factual information. A photograph can certainly capture every detail of a momentary even words cannot, but a photograph can do more than that. A personal photograph can portray, not necessarily accurately, the personality and the mood of the subject of the photograph.'

[19] For a seminal discussion on the public's right to know about the scope of state secrecy, see Thompson, 1999.

[20] Larrauri (2014: 67) also makes the point that resolving 'the tensions that confidential criminal records create with the publicity of judgments . . . is usually handled by arguing that although the judgment is public the criminal record is not.' And Cooper (2019) argues that publicity with respect to the identities of parties in a dispute is not necessary for justice.

identity of the accused and convicted would help to shed light on the kinds of incompetence, prejudice, and injustices we see routinely occurring in criminal systems. Such injustices *are* enabled by a lack of public scrutiny, whether this is due to secrecy or to the indifference of the media to anything but the most salacious or outrageous cases. But in most cases naming those affected would do little to improve practice.

To see why, consider a specific issue of controversy in contemporary legal practice in many countries. This is the increasing prevalence of guilty pleas and 'trial waivers' around the world, especially in Europe and the United States (Selbin et al., 2018). Getting people to plead guilty in order to waive the need for a trial is a procedure that is attractive from the perspective of the criminal justice system because it avoids the significant resource burdens of mounting a trial. But guilty pleas and trial waivers work poorly for suspects, who end up pressured to plead guilty to crimes they may not have committed or of which they stood a good chance of being acquitted, or the full consequences of which they do not understand.[21] These measures overwhelmingly affect people from racialized groups, those who cannot afford lawyers, and those who are vulnerable and less likely to understand their rights or the risks involved. Their use is enabled by the fact that plea bargaining and decisions to accept waivers take place in a confidential setting, for obvious reasons. But it is hard to see how greater public awareness of the names of those involved would address this issue. It would be more conducive to transparency to release details of cases and negotiations, than names. This would enable the public to scrutinize the extent to which decisions to accept a conviction are genuinely voluntary and informed. Similarly, a description of the demographic and socio-economic characteristics of the person involved would promote transparency, because it is these characteristics that tend to invite treatment that is prejudicial and discriminatory. The same can be argued for many other kinds of criminal injustice.

What are the implications of all this for actual practice? In his 2002 analysis of public access to official information in the United States, privacy scholar Daniel Solove advocates what he calls 'altering levels of accessibility' for public records. He argues that 'governments can make a public record available on the condition that certain information is not disclosed or used in a certain manner and by making access conditional on accepting certain responsibilities when using data—such as using it for specific purposes, not disclosing

[21] The campaign organization Fair Trials has done much to draw attention to the problematic nature of these processes.

it to others, and so on, certain functions of transparency can be preserved at the same time privacy is protected'. (Solove, 2002:1173).[22] A similar approach makes sense in the context of criminal justice. Respect for transparency, accountability, and open justice is compatible with a general presumption against permitting the publication of the names of defendants and offenders, with at least three caveats. First, defendants and others affected by the criminal justice system must always retain the right to name themselves and draw public attention to their case. Second, confidentiality should be lifted when the defendant is a public official or when their conduct concerns other officials or official business. Third, judges should in every case consider the extent to which naming the parties to a case would be in the public interest or conducive to the administration of justice, and should act within their discretion to do so. These measures would do much to remove barriers to the rehabilitation of people with criminal records, without undermining transparency and openness in criminal justice procedures. And they are not incompatible with giving some actors access to the full records, when doing so serves a public interest. For example, journalists, researchers, and others working to increase understanding and accountability of the criminal justice system could apply for the full de-anonymized records, and those could be shared with caveats. Private companies collating criminal history data to sell to employers and others would not qualify, as their activities neither enable accountability nor serve any public interest.

Openness in Courts but Confidentiality in Policing

The discussion above has focussed on the courts, but other areas of criminal justice that also produce criminal records tend to be far less open to the public than the courts across jurisdictions. There is, for example, no human right to be policed in an 'open forum'. The reason for this cannot be that police conduct is carried out less 'in our name' than that of prosecutors and judges. Nor can it be that the risk of official abuses of power by police is lower than the risks of abuse by prosecutors and judges. As Judith Shklar noted in her famous 1989 essay, *The Liberalism of Fear*, policing has always been used as a tool of brutality, oppression, and persecution. Over thirty years later, continued police killings of racialized citizens in the United

[22] More specific proposals along the same lines have been put forward by, amongst others, Sudbeck (2005).

States, United Kingdom, and France, as well as violent suppression of civil rights and environmental protest, show us that police power is still something to fear today. The diffident, mistrustful, and even hostile attitude of many citizens towards the police in their countries confirms this. The high risks of injustice in policing also support a very strong presumption of openness around misconduct proceedings following accusations of police abuses or corruption.

Some US legislators have adopted explicitly Benthamite reasoning to justify proposals for radical transparency around policing, akin to what is already established in the courts. Specifically, they have appealed to the high risk of police abuse and misconduct to defended laws mandating states to post information on all arrests online for anyone to access, and making police body-camera footage available to the public (Solove, 2002: 1170). Meanwhile, others have appealed to a more Millian concern for public participation to justify measures enabling the public to attend police incidents. In 2016, one US-based startup developed an app which enabled members of the public to tune their radios into local emergency calls, so they could choose to attend incidents themselves. Tellingly, the app was called 'Citizen' and its tagline was 'Can Injustice Survive Transparency?'. Concerns about the wisdom of inviting curious citizens to become involved in situations that are dangerous, unpredictable, and that require a professional emergency response led to the removal of Citizen from the Apple app store within days of its launch. But the very fact that the app could freely access the frequencies of police emergency lines and radios is itself remarkable.

Such examples serve to illustrate the problematic places to which devotion to transparency can lead us. However, the United States is a global outlier in its support of radical openness with respect to policing. In most countries, police accountability and the public right to know are achieved not through direct access to real-time information but by instituting official independent oversight mechanisms like ombudsmen and inspectorates, giving journalists regular updates about arrests and investigations, and involving members of the public as independent observers on ride-alongs, in custody spaces, and scrutiny panels. Individual rights to contest poor treatment at the hands of police are accommodated by making data, including recordings from body cameras and of interviews and interrogations, available to those directly involved, or to other bodies investigating wrongdoing, and instituting strong channels for complaint. Direct and real-time scrutiny by the public is not generally enabled or permitted, and the identities of suspects, victims, and witnesses alike are presumptively protected.

I want to argue that there are good reasons for these practices of privacy around policing. They relate to the obvious importance of confidentiality in encouraging people to report crime and of secrecy in enabling police to investigate it effectively. But they also protect the privacy of people in exceptionally sensitive and exposing circumstances. Police are often called to incidents in private and intimate spaces to respond to crises involving extreme human vulnerability. Domestic violence and child abuse, mental health crises and suicide attempts, fatal car crashes and drug overdoses are the routine business of police everywhere. But for the people involved, these awful events are likely to be the most personal, visceral, and demeaning moments of their lives. The dignity of those people would be inevitably violated by a practice of letting citizens and journalists attend incidents or access and repost footage or recordings online.[23] Their right to privacy and the importance of confidentiality in enabling the reporting of crime are therefore taken by most governments to outweigh the interests of the public in being able to directly scrutinize all exercises of police power. Even those scholars and lawyers who support the reasoning behind the doctrine of public fact—that information about acts which take place in a public forum can never be private—would not have grounds to support the presumptive publicity of police records, because much of the information that finds its way into such records, including arrests, cautions, risk assessments, and the laying of charges in fact happens in private spaces, at people's homes or places of work, or in a police interrogation room.

Conclusion

Political philosopher Bernard Harcourt points out that "seeing, monitoring, and recording . . .is quite different from sharing, releasing, revealing or publicizing" (Harcourt 2015). In this chapter, I have drawn on these and related distinctions to chart a path between public and private that respects both the need for openness, transparency, and accountability in the criminal justice system, and the dignity and privacy of those whose lives become entangled in it. I've defended a general presumption of confidentiality with respect to publication in open forums of the identities of those individuals, but have also argued for wide judicial discretion to determine where the balance between publicity and privacy should lie in specific cases. I've also provided reasons in support of

[23] For a useful discussion of the legal rights to privacy of people involved in humiliating, demeaning, or intimate activities in public, including with respect to policing, see Moreham, 2006.

existing rules and customs of privacy and confidentiality with respect to policing. Of course, not all defences of a general right of citizens to know about each other's criminal records appeal to the values discussed in this chapter. Some claim instead that sharing criminal records is justified as a kind of punishment for those who commit crimes or to promote public safety and protect the vulnerable against serial and predatory offenders. The next two chapters examine those arguments in depth.

5

Public Criminal Records and Just Punishment

Introduction 99
Untangling Public Criminal Labelling, Stigmatization, and Censure 102
The Communicative Justification for Public Labelling as Punishment 107
Communicative theory and the benefits of public labelling as punishment 109
Limitations of labelling as punishment for the communicative theory 110
The wrong kind of reaction to criminality 111
A civic duty to punish? 112
Non-punitive reactions to criminal labels 113
Unfair and disproportionate punishment 115
Would public commitment to communitive punishment solve the problems? 117
Forcing people to acknowledge and respond to criminality 119
Complex societies and the challenge to effective communication 121
Public Criminal Labelling as a Deterrent to Crime 123
Facilitating Punishment Through Exposure: The 'flypaper' Strategy 127
Conclusion 130

Introduction

Do people who commit crimes deserve to be exposed publicly as wrongdoers? Is the prospect of such exposure precisely what deters most of us from committing crime in the first place? In this chapter, we consider these and related questions, by examining the punitive justifications for making criminal records public. The idea that publicizing people's crimes is a justified way of holding them accountable is perhaps the most obvious line of defence for a right to know. If we believe it is important for legal systems to punish those found guilty of crimes and to punish them fairly, and if identifying or labelling those convicted of crimes publicly as criminals does just that, then we have a strong reason to make criminal records public. What's more, if publicizing criminality is justified as a form of punishment, then the considerable harms a public criminal record causes to those convicted (described in detail in Chapter 2) are, however unpleasant, not necessarily unfair.

The Crimes of Others. Katerina Hadjimatheou, Oxford University Press. © Katerina Hadjimatheou 2026.
DOI: 10.1093/9780198925149.003.0005

There are at least three different ways in which punitive rationales could be drawn upon to defend a general right to access criminal records. The first involves arguing that public identification or labelling of people convicted of crimes is a necessary and unavoidable part of the process of punishment. Such arguments claim that identifying offenders is just an essential part of what it means to publicly condemn (or, in the terminology of penal theory 'censure') someone. And if we can't punish *without* applying a visible criminal record or label, then a right to punish necessarily yields a right to know. The second kind of argument involves showing that labelling criminals publicly contributes to one or more of the justifying *aims* of punishment, specifically retribution (giving wrongdoers what they deserve) and deterrence (disincentivizing those who already have committed crimes, or who might be considering committing them, from doing so). The third kind of argument claims that publicizing criminal records—and specifically the names of those who have committed crimes—can facilitate criminal accountability by encouraging as-yet-unknown victims to come forward. Exploring these kinds of arguments also yields insights and conclusions that are relevant beyond retribution and deterrence, for example, to abolitionist approaches to criminal justice that advocate what is known as 'reintegrative shaming' or other kinds of community response.

In this chapter, I begin by arguing that stigmatization and the public labelling of criminals that triggers it are not in some sense essential to punishment, as some theorists have implied, but rather must be defended by appeal to their contribution to one or more of the justifying aims or functions of punishment. I then consider the communicative and the deterrence functions in turn. I focus on the communicative account of punishment because it is one of the most influential retributive accounts of punishment in scholarly circles today. I believe it can also offer the most convincing punitive case for a right to know about people's convictions. Deterrence is also worth considering, not least because it continues to be the criminal justice aim police and policy makers mention most frequently when they defend decisions to label people publicly as criminal. Deterrence theory is also enjoying something of a renaissance in recent scholarly justifications of punishment that take liberal political theory as their starting point (Flanders, 2017; Chiao, 2016). Neither the communicative nor the deterrence case for public labelling of criminals have been subject to much critical scrutiny in the academic literature.

In what follows, I reject both communicative and deterrent justifications for public labelling. I argue that the communicative justification for public criminal labelling fails because it delegates the right and the duty to punish to individual citizens. At best, this places demands on individuals to punish that are both unrealistic and unreasonable. At worst, it leads to inevitable disproportionality, that is, some people being punished less or more than they deserve. Disproportionality in punishment is difficult to avoid even with standardized punishments like incarceration or fines, because these deprivations are inevitably harder for some to bear than others. For example, people who are sole parents of dependent children are in general likely to suffer more from imprisonment than those who are not, for obvious reasons. But I will argue that the disproportionality that results from public labelling is harder to justify than the inevitable disproportionality that results from standardized punishments. This is because the former is likely to be the product of morally objectionable attitudes towards those labelled and their victims, whereas the latter is an unavoidable consequence of applying the laudable principle of treating like crimes alike. I close by arguing that many of the considerations put forward here apply also to other non-communicative retributive defences of punishment.

I also reject justifications for public labelling grounded in its value as a deterrent. To do that, I draw on recent empirical work in labelling theory to argue that public labelling aggravates reoffending and thus fails to deter the group most likely to commit crime, namely those who already have convictions. Some people defend shaming sanctions in virtue of their deterrent effects, and because my case against deterrence applies also to shaming, I do not consider the justice of shaming sanctions as a stand-alone issue here.[1] Defences of shaming sanctions that rest on the idea that shaming people is a fitting form of deprivation or suffering in its own right even if it does not produce any positive outcomes are, in my view, difficult to swallow, so I do not address them here.[2]

My arguments are relevant to considerations of whether publicizing criminal labels is justified as a 'collateral consequence' of punishment. Collateral consequences are burdens or penalties that accompany or follow legal punishment, but which are not specified in the criminal law or imposed as a formal aspect of the sentence (Lafollette, 2005). If fair and just processes of conviction and punishment unavoidably involve publicizing a person's criminal record, then public criminal labelling might be justified as a by-product of punishment. In what follows I will argue that punishment does not require publicity of criminal labels, and therefore that public labelling is not a necessary or unavoidable collateral consequence of punishment. My arguments also

[1] See Braithwaite's 1989 Crime, Shame and Reintegration.

[2] This position is defended by Moore (1989) but rejected by Nussbaum (2004), Kahan (2006) and Arneson (2007).

suggest that the harms of public criminal labelling raise issues of fairness and proportionality, which must be addressed if those harms are to be justified. As has been argued extensively in the context of debates about war, fairness, and proportionality considerations apply not only to actions and policies—like decisions about when to attack or how to punish—but also to the by-products thereof.[3]

I close the chapter by defending a distinct line of penal reasoning in support of publicizing criminal records. That argument, which I call the defence of the 'flypaper strategy', claims that publicizing criminal records is sometimes necessary to facilitate or enable criminal accountability, especially with respect to serial but 'hidden' crimes like rape, sexual assault, and other crimes of abuse.

Untangling Public Criminal Labelling, Stigmatization, and Censure

In Chapter 2, we saw that the harms and wrongs that have been associated with public criminal records arise in part because publicly identifying or labelling someone as criminal is stigmatizing. Before examining the communicative and deterrence potential of public labelling, I want to consider the claim that stigmatization is a defining and therefore inevitable feature of criminal punishment. This claim—that to punish *just is* to stigmatize—is important. It implies that, irrespective of which purposes one might believe justify punishment, wherever punishment is the appropriate reaction to an act, so is criminal stigmatization. If this is correct, then the fact that labelling someone as criminal stigmatizes them is by itself no reason not to label them *if it is morally legitimate to punish them*. I'm going to argue that this view mistakenly conflates censure, which is indeed a defining feature of punishment, with criminal stigmatization, which is not. If I'm correct, then the fact that punishment is the correct response to an act is not sufficient reason to publicly label and so stigmatize someone as criminal.

As discussed in Chapter 2, stigmatization involves the process of marking someone out in some visible and identifiable way as having a characteristic that is deeply discrediting (Goffman, 1963:3). The more discrediting the characteristic, the more stigmatizing the marking out; the more visible and identifying the mark, the more it dominates other (potentially redeeming) facts about the

[3] For a seminal discussion of this issue in the context of just war theory see Walzer's (2015: 151–159) Just and Unjust Wars . More recently these issues have been addressed in the context of collateral consequences of conviction by Hoskins (2019).

person.[4] Most stigmatizing acts of marking out are motivated by negative attitudes and reactions to some actual or perceived quality of the individual being labelled. But negative motivations are not a necessary or sufficient feature of stigmatization. Negative *reactions* on the other hand are essential to stigmatization. For example, it is possible that an act of marking out is intended to degrade but in practice has the effect of honouring: the act is then intended to stigmatize, but fails to do so. The reverse is also true, because an act of labelling can stigmatize unintentionally, in virtue of how others respond to it.[5] Therefore it is the response, not the motivation, that constitutes stigmatization. As we saw in Chapter 2 (and as sociologists have long argued), the negative reactions associated with stigmatization are what make it properly understood as *burdensome*. I would argue that status loss is the core or essential burden of stigmatization, acting as both the cause and one of the outcomes of the marking out. Discrimination and disadvantage flow from this primary burden as a person is both alienated and excluded from activities and opportunities open to the non-stigmatized (Link and Phelan, 2001).[6]

The extent to which criminal stigmatization actually occurs as a result of the imposition of a criminal label depends on how people in different relationships to a person interpret and react to their label. The imposition of an identical criminal label on two different people can lead to stigmatization of one but not of another. Whether and to what extent a label is stigmatizing is determined in part by the social status of the individual labelled. For example, positions of privilege occupied by some people in society can protect them from at least some of the status loss and disadvantage that would likely result for others similarly labelled (Link and Phelan, 2001). Money, power, and status can serve to insulate people from the losses and degradations of criminal stigmatization.

The extent to which a criminal label is stigmatizing also depends on the values of a person's relevant peer group. Someone who receives a criminal conviction may find that their status amongst immediate peers is enhanced, even as the conviction alienates them from the broader, disapproving public.[7]

[4] See Braithwaite 1989 for a criminological justification of the criterion of dominance over other features of a person.

[5] Thanks to Antony Duff for pointing out this to me.

[6] While status loss is inherent to stigmatization, it can occur without stigmatization. Jean Hampton puts forward a theory of retributive punishment as an infliction of status loss on the offender designed to deny the claim to superiority implicit in the criminal act and thus to vindicate the victim's equal worth (Murphy and Hampton, 1988: 125–128). Status loss in Hampton occurs as a result of the mastery of another, mastery that may include but is certainly not limited or reduced to the making of a status-degrading mark.

[7] Walker, 1980: 102–103. Differences between the extent to which different individuals experience an identical criminal label as stigmatizing seems likely to vary relative to the extent to which: the labelled

The extent of stigmatization also depends on how public the label is. Publicity is constituted in part by prominence and in part by reach, so a label is more 'public' the more people it is visible to *and* the more conspicuous it is, with conspicuous meaning hard to overlook or ignore. Other things being equal, the greater the number of people to whom the label is visible and the more negative their reactions to it are, the worse the loss of status is likely to be. At the same time, a label that is difficult to ignore, or dominates other visible aspects of a person, is more likely to provoke negative reactions than one which onlookers can pretend not to have noticed. For example, a criminal record that is only disclosable on application for certain sensitive jobs is less stigmatizing than a high-visibility 'convict' shirt or orange boiler suit of the kind offenders in some countries are forced to wear while carrying out community service penalties.

Some legal theorists claim or imply in their writings that stigma overlaps or is synonymous with censure (the expression of moral condemnation or disapproval in response to a criminal wrongdoing) and therefore inevitable whenever punishment occurs. Censure is commonly accepted to be a defining feature of punishment, with coercion, deprivation or 'hard treatment' being the other (Husak, 2008). For example, John Kleinig (1998: 273) states that 'punishment involves a stigmatizing condemnation of the punished'. Thomas and Thompson argue that 'censure and public shaming are intrinsic to the process of sentencing and press reporting is part of that censure' (2010: 346). And Andrew Taslitz claims that 'disesteem-imposition, even if not phrased quite this way, is a clear goal of our criminal justice system. The system assumes that conviction carries stigma with it and that the degrees of, and actual imposition of, various sentences reflect various degrees of disesteem' (Taslitz, 2009: 313, 414).[8] This conflation of stigma and censure is problematic because it leaves out at least two essential aspects of the former not shared by the latter, namely marking out and visibility. I have already argued that stigmatization necessarily involves marking someone out in a visible way. But criminal censure need not involve a process of marking out visibly.[9] This fact is concealed by talk about criminal labelling that implies that publicity is integral to it.

individual identifies with the disapproving group; their sense of status is determined by their position in relation to that group; how actually aspire to the goals in relation to whose attainment they are now at a disadvantage.

[8] Similarly, Mendlow (2022) talks about Lockean natural right entitlements to impose a 'stigmatising deprivation' but never explains the role of stigmatization, rather assuming it is an essential aspect of punishment.

[9] The question of whether stigmatization can occur without publicity was raised in a juridical context in relation to the case of Marper, where the referral by the Chamber of the ECtHR to the criminal stigmatization of unconvicted individuals whose DNA data was nevertheless retained by police was

To see how this problem arises, consider Liz Campbell's definition of criminal labelling as being 'depicted and censured openly as criminal' (Campbell 2013: 690, my italics). Campbell does not explain why openness need be so central, but the implication that criminal censure requires publicity overlooks the fact that it could—and indeed in many jurisdictions often does—happen in closed proceedings. Even in places which generally favour publicity in all areas of criminal justice, such as the United Kingdom and the United States, some categories of trials involve closed proceedings. This is the case, for example, for certain kinds of terrorism trials, and proceedings in juvenile courts. In closed proceedings, the official declaration of criminal guilt is witnessed by few people and the offender's anonymity is guaranteed. The fact that declarations of guilt and sentencing in such cases occur in private does not by itself render the censure any less condemnatory. Nor does it render the censure any less expressive of public disapproval, at least in the sense that 'public' can be taken to mean disapproval expressed in the name of the public via legitimate democratic mechanisms.[10] In other words, unlike stigmatization, which—other things being equal—increases with the publicity given to a stigmatic label, censure need be no less censorious if it is delivered in relative private.[11]

The points I am making here should not be taken to imply that public disapproval expressed in response to criminal labelling is not censorious; only that it is not necessary to the specific kind of censure that is itself a defining aspect of punishment.[12] Those who define the expression or direction of public disapproval towards a person through criminal censure as stigmatizing may be confusing the attitudes motivating the *imposition* of criminal censure with those

challenged by the UK government, which countered that stigma could not arise in the absence of a public articulation of suspicion (R v. Chief Constable of South Yorkshire Police, *ex parte* LS and Marper [2004] UKHL 94–122).

[10] This stands in contrast to the claims of some theorists that, in order to achieve its aims, censure must also be communicated to the public. For example, Ashworth and Zedner have recently claimed that it is 'inherent' to the exercise of censure that it be communicated 'to the victim (if any) and to the public at large' (Ashworth and Zedner, 2014: 14). While it seems obvious that an individual cannot be persuaded to repent unless they are told that what they have done is wrong, it is on the face of things far from evident why either persuasion to repent or repentance itself depends on communication of that message to the public at large. The rationale for public communication of censure becomes clearer when we consider the claim that all crimes are always crimes against the community and the claim that victims of crime have a right to take part in the persuasion of criminals to repent and in the acceptance of apologies and repentance.

[11] There is no inconsistency between this claim and the observation that being censured by more people may imply more censure. This is because the claim (and indeed the issue at hand) regards the impact on censure of its being done in public. It does not regard the related but distinct issue of the impact on censure of greater participation in the act of censure.

[12] Lippke (2018) argues in a related vein that 'it does not follow that shielding the identities of offenders from routine public scrutiny transforms their fines, probation, community service, jail or prison sentences into something unrecognizable as legal punishment'. (p. 203)

provoked by it. It is the public disapproval expressed by criminalization of an act that makes restrictions of liberty condemnatory and thus distinguishes them from other, non-punitive restrictions. The public or social disapproval that may be triggered by the criminal label imposed in response to censure is related, but distinct.

One source of the confusion detected here may be unconscious slippage between the censure and stigmatization involved in the criminalization of an act (the result of a legislative process), and the censure and stigmatization involved in the criminalization of a person (the result of a judicial or quasi-judicial process). Criminalization marks an act out as morally condemnable, and in that sense it attaches stigma to that act. It is also censorious to the extent that it directs censure towards those as-yet-unidentified individuals who commit the criminal act. Is stigmatization avoidable, given that legislating to make some activity criminal invariably involves stigmatizing those who engage in it? This, former kind of stigmatization is not avoidable. But neither is it the same as the stigmatization that is potentially harmful in the ways described in detail in Chapter 2.[13] Rather, it is an abstract kind of stigmatization, which necessarily accompanies criminalization but is—at least theoretically—proportionate to the seriousness of the crime. This abstract kind of stigma is therefore unresponsive to the contingent or contextual factors that determine the severity of the criminal stigmatization, factors such as the extent to which other individuals react negatively to the label.

It's worth pausing for a moment here to take stock of what has been proposed so far in this chapter. I have been trying to show that neither public labelling nor criminal stigmatization are essential to punishment. If this is correct, then the question of whether public criminal labelling is justified in any particular case cannot be determined by reference solely to the permissibility of punishing in that case. In other words, we can't answer the question of whether it is fair to publicly label someone as criminal only by asking whether they have been found guilty beyond reasonable doubt; guilt may be sufficient for punishment, but we still need to decide whether punishment calls for public labelling. In the next two sections, I consider the possibility that public criminal labelling fulfils one or more of the justifying functions of punishment and that this provides at least one important reason to think that it is precisely what punishment calls for.

[13] Simester (2021: 8) uses the term 'stigmatic convictions' to refer to those convictions understood by the public in general as conveying moral censure, but 'stigmatizing effects' to refer to public responses to conviction. This offers a potentially useful way of distinguishing the two.

The Communicative Justification for Public Labelling as Punishment

People convicted of crimes are rarely required to wear criminal badges or to carry signs publicizing their misdeeds as a form of punishment. This is true even in countries which embrace the use of social shaming as a kind of criminal sanction.[14] The absence of such practices from our modern landscape suggests that there are reasons operative in most criminal justice systems that count against the use of public criminal labels, at least highly conspicuous ones, as punishment. In his 1986 book, in which he lays the ground for his communicative theory of punishment, Anthony Duff considers the merits of just this kind of labelling-as-punishment, as an alternative to incarceration or other forms of hard treatment (Duff, 1986). Duff suggests that the reasons 'symbolic'[15] forms of punishment, such as criminal badges, are not considered appropriate by people who otherwise hold opposing views about what punishment should seek to achieve, relate to the inevitable inconsistency and arbitrariness with which members of the public will express their disapproval of those labels. This inconsistency means, he argues, that 'they will not distribute punishments equitably, or ensure that offenders receive the kind and degree of punishment they deserve' (1986: 149). Duff implies that if these problems of proportionality and coordination could be resolved, then public criminal labelling as punishment might have many advantages from a communicative perspective.

Duff's suggestions about the potential costs and benefits of public criminal labelling as punishment are worth contemplating, because they invite us to think about labelling in isolation from the other formal restrictions (like incarceration) it often accompanies. Doing so also helps to focus our attention on the reasons for and against public labelling as criminal punishment. And, as I will argue below, these reasons apply—albeit to varying degrees—to contemporary criminal labelling practices too. If it is true that conspicuous criminal labelling would fulfil effectively the communicative function of

[14] For example, Japan's criminal justice system traditionally prioritizes reintegrative shaming over carceral measures, an approach which involves the community but does not overtly label. See Sakiyama (2011).

[15] While Duff and others refer to this kind of public criminal labelling as a 'symbolic' penalty, thus implying that there is no hard treatment involved (and therefore none that must be justified), this seems to me to be misleading. The state's actions in labelling people publicly are symbolic, but they also amount to hard treatment, at the very least because forcing people to wear inevitably stigmatizing badges is a form of coercion.

punishment, and that its only downside would be potential disproportionality, then perhaps the arguments in its favour are stronger than Duff implies. After all, disproportionality is a problem that arises inevitably to some degree in connection with all kinds of punishments (Ryberg, 2004; Kolber, 2012). For this reason, it is generally treated more like a negative effect that we should seek to ameliorate when devising and implementing punishments, rather than a reason to jettison punishments entirely. And the communication of censure is widely acknowledged as an important or vital function of punishment even by those who reject claims that communication can be a complete theory of punishment (Tadros, 2011: 91). So if we can preserve the communicative potential of public labelling while reducing the risk of disproportionality, then we may appear to have a strong case for the justice of public labelling-as-punishment.

I think that such a case is actually difficult to make, and in the next section I explain why. I begin by acknowledging the communicative potential of conspicuous criminal labelling as punishment. Then I put forward some reasons for thinking that it is unlikely ever to be realized in practice. I argue that this would continue to be true even in a society in which most people subscribe to the communicative theory of punishment, because public criminal labelling is stigmatizing in ways that frustrate the kind of communication justified by the communicative theory. In addition, as Duff and others note, it leads to inevitable disproportionality. I argue that the disproportionality it leads to is indicative of unfairness and discrimination towards those thus criminalized, amongst other things. Both of those problems arise primarily because conspicuous criminal labelling inverts the norm common to—dare I say defining of—liberal societies, that punishment is something that should be carried out by the state on behalf of citizens, and not vice versa.[16]

[16] This norm is most obviously derivable from John Locke and Robert Nozick's individualist liberalism, in which the move from a state of nature to organized society involves individuals delegating their natural right to punish to the state (Locke 1999: 128–130; Nozick 1974: 112). More recently, Gardner (1998: 1) discusses this as 'the displacement function of the criminal law' as 'one of the central pillars of its justification'. In contrast, Duff's communitarianism conceptualizes the right to punish as an entitlement not of individuals but of the community. Nevertheless, both theories assert that punishment for crimes is a right exercised via the legitimate institutions of the state. And both deny that citizens, collectively or as individuals, retain a right to punish that can be exercised independently of the punishing acts of the legitimate institutions of the state (Duff, 2010). More recently, conflicting positions on the question of whether the state has an exclusive right to punish seems to converge on the view that only the state can impose sanctions that would otherwise be considered a violation of rights and freedoms (such as imprisonment) (Husak, 2016; Mendlow, 2022).

Communicative theory and the benefits of public labelling as punishment

Let us begin by describing what has become known as the communicative function of punishment. The communicative account of punishment states, roughly, that the primary aim of punishment should be to communicate public disapproval of the crime to the offender in such a way as to persuade them, by appeal to moral reasons, to repent (Duff, 2001:81–82). Moral reasons are reasons relating to what is wrong or right, fair or unjust, respectful or degrading, and so on. In the philosophy of punishment, they are often contrasted with threats and material incentives which motivate us by appealing to our self-interest rather than our conscience. In line with the communicative theory, both censure and hard treatment communicate disapproval to an offender on behalf of the political community (or, in Duff's terms 'polity'). Hard treatment is also a means by which offenders can do penance and repent, in something like a performance of contrition. On the communicative account, punishment is owed *both* to the victims of the crime *and* to the perpetrator. Victims have entitlements to have their wrongs addressed, and perpetrators deserve to be treated as moral agents with the potential for rehabilitation. Punishing is therefore a civic duty and not only a civic right. The communicative account is retributive (punishment is just because it is deserved) and so requires that some measure of proportionality be maintained between the seriousness of the crime committed and the severity of the penalty (Duff, 2005: 187; von Hirsch, 1993, ch.2).

How might public criminal labelling of offenders promote the communicative aims of punishment? Duff's account gives us some clues. For example, he points out that a consideration in favour of labelling-as-punishment via criminal badges is that, by inflicting 'a public and . . . lasting reminder of the offender's guilt' it can make offenders 'face up to' and take responsibility for what they have done, which is an essential step towards repentance (Duff, 1986: 148). This seems reasonable. It's hard to dispute that being forced to reveal one's crimes to every person encountered in daily life would make it difficult to ignore, deny, or minimize them. The prominence given to the criminal label over other facts about oneself would also likely force a person to takeseriously and reflect on their crimes, as would being faced constantly with public reactions to those crimes. The fact that it would remain the responsibility of the individual offender, rather than a punishing authority, to undertake reformative actions, may also encourage people to take responsibility for the state of their own moral compass, and to demonstrate that they have done so. For example, someone who has a public criminal label may understandably be keen to display evidence that they have reformed and are deserving of forgiveness and redemption, perhaps in the form of a certificate showing successful completion of a domestic abuse perpetrator programme, or a clean drug test, and so on. Something like this already occurs in some US states such as New York and Illinois, where people's criminal records are publicly accessible online. There, judicial authorities provide 'certificates of relief' or of 'good conduct' to help people with criminal records access jobs and housing they would otherwise likely be rejected for.

We can further channel the spirit of Duff's inquiry to identify additional ways in which conspicuous physical criminal labels might contribute to the communicative aims of punishment. One potential benefit of criminal labels is that they might enable a better 'fit' between crime and punishment than the currently standardized penalties devised by the state, such as fines and incarceration. Unlike those penalties, the powers of human expression enable reactions that are infinitely subtle and true to people's attitudes about a particular act of wrongdoing. In practice, these attitudes shift over time with changes in public morality, reflecting the norms of the day. One source of poor fit between standardized penalties and crimes stems from the weak responsiveness of the former to changes in attitudes towards the latter. If one of the fundamental aims of punishment is to express public disapproval for wrongdoing, and if the justification and moral authority of a specific punishment is drawn from its effectiveness in expressing that disapproval, then who could be better placed to deliver it in a way that reflects the nature and extent of that disapproval but the public itself? And what better opportunity to express remorse and demonstrate a commitment to reform than face-to-face with the community whose norms one has flouted? In this way, it might be argued that criminal badges would fulfil the communicative aims of punishment in a way that is both more faithful to those aims and maintains a better fit between crime and punishment than current, state-mediated penalties.

Limitations of labelling as punishment for the communicative theory

The potential of conspicuous criminal labelling to facilitate communication of disapproval, rational persuasion, and repentance is powerful. But there are at least two sets of reasons why we should be sceptical that this potential could ever be realized in practice. The first relates to the fact most people do not share the view that just punishment means the communication of censure in the form of rational persuasion. This means that their reactions to criminal labels are unlikely to be in the communicative spirit. We saw significant evidence of this in Chapter 2 where even overwhelming evidence of individual reform was not enough to prevent people being treated as dangerous, untrustworthy, or disgraced. The second relates to the nature of the relationship between offenders and individuals as citizens. As I'll argue in a moment, this relationship is not a sound basis for effective intervention of the communicative kind. Taken together, these reasons make it inevitable in practice that conspicuous labelling will facilitate public reactions to criminality that both undermine the communicative function of punishment and are unfair to those labelled.

The wrong kind of reaction to criminality

In most contemporary societies, people do not all share the view that punishment means rational appeal to moral reasons. What is more, in most politically, socially, and culturally diverse societies, people's views about what fair punishment looks like vary significantly. This means that someone compelled to wear a criminal badge would be likely to receive a variety of responses to their criminality. Some of these responses would aim to persuade. But others might celebrate the crime. (An example of the latter can be found in the case of Luigi Mangione, a young man who murdered a corporate health insurance executive in 2024 and then acquired status as a sex symbol—the 'hot assassin'—and hero to people across the USA [Winter, 2024].) Other responses aim to deter, incapacitate, humiliate, ridicule, avenge, or even harm. Fear of abuse or even retaliatory attacks by members of the public would, especially for those convicted of offences considered deeply shameful, be well grounded. As mentioned in Chapter 2, recorded incidents of violence against sex offenders in the United States[17] bear this out. So too do reports in the United Kingdom about offenders wearing high-visibility 'community payback' vests being verbally abused, beaten, and even shot at.[18]

On the other hand, positive reports of public responses to conspicuous criminal labels are not impossible to find. One notable instance involves the case of Michael Hubacek, convicted in the USA of manslaughter for a drink driving offence. Hubacek served only six months of the ten-year prison

[17] See, for example, attacks on sex offenders whose personal details were made public under Megan's Law in the USA (Levenson et al., 2007).

[18] (Travis, 2008; Fletcher, 2009).

sentence he was originally given. However, the judge used his considerable discretion in sentencing to instruct Hubacek to stand outside a high school once a month wearing a placard stating 'I KILLED TWO PEOPLE WHILE DRUNK DRIVING'. In interviews, Hubacek reported feeling positive about his labelling, to which he says '90%' of people' reacted kindly, saying things such as 'God bless you' and 'Things will be okay' (Ronson, 2015:83). We might find it reassuring to hear that public criminal labelling can prompt compassion rather than abuse. But compassion is not the same as rational persuasion by appeal to moral reasons. And it is the latter that the communicative theory demands. What's more, as we can see from the religious tone of one of the comments received by Hubacek, messages of compassion inevitably draw on people's own personal faith, ideology, or world view. This is problematic. Unless people communicate using appeals to humanity or other high-level values shared by people with a range of backgrounds and beliefs, their message will be articulated in terms of values that the offender cannot reasonably be expected to share. In other words, they risk communicating in ways that fail to resonate with the person their words are aiming to reach. On the other hand, it seems unreasonable to expect people to refrain from putting forth reasons that are genuinely their own, if we expect them to engage in good faith with offenders. There seems to be a tension between the desirability of the personal, authentic element for effective communication and the need for a more neutral, democratic perspective from which to censure.

A civic duty to punish?

Perhaps this tension arises because the communicative theory demands of citizens a 'civic' duty to punish, yet without also making them democratically accountable for their punishing actions. This notion of a civic duty to punish blurs the line between interpersonal duties we owe each other as members of society and the democratically assigned duties of those who carry out punishing functions on behalf of 'the polity'. In Chapter 4, we saw how important accountability is for the legitimacy and the fairness of criminal justice. The blurring introduced by the communicative theory is problematic because it risks lending democratic legitimacy and authority to people's own personal reactions to criminality, whatever these might be. It is not hard to imagine how empowering members of the public to communicate censure to offenders might also encourage people to feel self-righteous in their execution of this duty and in their expression of their views. All this would probably serve to further legitimize the ugly cancellations and social media pile-ons that have become so characteristic of public censure in our contemporary societies.

In most current penal systems, those who assign and implement criminal punishments are expected to act in accordance with certain professional standards, and are subject to scrutiny by democratic institutions such as parliament, specialist oversight bodies, and the media. Such scrutiny aims to reduce the risk that the punishments imposed in the name of the public are inflicted unfairly or in ways that fail to align with the norms of society.[19] For example, criminal justice officials such as probation officers or youth-offending workers are expected to refrain from expressing their own personal disgust about a crime to their clients. This expectation is fair. The role of the probation or youth-offending professional is to help reform people, not shame them, and because the officer accepted that condition of the job when they applied voluntarily to do it, it would be unprofessional to express disgust, even if that disgust were a reasonable response. The same cannot be said for individual citizens acting in their personal capacity, for whom prescriptiveness of this sort about what can and cannot be communicated would be an unacceptable interference with freedom of expression. In sum, as long as people are invited to react to criminality wherever they see it, they will sometimes react in ways that either fail to promote or actively undermine the aims of punishment as communication. Giving them a special right to do so risks encouraging these reactions to be made more stridently and even less helpfully.

Non-punitive reactions to criminal labels

A different challenge to the achievement of the right kind of censure through public criminal labelling would arise from people's non-punitive reactions to criminal labels. On a communicative account, explicitly punitive reactions would include people's verbal expression of disapproval as well as disapproval expressed through some action, such as the temporary suspension of a contract of employment. Non-punitive reactions are those actions or behaviours we adopt in response to knowledge of a person's criminality but which are not intended to censure or punish. Problematic non-punitive reactions might occur if people respond to labelled individuals in ways that deny that individual social benefits and exclude them from social activities in ways that are seriously detrimental to them. For example, I might be the kind of person who believes knowledge of people's criminal histories would be largely irrelevant to my decisions about who to associate with and how. Perhaps I believe that

[19] Owen Fiss expressed worries similar to these in relation to a legal movement in 1980s USA to encourage the use of private settlements as an alternative to court hearings, see Fiss (1984: 1085). The point here about efforts to avoid certain kinds of unfairness is not intended to deny for a moment the fact that many other things are deeply wrong with most penal systems and sentencing practices today.

many crimes are not morally wrong. Perhaps I believe in people's abilities to change and their right to a second chance. Perhaps, for these reasons, I am determined to treat people with convictions with the same kind of open mind and respect as I treat those without. Even so, I might well find myself struggling to achieve this and not react intuitively with fear, disgust, mistrust and so on, if knowledge of individual criminal histories were constantly thrust into my field of perception. Or my intuitive recoil from particular people might stem more from embarrassment, awkwardness, or fear of what others might think than a desire to punish. Nevertheless, as we saw in Chapter 2, both that response, and the anticipation of it, cause suffering and deprivation to the labelled individual.

Some might argue that the fact that behaviours such as avoiding people wearing criminal labels lack punitive intent means they cannot be conceptualized as punishment.[20] It follows, they may argue further, that such behaviours cannot be criticized as 'bad' punishment. For example, Dan Markel has pointed out that acts taken in response to crime convey a message but are not properly understood as punitive unless that message is intelligible to the offender (Markel, 2001: 2195). How does this apply to the issues we are now considering? Being avoided, excluded, or shunned communicates a message of public disapproval—a message that what one did makes one an undesirable associate. However, this message is not necessarily intelligible as punitive unless it is clearly signposted as such. Such signposting occurs explicitly during court proceedings, especially at the time of sentencing when judges make their remarks. Those remarks typically include some comment on the nature of the crime, the impact on any victims, the offender's remorse or lack thereof, and the need for public safety, deterrence, or some other justification for the sentence. Back in the community, where people do not routinely declare their motivations for their behaviour, a labelled offender would perceive little or no difference between an act of exclusion driven by a desire to punish and one driven by squeamishness or a fear of being stigmatized by association. Perhaps we must concede that this kind of collateral harm to the offender should carry no weight on the retributive scales, and therefore may not, strictly speaking, be an issue of punitive proportionality. Nevertheless, it must surely carry some weight in the broader criminal justice decision-making process (Gray, 2010: 1630, n46). As others have pointed out, the fact that some of the harms flowing from punishment may not be confidently defined as 'punishment' does

[20] See Markel and Flanders, 2010. Punitive intent is part of the definition of punishment according to Hart and others (Hart, 1959). David Gray claims, for example, that 'no theory of criminal punishment is obliged to justify... the unintended suffering that may incidentally result from punishment'. (Gray, 2010: 54).

not mean they should be disregarded or discounted when reasoning about the justice of different punishments.[21] We may think, for example, that a desire to avoid the extra suffering caused by non-punitive reactions to criminal labels can be a legitimate reason for preferring another form of punishment with less weighty and inevitable collateral harms than public labelling, assuming such a punishment can be found.[22]

What does this mean for communicative justifications for the public labelling of people with convictions? The extra suffering imposed through public labelling seems difficult to reconcile with the communicative aims of punishment. To remind ourselves, these are to communicate public disapproval of the crime to the offender in such a way as to persuade them, by appeal to moral reasons, to repent. Avoiding, excluding, and shunning may communicate disapproval, repulsion, or fear but they do not constitute rational persuasion. The inevitable shrinking away from people bearing the criminal mark isolates individuals from the moral community, rather than reconciling them. What is more, fear of the public reaction to one's criminality is a powerful incentive to withdraw voluntarily from social interaction, as attested to by recent sociological work on 'system avoidance' and 'social withdrawal' described in detail in Chapter 2. It may also drive people to seek the company of those more favourably disposed to criminality.

Unfair and disproportionate punishment

In addition to failing to bring about the kind of communication that is justified, labelling-as-punishment is unfair to offenders. People considering whether to commit criminal acts should know in advance what their punishments if caught will consist in, roughly speaking. Otherwise their decision about whether to commit the crime cannot be said to be properly informed, or, it follows, autonomously taken. The unpredictability of public responses to criminal labels makes them unfair as a form of punishment for at least this reason. People who have committed minor offenses of the kind prompting a sentence of community service could hardly anticipate being shot at, as described above. Nor could Kieran, the teenager convicted of a public decency

[21] Both Nathan (2022) and Hoskins (2023) offer excellent discussions of this and related points.

[22] Moore gives us a different but related reason to be sceptical about the benefits of giving citizens the right to punish. His concerns relate more to the effect of punishing on our own moral characters than the effects on those we punish. He argues: 'The giving of punishment is dangerous to virtue. Doing so easily can give rise to those dark emotions that Nietzsche lumped together under the French term ressentiment, emotions of resentment, projected guilt, sadism, envy, and so on. Giving the power of punishment to the state alone does not eliminate that danger... But it does reduce such danger because institutionalized punishment can reduce the opportunities for sadism, abuse, and the pleasure of giving pain that can corrupt our virtue' (Moore, 2010: 48).

offence and described in Chapter 2, have expected his neighbours to launch a campaign of false reports of child abuse against him to police. In Chapter 2, we saw too how the uncertainty about how others will respond to a criminal record is itself a source of psychological and emotional harm for people with convictions, even leading them to withdraw from potentially exposing encounters entirely, in an effort to regain a modicum of control.

A further reason why unfairness would arise is that inequalities of status would come to determine those responses, thus making proportionality difficult to achieve. The concern here is that people who are equally culpable of equally serious crimes would be punished more or less severely because of the unequal and stratified character of most modern societies. People's moral judgements of and reactions to others are influenced by the social status and other attributes of those judged. For example, research shows that people's preconceptions and personal prejudices come often to influence their performance as jurors. We also know that juror bias is difficult to address, either by raising jurors' own awareness of it or by introducing pre-appointment vetting schemes (Roberts, 2012). There is no reason to believe that bias would be any less likely to influence the reactions to criminals of the general public. There is a real risk that, in our deeply imperfect societies, the identity of the criminal rather than the nature of the crime would too often come to determine the extent, the nature, and severity of punishment. Looking back to the case of the murderer Luigi Mangione, many have commented that his youth, good looks, social privilege and whiteness appear to have insulated him from the opprobrium meted out to less fortunate perpetrators of homicide. At the time this book is being written, his every appearance in court is attended by a devoted fanbase numbering in the hundreds, and his legal team have received over two hundred and fifty thousand dollars in crowdfunding. Such a situation sits uncomfortably with well-established and widely held intuitions about fairness and desert, in particular the intuition that people should be punished for what they do rather than who they are.

Earlier, I mentioned that the problem of disproportionality is one faced by all theories of punishment. I now want to argue that the disproportionality just described—where one's status or identity comes to determine the severity of the punishment—is harder to justify or tolerate than the disproportionality that results from imposing an identical penalty on two individuals who turn out to react to or experience it in different ways. Standardization in criminal penalties (i.e. imposing set penalties for certain crimes) is itself an attempt to prevent bias and discrimination in sentencing; to ensure that sentencing is subjected to democratic oversight; and to make sure that both offenders and victims-to-be are aware of the kinds of punishment that can be expected for specific crimes. Some people will suffer more from incarceration or other punishments than others. Fines hit poorer people harder[23] and prison is worse for people whose incarceration means they can no longer care for their children. In most countries, these differences in the impact of punishments can be taken into account by a judge when sentencing, alongside other factors like culpability, remorse, and so on. But the discrepancies in the experience of hard treatment that will inevitably remain do not by themselves imply than anyone has thereby been wronged. In contrast, people *are* wronged when they suffer punishments that are determined even in part by personal prejudices towards them. Wrongs also occur when prejudicial preferences result in an offender receiving public sympathy and even being lauded for their crimes rather than held accountable. Combining public criminal labelling with a civic duty to punish would not only open the door to such wrongs, but also risk validating and even valorizing them.

Would public commitment to communitive punishment solve the problems? The problems with conspicuous labelling that I have just pointed to are not problems internal to the communicative theory. Rather, they are problems that arise mainly because not enough people actually subscribe to that theory. If most people genuinely did support the idea of punishment as communication, then the problems of uncertainty faced by the offender, risk and fear of insult or abuse, parallel trepidation felt by members of the public, disproportionality, and the tendency of labelling to marginalize rather than reintegrate may plausibly be reduced significantly. Assuming this could actually be achieved, would conspicuous criminal labelling then be justified? There are compelling reasons to think not.

Recall that the aim of communication is to engage the offender in moral reflection and rational persuasion that will help them recognize the wrongness of their actions, repent, and seek a reconciliation with the society whose norms they have transgressed. The effectiveness of any such communication ventured by a citizen is likely to depend to some extent on their knowledge both of the particular case and of the individual in question. Without sufficient knowledge of the case, or sufficient understanding of the limits of one's knowledge, it would be all too easy for people to censure inappropriately. The detailed evidence and context presented to a judge or jury in a criminal trial serves not only

[23] Though, as helpfully pointed out to me by Duff, some mostly northern European countries operate 'day fines' which seek to be proportionate to the means of the offender, see Drapal(2021).

to promote fair verdicts but also to inform fair sentencing. Could sufficient detail be made available to the public to enable them to respond appropriately to a criminal badge? It is hard to see how this could be achieved. And even if it were possible to somehow surmount this difficulty, releasing detailed information may violate the rights of victims, witnesses, the perpetrator's family, and so on. Perhaps well-motivated citizens could still communicate censure formally, and in a way tailored to the extent of their knowledge of the case. At the end of the day, the extent to which one finds this likely or even plausible may come down to the faith one has in the ability of ordinary strangers to provide reliably right responses to criminality.

But there is a different reason that the power of civic communication to effectively censure may be limited. Communicative theory speaks of 'civic duties' to censure. This seems to assume that 'citizens' as such stand in the kind of relationship to each other that makes effective communication leading to moral reform a genuine possibility. Yet empirically informed analyses of reintegration suggest that moralizing about crime is best left to those close to the offender both in personal relationship and in terms of peer group (Braithwaite, 1989). Closeness is important partly because those who know and can relate to the offender are, generally speaking, better able to put their crimes in context and thus to intervene in ways more likely to resonate with that person. But it is also important because offenders are more likely to respond appropriately to those they consider peers, allies, or close associates, whose opinion they care about and whose acceptance and approval they are motivated to secure.[24] Of course, those close enough to an offender to engage in the right kind of communication with them would not typically need to see a label to find out about their criminality. The label is for everyone else. Yet it is 'everyone else' who is least well placed to communicate censure in the right way.

More generally, asserting a universal civic duty not only to know about each others' crimes but also to punish them seems excessively burdensome (or what philosophers call 'overdemanding'). For many of us, faced with the presence of individuals guilty of serious crimes, it would require significant effort merely to control one's emotional reactions to the label, let alone to engage the person concerned in rational persuasion to reform. Members of the public may

[24] This need not contradict claims made above about the advantages of leaving censure to an authority that is accountable democratically, such as the judiciary, for two reasons. First, because the judiciary will typically have been given a great deal of information about both the specific incidents under consideration and the individual accused, and so will still be better placed than 'citizens' to deliver appropriate censure. Second, because the fact that a criminal's peers might be best placed to deliver effective censure does not mean that they will generally be motivated to do so such that they could be relied upon to fulfil the function of a punishing authority.

understandably fear those with a history of violent crime or abusive behaviour, especially as they would not know how such individuals might react to public censure. Indeed it would be difficult to know how to react even to less disturbing breaches of the law, partly because of the inevitable awkwardness that would come from engaging strangers or people we hardly know in discussion that is deeply personal, concerning as it does the state of their moral conscience. It seems unreasonably demanding of people to insist that they nevertheless *must* engage directly with such individuals on the subject of their crimes.

But perhaps we could make such engagement what Immanuel Kant called an 'imperfect duty', that is, something that—like giving to charity—we each must do sometimes and to some extent, but not in every possible case or to the fullest extent possible.[25] One might argue that, as long as we communicate appropriately with some offenders some of the time, we can consider ourselves good citizens, on the communicative account. This solution would succeed in reducing the arguably unreasonable burdens and demands of punishing on citizens. But it also raises further problems. For it may well end up resulting in a situation in which people whose crimes are relatively banal or unthreatening receive a great deal of appropriate communication, while those whose crimes are most repellent receive little or none. Equally, it could lead to a situation in which the civic duty to punish is in practice performed overwhelmingly by the eager few, thus letting the rest of us off. It is not difficult to imagine the enthusiasm with which some religious groups on a mission to save souls, or some self-styled rehabilitation gurus and their followers, might come to dominate the practice of public censure. Such groups are unlikely to be able to represent the public faithfully or effectively, even if they genuinely try to adopt a rational persuasion approach to punishment.

Forcing people to acknowledge and respond to criminality

A further difficulty that would arise with criminal labelling as punishment stems from the fact that it forces knowledge of criminality upon citizens, creating a de-facto *requirement* to know. Even if people were not required to respond punitively to knowledge of criminality, the mere fact that such knowledge is imposed on them seems problematic, at least for those amongst us who would genuinely prefer not to know. Why might some people prefer not to be alerted to the crimes of others? One reasonable explanation might be that giving criminality such prominence in public risks destabilizing widely valued

[25] For an account of Kant's distinction between perfect and imperfect duties, see Hill (2019).

conventions of concealment that constitute what Thomas Nagel has called 'one of the conditions of civilisation' (Nagel, 1998: 3). Non-exposure of criminal history in everyday interpersonal interactions, combined with the knowledge that criminal justice is being done elsewhere, on our behalf, helps to maintain the kind of civilized atmosphere that enables people to go about their collective business in an ordered and peaceful manner. But the prominence of a criminal badge would make an individual's criminal history impossible to avoid or ignore. Imagine being regularly faced—in our daily interactions at the supermarket, on public transport, at the park with our children—with murderers, rapists, child abusers, terrorists, robbers, pimps, drug dealers, thieves and dangerous drivers. Of course, we all *are* faced regularly with such people today, but the fact that we—generally speaking—don't know who among us they are, enables civilized interaction to take place.[26]

One might argue that both the issue of the excessive demandingness and the previous concern about people's natural awkwardness, anxiety, and/or fear could be addressed by the production of communicative scripts for offenders and censurers. These scripts would be generally known by all and could be recited when appropriate in a kind of civic ritual of censure and repentance. A script or a choice of scripts could alleviate some of the uncertainty and fear on both sides and facilitate communication. But ritualistic exchanges can all too often become mechanical and easy to enact without genuine personal conviction. Even an optional script risks substituting meaningful communication with the worn-out rehearsal of empty phrases. Similar issues undermine the potential of ritual removals of criminal labels, which some have argued could be introduced as a way of celebrating reform, representing reconciliation with the community, and opening the door to reintegration. Legal proposals to introduce such rituals have been tabled in the United States to address the harms associated with the enduring publicity given to criminal records there (Colgate-Love, 2011). Even if replacing one label with another label could actually achieve this, by the time the ritual is performed the process of exclusion and withdrawal is likely to have raised significant and lasting barriers to genuine reintegration.

Robert Nozick reminds us that 'if a principle is a device for having certain effects, then it is a device for having those effects when it is followed; so what actually happens when it is followed, not just what it says, is relevant in

[26] 'The point of polite formulae and broad abstentions from expression is to leave a great range of potentially disruptive material unacknowledged and therefore out of play' (Nagel, 1998:1). Here Nagel is discussing social conventions of privacy, but his points are relevant to people's criminal histories and judged propensities.

assessing that principle as a teleological device'[27] (Nozick, 1974: 38). In this section, I have been trying to show that what actually happens when we use radical publicity in the form of conspicuous labels is most likely something other than the kind of punishment endorsed by the communicative theory. For this reason, public criminal labelling as punishment is difficult to justify on communicative grounds. Indeed, it would continue to be difficult to justify even in a society in which most people were genuinely committed to the communicative account of punishment. The explanations for this, which include concerns about inevitable unfairness, disproportionality, and the challenges to effective communication faced by even well-meaning individuals, all stem from the fact that labelling-as-punishment transfers some of the right and duty to punish from authoritative institutions to citizens. Such a move is problematic, in particular, for those of us who live in complex mass societies in which anonymity is common and values and ideologies vary widely even between neighbours. Transferring the right and duty to punish from the state back to citizens seems to hold most potential if implemented in small, tight-knit, morally homogenous communities (perhaps similar to Aristotle's concept of *polis* in which there are few boundaries between citizen and state). In such places, people already know each other well, which means that awkwardness and fear are reduced and crimes can be understood in the context of a particular life story. In such places, it is easier to ensure that people who abuse their right to punish by shaming, humiliating, or harming offenders are held accountable, as their actions are more likely to be witnessed or identified early.

Complex societies and the challenge to effective communication

Enacting a civic right and duty to punish seems far less likely to be successful in complex societies populated by disconnected and sometimes mutually suspicious groups and individuals who often do not relate to each other. Against this background, any faith in 'citizens' as such to take on this reformative role seems misplaced. Alternatives are presented by current efforts in the field of restorative justice and transformative justice. The former aims to connect offenders with specially trained professionals and therapists who can facilitate effective communication and engagement between offenders and the people they have harmed, as well as guide and nurture it once it is in place. Transformative justice is an approach to community intervention that seeks to hold accountable and rehabilitate those who harm others, while healing and promoting the recovery

[27] By teleological device, Nozick just means a rule or norm that we install to bring about a desired end or state of affairs.

of those harmed, in ways that do not reproduce violence, discrimination, and disadvantage (Brown, 2019). Both these alternatives to state punishment can and do enact communicative forms of criminal justice. But neither necessitates or typically involves labelling criminals publicly or otherwise publicizing their criminality, beyond the confines of the relationship or community in which justice is pursued. For example, research with victims of crimes of violence and abuse suggests that the goal they most commonly seek is 'exposure of the offender as an offender' and that for them it is more important to 'deprive the perpetrator of undeserved honor and status than to deprive them of either liberty or fortune' (Herman, 2005: 90, see also Miller, 2011). However, the context in which this is sought is the shared community, specifically the friends and family who had acted as bystanders and who, often in cases of sexual and domestic violence, had previously enabled or validated the perpetrator rather than supported the victim. And the reintegration envisaged is as much about the community's treatment of the victim as it is about the moral reform of the perpetrator. General publicity in the form of labels, badges, or publicly accessible criminal records is unlikely to achieve this kind of repair and redress.

Towards the beginning of this chapter, I wrote that taking seriously the idea—entertained briefly by Duff—of criminal badging can help us to think more clearly about the potential for contemporary criminal labelling practices to be justified as punishment. But, it might be argued, all the points I have made thus far against the view that labelling may be justified as punishment on communicative grounds—points about the likely disproportionality, excessive demands on individuals to communicate disapproval, barriers to reconciliation and reintegration, and unfairness—have all been discussed in relation to criminal labels that are used *in place of* other kinds of punishment; that attach physically to the offender, like clothing or a badge; and that are therefore *extremely conspicuous* in a way that makes them both dominant in relation to other characteristics of the offender and very difficult for others to ignore. But many contemporary criminal labelling practices—such as the maintenance of criminal record repositories or the sharing of criminal record information with employers, landlords, and educations providers—do not involve such conspicuous marking out. Many, like the naming of offenders in trial proceedings or the practice of making offenders wear identifying boiler suits, are limited to a certain place and time. And most take place alongside other, formal sanctions, such as incarceration or community service.

It is true that the stigmatizing potential of mugshots on posters, high-visibility work vests, or mentions in the local paper, or on a police-hosted website pale in comparison to that promised by a physical criminal badge. But this is no reason to think that these forms of public labelling are any easier to justify as punishment on communicative grounds.[28] And in any case, current differences between readily available criminal labels, such as listings in online databases or on police websites, and highly conspicuous labels such as criminal badges may shrink and even disappear in the near future. Processing speed, computational power, and the ubiquity of personal devices means it is ever-easier for information about people we encounter to be collated and presented to us automatically. For example, it is not far-fetched to predict that we may soon use wearable devices equipped with facial recognition set to provide summaries of online information about anyone the wearer encounters, in real time. If that is indeed where we are headed, then criminal records that can currently be revealed by an Internet search will soon become far more conspicuous, almost by default (Tunick, 2013).

Public Criminal Labelling as a Deterrent to Crime

But perhaps the justification for labelling-as-added punishment is to be found in its deterrence or crime-reduction function, rather than its potential in communicating censure. Deterrence has long been considered a core aim of criminal penalties, acknowledged as such by Enlightenment thinkers including Adam Smith (1776/2002:2.1.1.6), Jeremy Bentham (1789/2009), and Cesare Beccaria (1764). And deterrence theory has recently enjoyed something of a revival in the philosophy of punishment too (Ellis, 2003; Chiao, 2016; Hsin-Wen Lee, 2017). More generally, it is often taken to be obviously true that the prospect of being publicly marked as criminal induces fear and shame and thereby deters people from committing crimes (Arneson, 2007; Kahan, 2006). As legal philosopher H.M. Hart observed: '[A legislator] will be likely to regard the desire of the ordinary man to avoid the moral condemnation of his community . . . as a powerful factor influencing human behaviour which can scarcely with safety be dispensed with' (Hart, 1958: 409). Deterrence continues to be politicians' favoured rationale for novel penal initiatives, especially those which publicly name and shame offenders. Police too cite deterrence as the reason for posting mugshots and other identifying descriptions of suspects and offenders in the media. For example, in 2002 one UK police force launched a poster

[28] As far as I am aware, Duff himself does not attempt to justify such actual examples of public labelling on punitive grounds. Where he does defend publicity in criminal justice, this is primarily in terms of the importance of public participation in criminal justice processes, though considerations of transparency and deterrence are also given weight (Duff, 2001: 148).

campaign to deter prolific offenders from coming to the area to commit crimes. They hired advertising space in streets and shopping centres and filled them with oversized photographs of local offenders. The photos were subtitled with the offender's name, the nature of their offence, the sentence, and the warning 'If you come to Brentwood to commit crime, expect to do the time!'.[29] The aim was to warn these usual suspects that the police would be watching and waiting to catch them out if they continued their wayward path. But does the prospect of being publicly labelled a criminal in fact deter? The question is an empirical one, so we need to look at the evidence. In the rest of this section, I draw attention to some recent research on the topic that suggests deterrence is unlikely to justifying public labelling.

As discussed in Chapter 2, sex offender notification laws in certain US states (popularly known as Megan's Law) proactively inform members of the public about the presence of people convicted of sexual offences in their neighbourhood. Methods of notification vary and can include media releases, mailed or posted flyers, dedicated websites, door-to-door contacts, and community meetings. Sex offender notification is highly controversial, and perhaps because of this there is a significant body of research examining its impacts both on individual reoffending (specific deterrence) and offending rates in the community at large (general deterrence). The findings from these studies show that notification has no discernible effect on general reoffending (Lasher and McGrath, 2012)[30] but actually increases specific reoffending (Prescott and Rockoff, 2008; Hamilton and Fairfaz-Columbo, 2023). In other words, community notification achieves precisely the opposite outcome than that for which it was introduced. Interestingly, this evidence has done nothing to shift entrenched public beliefs in the effectiveness of publicly labelling sex offenders (Hamilton and Fairfaz-Columbo, 2023).

Labelling theory provides further grounds for doubting the effectiveness of public labelling as a deterrent. It is a strand of criminological research that analyses the impact on reoffending (or 'recidivism') and delinquency of criminal labelling. Its proponents typically define labelling as the application of a public criminal record. In a 2007 paper, Chiricos et al. examined, in a US context, the relative impact on recidivism of felony convictions that are accompanied by a

[29] See Ellis v. The Chief Constable of Essex Police [2003] EWHC 1321.

[30] The study does not distinguish between the notification elements of the laws, discussed here, and their registration elements, which require people with convictions to report changes in their circumstances to police. It is entirely possible that isolating the registration requirements, which are linked to police duties to monitor sexual offenders, from the notification elements and focussing only on the impact of the latter would indicate even less of a possible deterrence effect.

publicly accessible criminal record and those in which the judge restricts the publicity of the record. Individuals whose conviction did not result in criminal labelling lost no civil rights (to vote etc.) and could legitimately fail to declare the conviction on employment applications and elsewhere. Analysis of reconviction data for 95,919 men and women supported the conclusion that those with a public record are significantly more likely to reoffend in two years than those without (Chiricos et al, 2007). Longitudinal studies have produced similar findings. For example, a 2018 empirical study in certain US states found that the existence of websites making criminal records public online leads to an increase of approximately 11% in reincarceration amongst those leaving prison with at least one prior record for a serious offence (Luca, 2018).[31]

The explanations given by researchers for how and why labelling increases reoffending centre on the difficulty of desisting from crime when, as is often the case in the United Sstates and Europe, one's criminal record prevents or obstructs one finding a decent job, getting an education, renting accommodation, obtaining insurance or loans, or being eligible for welfare benefits.[32] If this is correct, then it is likely that limiting the public accessibility of criminal records reduces both the harms of stigmatization to offenders and the harm to society of increased crime.

As all this suggests, the evidence on deterrence is weighty. But it is important to acknowledge that there are methodological limitations to existing studies from labelling theory, which should make us cautious about taking them as conclusive evidence for the claim that making criminal records public increases offending more than it deters. Two features of the research in particular are worth keeping in mind. The first is the fact that studies tend to compare rates of reoffending for people who have been incarcerated and labelled publicly as criminal with rates of reoffending by those who have been convicted but have not been incarcerated or labelled publicly. That makes it difficult to isolate the effects of labelling from the effects of incarceration. And that, in turn, limits the extent to which we can draw strong conclusions from that literature, especially as a range of studies appear to show that longer periods of incarceration are correlated with higher rates of reoffending anyway (Cullen and Jonson, 2014).

[31] See also Bernburg et al., 2006. It is not addressed in the paper whether some of this phenomenon could be explained by jurors looking defendants up online and therefore becoming aware of their previous records, which could increase willingness to convict.

[32] Criminal record data is made available to employers in the UK and EU countries and those with a criminal record are in many countries barred from a wide range of public sector and licensed positions (Larrauri, 2014).

The second limitation with empirical studies of labelling and deterrence is that they do not attempt to measure general deterrence but merely specific deterrence, that is, the likelihood that someone convicted once will be convicted again. This is not a problem if the ultimate aim of deterrence is to reduce the total *overall* number of crimes committed, because we know that most crimes are committed by the same people. So a measure that deters existing offenders will still reduce overall crime significantly. But if the aim of deterrence is *both* to reduce the overall number of crimes *and* to reduce the overall number of people criminalized in the first place, then it is a limitation. Because in this case we would want deterrence measures to be targeted both towards those who would otherwise be convicted as well as those who already have convictions. Because the research cited above only reports rates of *re*offending, it cannot tell us whether giving people a publicly visible record deters would-be offenders. To be completely conclusive, studies seeking to contest the hypothesis that labelling deters all-round would need to show that labelling reduces first-time offending by more than it aggravates reoffending. This has yet to be done. But even taking into account these limitations and being suitably cautious about just how much the studies prove, the research still shows clearly that, if a public criminal record has *any* effect on a person's behaviour, the effect is to increase reoffending. At the very least, this suggests we should be very sceptical about any attempt to justify the general public labelling of criminals in terms of deterrence.

Having said that, there may be exceptional cases in which a public emergency or pressing security risk might justify limited publicity to prevent harm. A potential example of the latter can be found in the UK government's response to the rapid spread of racist riots across the country in the summer of 2024. The riots were a reaction to the mass murder of a group of children by a 17-year-old black boy in the town of Southport. Fuelled by misinformation about the boy's migrant status and alleged terrorist agenda, groups of anti-migrant and white nationalist activists attacked refugee accommodation, mosques, and non-white members of the public, causing serious harm to people and properties, social disorder, and fear. In an attempt to stop the spread and escalation of these gatherings, the government ordered police around the country to make an example of the protesters. Widespread arrests and charges followed. But police also posted photographs and descriptions of the people they had charged online, on national broadcasters, and in the press, in an effort to de-escalate the situation and stop the riots spreading further, by warning others of the seriousness of the consequences and discouraging them from joining in. This kind of deterrence was an exceptional and temporary measure, targeted to a specific crime at a specific place and time.[33] Even if we decide that it was justified all things considered, and that less stigmatizing warnings would not have been just as effective—and there is at present no evidence either way—it would still only suggest a small range of circumstances in which it would be justified to publicize criminal records for deterrence.[34]

Where does this leave us? With the conclusion that *if* punishment is justified in virtue of its deterrence or crime-reduction effects, then *adding* a public criminal record to other sanctions is unlikely to be justified as punishment. This conclusion is relevant both to the kind of discretionary labelling imposed by the judge in the case of the sandwich-board wearing Hubacek and to labelling legislated by elected representatives devising new or existing sanctions.

Facilitating Punishment Through Exposure: The 'flypaper' Strategy

Before concluding this chapter, I want to consider one punishment-related reason why we might think it fair, even required, to publicize a person's criminal records. Unlike deterrence or reintegrative shaming, this justification for exposure is hardly ever discussed in public or academic debate. But I'm going to argue that it provides a much stronger ground for a right to know than punitive rationales. What I have in mind is the idea that sometimes exposing a person's criminal history to the public can facilitate criminal accountability and ultimately punishment, by encouraging as-yet-unknown victims to come forward to report their crimes. This approach to getting justice is sometimes informally referred to as the 'flypaper' strategy, because it involves putting a name out and seeing what 'sticks'. Let's consider a real example.

In 2009, London cabbie John Worboys was convicted of drugging, raping, and sexually assaulting 12 women. Worboys would pick up female clients, tell them he had just won large sums on the lottery or at a casino, and then invite them to toast his success with a glass of champagne. If they declined, he pestered them until they agreed. The champagne was spiked with sedatives. After a series of police blunders and failings, Worboys was eventually charged and

[33] The measure did not require a departure or derogation from policing regulations. The College of Policing guidance on police relations with the media and the naming of arrested suspects states that, although there is nothing to prevent police forces naming suspects where there is a policing purpose, the names of arrested suspects should not be released by the police to the press or public save for exceptional circumstances (College of Policing, 2023: para.4.2–5).

[34] Thanks to Harvey Redgrave for bringing this example to my attention.

sentenced to a minimum of eight years and a maximum of whole life. The judge said his release would be dependent on an assessment by the parole board that he no longer posed a threat to the public.

Just eight years later, despite Worboys' continued refusal to take responsibility for his crimes, the parole board decided to release him. The victims whose drugging and assault he was convicted for were dismayed and furious. So were the police. They had received over 80 reports about Worboys from members of the public, though only 12 of those had made it to court. He was getting off lightly for the crimes he had been convicted for and he was getting away with the rest of them. The police went to the press and released an appeal for more of Worboys victims to come forward to support further prosecutions against him. Four women did. The case was successful. This time, he was sentenced to two life sentences, meaning he will never be released (Siddique, 2019).

Worboys is now a household name in the United Kingdom, but police also use the flypaper strategy with lesser-known serious offenders who they believe are guilty of more crimes than they have been charged with or prosecuted for. The aim is to increase accountability and reduce impunity, by seeking to ensure that people are punished for (all or more of) their crimes. So the flypaper strategy is more about what we might call *getting justice*, whatever that might consist in, rather than obtaining retribution, communicating censure, or deterring others. Still, to the extent that it is about securing criminal accountability, it is a punitive rationale, and so worth considering alongside these other kinds of reasons.

At the time this book is being written, the flypaper strategy is used exclusively with respect to perpetrators of serial sexual, domestic, and related crimes of abuse. The reasons for this will be obvious to readers with even a cursory familiarity with the research around the perpetration of such crimes, or the criminal justice system's response to them. Nevertheless, they are worth summarizing here. Crimes of abuse, such as sexual assault and rape, domestic abuse, and child sexual abuse, share some distinctive characteristics. The special features of these crimes are discussed at length in Chapter 7, but for current purposes, just one of them is pertinent. That is the tendency for victims to be discouraged or inhibited from seeking criminal justice in a variety of ways. This reluctance may be prompted by the behaviour of the offender themselves, but it may also be a rational response to a demonstrably ineffective and retraumatizing criminal justice system. Research shows that victims of these crimes explain their non-reporting in terms of shame; fear; a sense of powerlessness; lack of trust in the criminal justice system to treat them with respect and protect them from harm; having been manipulated into a sense of loyalty to the offender; blaming themselves for the abuse; believing it is not serious enough to complain about; having been convinced that they lack credibility and won't be believed; and worries that reports will affect their children or other aspects of their family life.[35] Worboys' victims themselves described these considerations as weighing on their decisions.

Victims' concerns about the potentially negative response from the criminal justice system are well-founded (Ministry of Justice, 2024a). In England and Wales, only 2.7% of rapes reported to the police result in a charge let alone a conviction, and even those cases that do go to court routinely take years to be heard (Rape Crisis, 2024). In 2020, the government's Victims' Commissioner declared that rape had been effectively decriminalized in the United Kingdom (Victims' Commissioner, 2020). The story is the same when it comes to domestic abuse: only 3.5% of reported crimes result in a charge and only 2.8% result in a conviction.[36] In short, perpetrators offend with impunity and victims are denied criminal justice.

Problems of impunity with respect to these kinds of crimes become even worse when perpetrators are wealthy and powerful individuals. Status and money can help abusers both to secure the cooperation of bystanders and to deploy the civil legal system to literally silence their victims through the imposition of injunctions or non-disclosure agreements (Robinson and Yoshida, 2024). Where impunity is rife and power dynamics exploitative and unequal, where victims are shamed, threatened, and silenced, should suspects or convicted criminals be publicly named to encourage others to come forward? The answer must be 'yes', but also, 'it depends on the features of the specific case'. In the case of Worboys, a conviction had already been secured and there was little doubt that this was a very dangerous man who felt no remorse. But other cases might be less straightforward.

I am not able to give a full and in-depth defence of the flypaper strategy here, but it seems reasonable to propose that it is more likely to be justified the more serious the crime; the more certain it is that there are additional as-yet-unknown victims; the more urgent the need for accountability; the more vital victim testimony is to securing that outcome; and the less likely the exposure is to interfere with the administration of criminal justice. Flypaper is unlikely to be justified for relatively minor crimes like drug dealing or theft,

[35] For some recent examples of studies in what is a vast body of empirical research, see Stewart et al. (2024) on reasons for not reporting sexual violence and Birdsey and Snowball (2013) on reasons for not reporting domestic abuse.

[36] See 2024 statistics from the Office for National Statistics, reported in the BBC (Cuffe and Leigh, 2024).

even if there is serial offending and impunity. Police typically do not rely on victim cooperation and testimony to investigate or secure prosecutions for these crimes. If a person is already serving a life sentence, then they are at least being held accountable, even if not for all of their crimes. If police lack the grounds for believing that there are other victims who have not yet come forward, then the exposure serves no purpose. And if a person is just a suspect and not (yet) convicted, then exposure might prejudice the administration of justice. This is why, in such cases, police tend to appeal to as-yet-unknown victims to come forward by describing the suspect, their behaviour, and their modus operandi, but without naming or otherwise identifying them. At the same time, if a person has already been publicly identified as criminal, for example through a high-profile conviction, the less harm the additional exposure involved in a flypaper act is likely to cause. Decisions about whether and when to use the flypaper strategy and accountability for those decisions should ultimately lie with police, but they should be subject to regular oversight and scrutiny to ensure an acceptable balance is being struck between the need to punish the guilty and other aims of criminal justice, including procedural fairness and rehabilitation.[37]

Conclusion

In Chapter 2, I argued that the strong evidence of the harms and wrongs of public criminal records makes a robust justification for them necessary. In this chapter, I've argued that such a justification cannot be found in the need to censure people who commit crimes. Neither can it be found in the communicative or the deterrence purposes of punishment. On the other hand, it may be justified as part of a flypaper strategy designed to increase criminal accountability, depending on the circumstances of the case in question. The arguments put forward here should matter to anyone thinking about the justice of publicly labelling or identifying offenders as a punishment for crime, whether or not they subscribe to the specific theories I've discussed. In the next chapter, we turn to consider what I argue is the strongest justification for a right to know, namely the need to prevent harm.

[37] As currently happens in the United Kingdom, where an Independent Monitor is appointed to inspect annually the police disclosure of information to the public.

6

Sharing Criminal Records to Prevent Harm

Introduction	131
The Proposal: A Harm-Prevention-Based Right to Know	135
A Defence of the Proposed Right to Know	136
Justifying the need for 'reasonable grounds for belief'	136
The role of vulnerability	137
Defining 'significant risk of criminal harm'	138
Demonstrating 'significant risk of criminal harm'	140
The importance of individual risk-assessment	140
Information considered in the risk assessment must be relevant	141
Information should be current	142
Information should be reliable	143
The Kinds of Criminal History Information That Can Be Disclosed	144
The Right to Be Informed: 'upon request' and 'proactively'	145
The Rights of Subjects of Disclosure to Be Informed	146
Who Can Claim a Right to Know?	147
Professionals and practitioners managing criminal risk	147
Gatekeepers to vulnerability	148
People at risk and those who care for them	148
The Libertarian Objection	149
Conclusion	151

Introduction

Should people have a right to know about someone's criminal history if that information will help them protect themselves, or those to whom they have a duty of care, from criminal harm? Even the most ardent critics of the current expansion in access to criminal records accept that disclosure is sometimes morally required to protect the public. Take James Jacobs, whose book *The Eternal Criminal Record* has done more than any other publication to draw attention to the devastating injustices inflicted on people and families by public criminal records in the United States. Jacobs argues that in cases where 'making criminal records publicly accessible facilitates victimization avoidance' it is therefore justified for protective purposes (2015: 220).[1] And Unlock, the UK-based NGO that campaigns against the over-disclosure of criminal

[1] Other notable admissions of a harm-prevention rationale for disclosure by otherwise diehard opponents of publicity include Chin (2012:1808) and Larrauri, (2014: 395). See also Zand-Kurtovic and Boone (2023), Corda (2016: 55), Henley (2019), Lippke (2018, 2025).

The Crimes of Others. Katerina Hadjimatheou, Oxford University Press.
DOI: 10.1093/9780198925149.003.0006

records, supports sharing criminal records with employers when the crimes in question are 'relevant' to the role a person is applying for. In fact, support for disclosing criminal records for public safety and the protection of the vulnerable is the *only* issue on which a genuine consensus can be found in the debate over public access to criminal records.

This consensus has shaped laws and policies on criminal record disclosure around the world. Most, if not all, countries have some kind of legal provision for disclosing criminal records to employers and organizations that might otherwise unwittingly provide dangerous people with new opportunities to commit crime. Many have established entire agencies devoted exclusively to filtering and sharing criminal records in this way.[2] These initiatives are supported by domestic and international human rights laws. For example, the European Convention on Human Rights expressly recognizes that interferences with the Right to Privacy (Article 8), that might normally be considered violations of the law, can be justified if necessary for 'national security', 'public safety', and 'the prevention and detection of crime'. Public opinion, too, is in favour where recorded. A large US survey conducted in 2001 found that 'where there is a public safety or crime prevention interest' a substantial majority of members of the public supported the sharing of criminal history information outside the criminal justice system (Department of Justice, 2001: 5).

This solid consensus might appear to provide a strong starting point from which to defend a right to know. But strong consensuses can also end up stifling debate and making it harder to reach nuanced and informed positions. The dangers are both political and testimonial. On the one hand, there is a risk that 'protecting the vulnerable' becomes a trump card no one feels able or dares to challenge. On the other, our strong agreement on the justice of sharing records to prevent harm *in principle* might lead us to ignore the evidence on whether it actually works *in practice*. In both cases, appeals to public safety risk becoming a way of evading the real moral questions and shortcutting debate.

Nearly anything can be justified in the name of preventing harm or protecting the vulnerable, if the harm and vulnerability are severe enough.[3] Though the consensus on the importance of public safety is indeed strong, it is also quite narrow. And it is focussed on a relatively small range of extreme cases. For example, we probably all agree that police should alert the public

[2] In the United Kingdom, we have the Disclosure and Barring Agency, for example, whereas the Netherlands' equivalent is Justis, France's is Casier Judiciaire, Germany's is Führungszeugnis, Italy's is Procura della Repubblica, Spain's is Antecedentes Penales, and Portugal's is Registo Criminal.

[3] As just war theorists and trolley problem enthusiasts have shown so effectively.

when a serial killer escapes from a local prison. But we might disagree about whether local shopkeepers should be similarly alerted when a convicted shoplifter is released. We probably all agree that schools should be able to find out if teachers they employ or are considering employing have a history of abusing children. But we might well disagree about how much detail of that history they should have access to, whether the disclosure should include allegations as well as convictions, or how far back in a person's history the disclosure should reach. In other words, there may be a strong consensus in favour of a right to know for protective purposes, but there is likely to be much less agreement on the question of who can legitimately claim that right, to what information, and under what circumstances.

The aim of this chapter is to provide the intellectual groundwork for such an agreement. It does this by proposing and defending a right to know for harm-prevention purposes. It defines this right via a set of criteria that would need to be met for a disclosure to be justifiably made. And it argues that this right to know would, if implemented, protect the public from criminal harm without unfairly stigmatizing people with criminal histories. I will argue that my proposed right to know has three advantages. First, it is general enough to apply to any context in which a criminal record is shared or disclosed to protect public safety. Second, it is detailed enough to provide clear guidance for decision making in specific cases as well as on disclosure policies more broadly. Finally, it respects important moral principles, notably those of proportionality and necessity, equal treatment, dignity, and the presumption of innocence. Following my criteria for a right to know would enable us to align our practices around criminal record disclosures more closely to these norms, and therefore to be more faithful to them than (in most places) we currently are.

Previous discussion about the fair disclosure of criminal records for harm-prevention purposes has tended to focus on discrete arenas like employment and volunteering, access to public services such as housing and education, and public notification of sex offenders. The value of my criteria lies at least in part, therefore, in their provision of consistency and coherence across these previously disparate domains. But this chapter offers more than just an exercise in tidying things up and making things consistent. The generality of my criteria means they are also applicable to newer and less well-theorized arenas of criminal record disclosure. In Chapter 7, I show how the criteria support the disclosure of even non-conviction records, like police reports, to prevent predatory crimes and crimes of abuse, even while the arguments in this chapter suggest that disclosure practices in the context of employment, education, and public services should be constrained far more tightly than they currently are in most countries. Taking harm prevention seriously, as I argue my right to know does, therefore implies significant and, for some countries, radical changes to criminal record disclosure practices.

While my proposal for a right to know is relevant to all countries to some extent, practices of criminal records collection, retention and sharing vary so widely between jurisdictions that parts of the discussion will be more relevant to some than others. Certain countries—like the United Kingdom, most of Europe, and the West—have digitized all kinds of criminal records, from police records to court records, records of cautions, restraining orders, and other preventive measures as well as convictions. Others have digitized only some kinds of records and others still none. Many countries delete police records automatically after a set time or if charges are not brought, whereas others retain them indefinitely. The considerations that weigh in favour of and against recording and retaining information about reported and proven criminality are distinct from those relating to the sharing of information authorities already hold. While my arguments in this chapter are relevant to the former, my main aim is to examine what we are justified in doing with criminal records when and if we keep them. This means they are relevant to questions of reform to *existing* practice in countries like the United Kingdom, where records are retained and re-used routinely, but more useful in informing *future-facing* innovations in countries which, like Botswana, are only now moving towards digitization.

Throughout this chapter, I use the term 'disclosure' to describe the sharing or publication of criminal records that takes place to prevent harm. That term, which is associated with UK practice, implies that at least some of the criminal records that are relevant to preventing harm are not already publicly available. This is true of all jurisdictions, even US states in which police and arrest records are routinely published online. Even there, intentional sharing with specific people or agencies over and above general publication takes place in contexts like employment, access to housing, and insurance. And even there, details of criminal behaviour and modus operandi, which are recorded by police when they attend a call out, are not shared with the public. In most jurisdictions, police records and non-conviction records are confidential and protected from publication by laws including the right to privacy and the right to rehabilitation. As we will be discussing the sharing of precisely these kinds of records in this and the next chapter, the term disclosure seems appropriate.

The Proposal: A Harm-Prevention-Based Right to Know

My argument in a nutshell is that criminal records *should* be shared to prevent harm,[4] but only on a need-to-know basis. This means that a right to know should extend only to those people whose position, role, or circumstance gives rise to a duty or opportunity to protect the vulnerable or prevent criminal harm and only to the kinds of criminal history information those people need to achieve such protection. The criteria for claiming a right to know are the following:

If:

a) A person's criminal record (including non-conviction records) and behaviour provides the relevant authorities with reasonable grounds to believe that the person poses a significant risk of criminal harm to an individual, group, or population *and*
b) knowledge of that person's criminal history would allow the individual, group, or population to take precautions against that harm, whether to protect themselves or to protect a person/s to whom they have a duty of care, *then*
c) that individual, group or population has a right to be informed only about those aspects of the person's criminal history which, if known, would enable them to take protective measures.

The subject of a criminal record disclosure should be informed in advance of the disclosure and its content unless doing so would incur unreasonable costs or increase the risk of criminal harm.

'Relevant authorities' are just those authorities with responsibility for maintaining and disclosing criminal records. Typically, they include police and other criminal justice agencies, criminal records agencies, and social services including child protection.

[4] 'Harm prevention' and 'prevention of criminal harm' should be understood as distinct from 'crime reduction'. The latter tends to refer to deterrence, incapacitation, or other measures that act on an individual or on people in general to reduce their incentives or opportunities to commit crime, irrespective of whether that crime actually harms anyone. My interests are not in the field of crime reduction but rather in that of what UK policing calls 'public protection', that is 'the deployment of... powers and expertise to reduce the harms of crime by protecting those most vulnerable to victimization' (Kemshall and Wood, 2007).

A Defence of the Proposed Right to Know

Justifying the need for 'reasonable grounds for belief'

How certain should we need to be that a criminal record evidences risk before a disclosure is permissible? Any account of a right to know needs to specify the point or level of certainty—the 'epistemic threshold'—required for a belief to be considered strong enough to warrant authorization of a disclosure. I have proposed that the threshold should be 'reasonable grounds for belief' but others have defended much lower or higher thresholds. For example, until 2013 police chiefs in the United Kingdom were permitted by law to disclose any information in police records which they considered was relevant to public safety and which 'might be true' (The Police Act, 1997). This threshold seems much too low to be fair to those with criminal records. That's because almost anything 'might be true', so implementing this standard would permit the disclosure of a wide range of information including many that most of us would think should not be shared further. It would, for example, allow the disclosure of allegations of criminality that police believe strongly to be unreliable—so long as these are not entirely implausible. We owe it to people with criminal records to insist at the very least that disclosures will only be made when there are good reasons to do so. Disclosing something merely because it indicates relevant risk and might be true is not a good enough reason.

At the other end of the spectrum of thresholds, some have argued that we should not allow the disclosure of any criminal record information that might *not* be true. For example, scholars like Larrauri (2014) and Weaver (2018) argue that it would be unjust to stigmatize someone as criminal unless the criminality has been proven 'beyond reasonable doubt', that is, through a criminal conviction. Doing so, they argue, would undermine the presumption of innocence, which is a basic civil right. I disagree with this position and later in the chapter will explain why it does not provide a convincing objection to my proposed right to know. For the moment, I will say that this might be a reasonable position to take if having a criminal conviction were the *only reliable indicator* of significant risk of future criminality. But that is not the case. Most serious criminal behaviour of the kind we all want people to be protected from never actually results in a conviction. In fact the minority of crimes reported to police result in a conviction. But, as I will argue in detail later, this is particularly true of predatory crimes, including serious and violent abuse of adults and children—precisely the kind of crimes we hope criminal records checks or disclosures would help to prevent. The problem is that adopting 'beyond reasonable doubt' as the standard for disclosure would inevitably enable people who have police records—and often multiple records—for serious violent crimes against vulnerable people, to gain access to further victims through their work, volunteering, and other activities. Not only would that be unjust to those past and future victims, it would also be irrational. Because it would require us to treat people who we have good reason to believe pose a real risk, as if they posed none at all.

One reason for choosing 'reasonable grounds for belief' as the lowest epistemic threshold we should reach before permitting a disclosure is that it is continuous with thresholds normally applied in the United Kingdom and other countries to justify preventive interferences with a person's freedom or rights, such as police searches. In the United Kingdom, it is also the current threshold regulating the disclosure of non-conviction information such as police records of reported crime (Disclosure and Barring Service, 2024: Principle 2). What qualifies as 'reasonable' is obviously subjective and open to debate. But criminal justice practitioners, judges, and courts are well practiced in working with and deploying the concept of reasonableness in their daily work.

The reason I defend 'reasonable grounds for belief' as the 'lowest' rather than the *only* threshold is that, in practice, our tolerance for risk varies according to the severity of the potential harm and the vulnerability of the potential victim. So it seems sensible to leave open the question of whether for some less serious kinds of criminal harm it may be proportionate to apply a higher threshold. One such threshold might be the belief that 'on the balance of probabilities' one person poses a risk of harm to another. 'On the balance of probabilities' is the threshold that normally has to be met in order to impose preventive measures such as restraining orders in a civil court. Another threshold, which was proposed by Grace in his 2014 discussion of criminal records and privacy, is 'reasonably certain', which is slightly higher than 'on the balance of probabilities'. We might think that it is only fair to disclose a previous offence of shoplifting or drug dealing if one is reasonably certain the person will use a position to repeat that crime, while at the same time thinking that we should take fewer chances with people who might pose a risk of murder or abuse. My criteria allows for these details to be worked out in relation to specific cases.

The role of vulnerability

Having said that, we can also capture a chunk of the cases in which we might want to take fewer chances in the category of 'vulnerability'. Vulnerability does not feature explicitly in my criteria because, even though it is an important consideration in assessing whether the risk posed by a person justifies a disclosure, the presence of vulnerability is not necessary for disclosure to be justified. Vulnerability might be an attribute or position of a potential victim. For example, of children, adults with cognitive or physical disabilities, or those who find themselves in a position of relative weakness with respect to the authority or power of the person with the record. But vulnerability could also be a feature of a place or context. For example, nuclear energy or weapons facilities, chemical laboratories, national security roles, major transport and infrastructure sites have certain vulnerabilities in the sense that they provide people who access them with extraordinary opportunities to inflict serious criminal harm on persons, governments, or populations. We care a lot about protecting vulnerable people because they tend to be targeted for violence and abuse, and because they are less able to defend and protect themselves. We care about vulnerable places and things because failing to protect them exposes us all to serious harms. In the United Kingdom, the law allows police to share more detailed and older criminal record information with employers offering roles that give people responsibility for or access to vulnerable people, places, or things, than with employers who do not. My criteria allow for these distinctions.

Defining 'significant risk of criminal harm'

My criteria specify that a disclosure should be supported by a reasonable belief that a person poses a 'significant risk' of criminal harm. 'Significant risk' is not intended as a statistical term but merely implies a credible likelihood of offending. 'Criminal harm' means harm to a person or agent resulting from criminal behaviour. Someone who has a criminal record for possessing marijuana for personal use poses no risk of criminal *harm* to anyone in almost any conceivable scenario.[5] Someone who has a criminal record for stealing from their workplace, but who is applying for a position in a company that provides them with no opportunity for future theft, poses no risk of *criminal* harm to that company, though their history may indicate that they are less trustworthy than other candidates.[6] In neither scenario would it be justified to disclose the criminal record on harm-prevention grounds.

[5] The only cases in which it would are those in which the possession indicated a dependency on substances and the person was applying for a job operating potentially dangerous machinery or vehicles.

[6] This criterion would also count against disclosing criminal history information about activities that should not have been criminalized in the first place. For example, the case of Rotaru v. Romania (2000) relates to a legal challenge brought against the Romanian Intelligence Service for sharing the criminal

In decisions about when to disclose what to whom, an individual risk- assessment should take into account both the severity of the potential harm and the risk that the harm will in fact occur. The former involves thinking about the vulnerability of the people or context to which the person with a criminal record is seeking access, whereas the latter involves assessing how likely it is that the person will engage in the harmful behaviour given their individual circumstances. My criteria do not specify a threshold of severity for criminal harm. Rather, proportionality should be sought between harm prevented, the practical costs of disclosure, and the burdens imposed on those with records.

My criteria do entail that the risk of criminal harm must be posed by *the individual about whom the disclosure is made*. Readers would be forgiven for assuming that this is so obvious it need not be stated. But actual disclosure practices in some countries have diverged from this in recent years, especially in the context of employment. For example, recent research in Canada described a case in which Ontario police disclosed records of a female job applicant's criminal *victimisation*, leading ultimately to her rejection by the prospective employer (Maurutto et al., 2023:1377). The woman had a restraining order in place against her abusive ex-partner. When she applied for a job in a daycare centre, the record of the restraining order was shared with the employers, on the ground that there was a chance her ex-partner would harass her at work, putting the children and staff at risk. As the risk of criminal harm in this case was posed not by the woman but by her abusive partner, and the record was his rather than hers, my criteria would rule out this kind of disclosure.

Baldwin discusses a related but slightly different case, in which a mother lost her job in a school because her son had a violent criminal past. He argues, in relation to that case, that 'it is remarkable that an applicant can be subjected to a . . . disclosure relating to the activities of other individuals. This is a form of *guilt by association* which should, frankly, be an unacceptable form of vetting in any circumstance (2012: 162)'. Baldwin is correct, but it is worth taking a moment to spell out the reason why stigmatization-by-association is unacceptable. Let's consider again the example of the woman rejected by the daycare centre. The reason the rejection was unfair was not that employing the woman posed no risk of criminal harm to the children and staff at the daycare centre. On the contrary, employing her would likely, other things being equal, have

record of a citizen whose file contained information about his conviction for 'insulting behaviour'. The man had, as a student, written two letters of protest against the abolition of freedom of expression when the communist regime was established in 1946. (Cited in Baldwin, 2012: 160) posed such a risk. Rather, the reason is that the woman herself bore neither causal nor moral responsibility for that risk. She played no role in creating the risk and held no power to reduce it, therefore, she should bear none of the costs of protecting people against it.

Those costs should instead have been borne by the two agents who were responsible for that risk, namely, the woman's ex-partner and the police. The women's ex-partner was responsible because he had chosen to illegally abuse and threaten her. The police were responsible because they had through their failure to ensure her protection fallen short in their professional duty to prevent him from doing so. In other words, the abusive partner and the police *had jointly made it the case* that employing the woman posed a risk of criminal harm to those attending the daycare centre. Displacing the costs of managing the risk onto her shoulders was especially unfair in light of the fact that the police themselves could have taken protective measures to reduce the risk, such as warning the abusive partner against visiting the daycare centre and preparing to arrest him in the eventuality that he did.

Demonstrating 'significant risk of criminal harm'

The importance of individual risk-assessment

Assuming then, that the disclosing authorities are sharing information about a person who themselves poses a 'significant risk of criminal harm', how should this risk be established and demonstrated? As others have argued before me in relation to the imposition of different kinds of preventive restraints, the decision-making process should involve an individual risk-assessment (Hoskins, 2019: 175; Duff, 1998). Individual risk-assessments stand in contrast to profiling exercises. The latter assess risk on the basis of statistical trends and group characteristics (e.g., the fact that a person shares sex, age, or ethnic attributes associated with crime). The former consider the particular risk posed by the specific individual given their personal history and circumstances.[7] Individual risk-assessments are already the established approach to criminal justice decision-making used by judges, juries, and parole boards. They are, unlike profiling exercises, compatible with respect for the autonomy and agency of individuals, as well as their culpability.

[7] For example, the fact that someone was acquitted of a crime should not be taken at face value as conclusive evidence of a lack of risk. An individual risk-assessment would reveal, for example, if the trial collapsed due to a key witness withdrawing their testimony after suspected intimidation or fear.

Risk assessments also stand in contrast to policies that permit disclosure of certain kinds of information just because they fall within a specific category. For example, a policy or regulation that permits disclosure of unspent records should not entail an automatic disclosure of all unspent convictions just because they are unspent. Some of the convictions in a record may be relevant to the particular context in ways that suggest risk, but others may not. Relying solely on categories like 'spent' or 'unspent' to make decisions about disclosure does not amount to a risk assessment. Doing so, for example, in the employment context, displaces the responsibility for such an assessment onto the employers, and evidence shows that they often shirk that duty by reflexively excluding any candidate with a 'live' record.

Risk assessments may differ in their rigour and depth depending on vulnerability. In most cases in which disclosure of criminal records might be considered, individual risk-assessments may be relatively cursory, involving the application of evidence-based rules of thumb and formulas for making routine disclosures, based on analysis of many cases over time. Where the vulnerability is low, it is also reasonable to limit these assessments to records of convictions or unspent convictions. But where the vulnerability is high, knowledge of criminal typologies and offending trajectories, as well as the skills to apply this knowledge to the case in question, are also necessary to enable sound judgements of risk. And non-conviction records such as police reports should also be considered in that risk assessment process.

Information considered in the risk assessment must be relevant

Information which is disclosed must be directly relevant to the purpose for which the disclosure is being sought, for example, there must be, in Henley's words, a demonstrably 'close nexus' between 'the nature or circumstances of an offence and the purposes of any enquiry about criminal background'.[8] A paradigm example of 'close nexus' is provided by the real case of the St Albans Poisoner, a serial killer who became infamous in England in the 1970s, well before criminal records were digitized or subject to disclosure. The poisoner, whose name was Graham Frederick Young, murdered three people, was suspected of killing a fourth, and attempted to kill two others. Young was first incarcerated at 14, after having been found guilty of poisoning his father and sister. He had a long-standing obsession with chemicals and poisons which continued while he was in prison. After being released at the end of his

[8] Henley (2019: 334). For important articulations of similar arguments, see also Aukerman (2005: 39–49) and Corda (2016: 36).

sentence, he applied for jobs in a forensic science laboratory and a pharmaceutical training school, both of which would have given him ready access to poisonous substances. Neither application was successful, but eventually he did find work in the storeroom of a laboratory that used toxic chemicals to manufacture lenses for the military. Within 6 months of starting his new job, he was arrested for poisoning three of his workmates and killing two of them. He spent the rest of his life in prison. The nexus between Young's criminal history and his employment could not have been closer.

In contrast, the case of P, which was fought in the UK's Supreme Court in a 2017 legal challenge[9] to the government's criminal records policy, illustrates the injustice of disclosing when there is no close nexus. In 1999, P received a caution for stealing a sandwich from a shop and, a couple of months later, a conviction for stealing a book and failing to surrender to the bail granted for that offence. She was 28 years old, homeless, and suffering from schizophrenia spectrum disorder. Sixteen years later, after having received treatment successfully and committed no further offences, P qualified to work as a teaching assistant. Because the rules on working with children meant she was obliged to disclose *all* criminal records to prospective employers, she could not secure a job. P's criminal record had not indicated any risk to children in the first place, so the 'close nexus' test was not met. The fact that she was ever made to disclose it, let alone decades later, served no purpose at all, let alone that of protecting vulnerable people from harm.

Information should be current

'Recency' is often stipulated as a criterion of relevance in the context of criminal record disclosures, because, in general, the older the information, the less likely it is to indicate actual risk. But 'currency'—which I define as 'recent enough to be relevant to the present purposes'—recognizes better that the extent to which recency indicates risk varies according to a range of factors. Most people with criminal records do at some point 'age out' of crime and stop offending or 'desist'. Implementing a process of risk assessment that includes consideration of currency recognizes better that 'redemption times' (the amount of time that must pass for a person's risk of offending to align with that of the general population) differ across crime types and across repeat or one-time offenders. Professionals making decisions about disclosures should take these differences into account.

[9] R (on the application of P) (Appellant) v. Secretary of State for the Home Department and others (Respondents), UKSC/2017/0170.

As well as ensuring that risk assessments are based in evidence and not mere speculation, the requirement for currency embeds into the decision-making process respect for individual agency. It does so by ensuring that processes recognize and are responsive to the fact that people are moral agents with capacities to improve and reform. Recognition of the enduring potential for rehabilitation of offenders has been judged by European Courts to be a positive obligation of states that is 'grounded in human dignity' (Meijer, 2017: 161). Hoskins puts forward a powerful philosophical argument in support of such recognition in policies and practices managing people with convictions. He argues that preventive interventions that 'fail to take seriously the prospect of offenders' reform', or communicate to individuals and the community 'that the state does not really regard their redemption as a genuine prospect, or at least not a prospect that is worthy of its concern', express 'contempt' for people and are therefore incompatible with respect for their dignity (Hoskins, 2019: 168, 116). This seems correct. While it is entirely plausible that some people's criminal records will remain current for their entire lives, for most people a track record of no contact with the criminal justice system will at some point qualify as evidence of reduced risk of criminal harm.[10]

Information should be reliable

The relevant authorities should assess, be satisfied with, and be able to demonstrate the reliability of the information that goes into a disclosure. This is implied in the threshold of 'reasonable grounds to believe' discussed above, but it is worth exploring in a little more depth here too. The question of reliability is not often addressed in the literature on criminal records, but it is arguably important enough to be included alongside close nexus and currency as a necessary consideration in the risk-assessment process for disclosure. Assessing the reliability of evidence and intelligence is of course something police do constantly, when making decisions about whether to investigate a crime, make an arrest, pursue a prosecution, or not. Other relevant authorities, such as social workers, may be both less confident and less competent in this arena. One of the benefits of establishing an agency or government department tasked with the management of disclosures is that professionals working there can develop such expertise. This is especially important where the disclosure relates to non-conviction records, because the behaviours such records attribute to a person have not been proven in a criminal court.

[10] Though my focus in this book is on public access to criminal records, these points could clearly also be drawn on to argue in favour of policies of expungement for some kinds of records.

Decision-making processes with respect to the disclosure of non-conviction records to members of the public must involve assessments of reliability over and above those necessary for convictions, because there is a greater likelihood that the reports captured in the records may be erroneous. In fact, and perhaps surprisingly, the risk of false allegations may in some cases be *higher* when someone already has a prior criminal record. We saw how this can occur in Chapter 2 when we considered the case of Kieran, the young autistic man who as a child had been convicted of an offense of 'outraging public decency'. Kieran had been supported by a youth offending service caseworker to rehabilitate and reintegrate successfully. But his vigilante neighbours subjected him to a campaign of harassment and malicious and false allegations of sexual offending, which police were obliged to record every time. A proper risk assessment of someone like Kieran should be rigorous enough to identify the allegations as malicious and discount them as indicators of risk of criminal harm.

The Kinds of Criminal History Information That Can Be Disclosed

On my account, a right to know extends to 'those aspects of a person's criminal history which, if known, would enable others to take protective measures'. Although the right extends to those aspects *only*, this still leaves open the possibility for disclosure of any *kind* of criminal history information. My criteria allow in principle for a disclosure to include information both about previous convictions and about behaviour that did not result in a conviction. It also permits the disclosure of outcomes of formal risk assessments, the imposition by a court of preventive orders, and so on. The disclosure itself might include a summary in the form of a certificate of conduct, a judgement of risk level, or actual details of the criminal behaviour recorded. Just how much and what kind of information it is permissible to share in any particular case depends heavily on the purpose for which it is being disclosed and the nature of the risk posed. The disclosure of non-conviction records such as police reports and allegations is particularly controversial, and I will defend my endorsement of it in depth in a moment.

As well as excluding the sharing of information that does not enable preventive action, my criteria should be interpreted as requiring that information should only be shared in the least intrusive and stigmatizing way compatible with the prevention of harm. This is implicit in my criterion C. Too often people with criminal records are treated as if their pasts make them fair game for any future exclusion or deprivation, as if they have forfeited any right to basic concern. This condition serves simply to require that efforts to achieve the protective potential of a disclosure do not cause unnecessary harms.

While I do not wish to be too prescriptive here about precisely what form disclosures should take, the Dutch approach, which allows sharing of information with employers only in the form of generic certificates of conduct, promises to be both less stigmatizing for people with criminal records and less demanding for employers than those which disclose, for example, a list of convictions. There is, as already discussed in detail in Chapter 2, a great deal of evidence that employers are neither confident nor competent in assessing risk and making sound decisions about who they can safely employ. Ultimately, they have been shown to assume mistakenly that any record of criminal history must be relevant and to respond irrationally and unfairly when faced with them. But in many cases where there is an actual risk of harm, preventive action can be taken without knowledge of the precise behaviour or conviction included in a record. For example, the Netherlands' approach of specifying the level of risk for employers in advance should support more confident decision-making.

The Right to Be Informed: 'upon request' and 'proactively'

As I specify it, the right to know is a right to 'be informed'. This leaves open the possibility that it is a right to be informed *upon request* or a right to be informed *proactively*. Either is possible, depending on the circumstances. 'Upon request' disclosures are justified when the individual, group, or agent who can take protective action has either the duty or the discretion to request the information. For example, employers hiring people to care for vulnerable adults have a moral (and in many places a legal) duty to find out whether the people they employ pose a significant risk of criminal harm to those within their care.

A right to be informed via a proactive disclosure would only apply when the risk is high, the criminal harm is serious, and the person who can take protective action could not be expected or relied upon to ask for the information themselves. To illustrate how such considerations might operate in practice, we can take a real example. In 1997, the Supreme Court released a landmark legal decision which became a test case for a 'need to know' justification for criminal record disclosures in the United Kingdom.[11] The case related to a

[11] See R v. Chief Constable of North Wales Police, *ex parte* AB [1997] 3 WLR.

disclosure about child sex offences made by police in North Wales. The disclosure was made to the owners of a campsite in a popular holiday destination. Police visited them and warned them that one of the camper vans on their site housed a couple who posed a danger to other campers, in particular children. The couple had recently been released from prison. They had both served sentences of over 10 years for multiple, serious, and violent child sexual abuse. Upon release, both had been assessed as extremely high risk by psychologists and parole officers. At the time of the police visit and the disclosure, the couple had been living in the holiday campsite off-season. They moved there after being forced out of multiple lodgings by neighbours who had become aware of their convictions from historical press reports and subjected them to harassment. They had given up on attempts to secure stable accommodation and had instead bought a camper van. When school holidays came around and the popular campsite was about to be inundated by families with children, police asked the couple to voluntarily move their camper van off the site. When the couple did not, the police informed the owners of the campsite of the couple's history. The couple were promptly evicted.

Was it permissible for the police to inform the campsite owners? According to my account of the right to know, yes. The couple posed a significant risk of criminal harm, and as far as we know there was no less intrusive way for police to address this than to disclose the risk they posed. The only alternatives immediately open to police would have been to install a surveillance team to monitor the couple's movements for the duration of the school holidays, to watch and wait and take the risk of them committing another crime, or to forcibly remove them from the site. The first option would have been extremely resource-intensive and in any case imperfect. The second would have exposed the children at the campsite to unacceptable risk. The third exceeded the legal authority of the police. Informing the campsite owners did not by itself solve the problem of the risk posed by the couple. At best it was an exercise in disruption and at worst it was a short-term displacement of risk. But it did allow the owners of the site to exercise their duty of care to their guests and protect their children from serious risk of criminal harm.

The Rights of Subjects of Disclosure to Be Informed

The North Wales case also helps illustrate the last requirement of my proposed right to know, namely that subjects of a criminal record disclosure should be informed in advance of the disclosure and its content unless doing so would incur unreasonable costs or be likely to increase the risk of criminal harm. Informing people of their imminent exposure or labelling is important because it allows them to make representations (i.e., provide evidence of reform, contest the content or basis for the disclosure) or otherwise prepare in ways that enable them to maintain some dignity. The police in North Wales met this condition by warning the couple that they intended to inform the campsite owners and giving them the opportunity to respond or react in advance.[12] Advance notification would not be appropriate in cases where it may prompt reprisals or other actions that expose vulnerable people to increased risk of harm. We will consider such cases in a moment, when we discuss disclosures in the context of preventing crimes of abuse.[13]

Who Can Claim a Right to Know?

In practice, the criteria and conditions set out above provide three categories of people with a right to know.

Professionals and practitioners managing criminal risk

First, professionals within the criminal justice system whose role includes the management of risk posed by people with criminal histories, for example, psychiatrists, probation officers, police, parole boards. This aligns with current practice in most countries and should be relatively uncontroversial. It seems safe to assume that most people would accept that such professionals need to have access to a broad range of criminal history information to make their assessments and fulfil their daily duties, and to inform decisions about risk that are reliable and safe. Making detailed information available to such professionals is only minimally stigmatizing (if at all) because it is not shared beyond the relatively closed context of the criminal justice system.

[12] Of course, we can have a parallel debate about whether the state through social or other services should have done more to provide them with safe possibilities for accommodation and whether it was reasonable to expect them to live a peripatetic lifestyle with all the insecurity and other shortcomings that entails.

[13] In Kentucky in the United States, anyone can do a criminal records check by paying a small fee for a court records search that would also reveal cases that were dropped and prevention orders. But the subject of the request is notified in writing that the request has been made, which brings a risk of reprisal for those who make it.

Gatekeepers to vulnerability

The second category is people whose professional role puts them in a position of care in relation to people or things that are vulnerable to criminal exploitation, abuse, or attack, or as gatekeepers for access to such people or things. This category includes most professional bodies, because professional bodies play an important social role in licencing people to take up positions of power and trust. In addition, it includes employers of those working or volunteering with children or vulnerable adults, including in care homes, social services, prisons, police, schools, hospitals, and so on, as well as those working with dangerous materials, such as weapons, chemical and nuclear research, matters of national security, infrastructure, and large sums of money. Plausibly, it could also include services like online dating sites, which are often targeted by serial romance fraud, sexual, and domestic abuse offenders to scout for victims. These platforms have a duty to recognize that their services provide dangerous people with the opportunity to invent a persona that enables them to continue offending, and to take protective measures to reduce the risk. In some cases, people will already be barred from working or volunteering in specific roles or from opening accounts on certain platforms, and a records check will consist merely in a verification of barred status. Given that most countries that disclose records to employers do so in a wide range of cases where there is no vulnerability at play, this category represents a significant reduction in the range of cases in which disclosure would be permitted.

People at risk and those who care for them

The third category includes members of the public (or those responsible for their care, if the person lacks capacity) who are at risk of criminal exploitation, abuse, or attack by specific individuals. Examples include people in a local area at risk from a violent and dangerous fugitive or as-yet-un-apprehended serial rapist or killer. More controversially, it also includes schemes set up to enable people vulnerable to violent and abusive criminality from specific individuals to receive detailed information about the risk that an individual poses, even if they have never been convicted of a crime. I will provide detailed arguments defending this proposal in a moment.

There are some cases in which fulfilling some people's right to know might unavoidably mean sharing criminal history information with entire populations. For example, imminent threats to the public from dangerous individuals or groups, such as fugitives or terrorists, at large in a place or community would in some cases justify alerts through the press and broadcasters to allow people to take protective measures. It is also conceivable that warning one group of people about a danger might only be achievable in practice by making the warning available to everyone. However, this kind of case is exceptional and analogous to an emergency measure, a departure from normal practice.

The Libertarian Objection

Before looking more carefully at the sharing of non-conviction information to prevent crimes, I want to address one immediate objection to the way I have defined these categories, and this latter category in particular. Libertarian thinkers would contest both the narrowness of my proposed categories and the significant decision-making role I assign to 'relevant authorities'. Libertarians hold that individual citizens should be empowered through free access to information to exercise their own personal choices about how much risk they are prepared to take. They argue that *everyone* is potentially in a position to protect themselves and others from the criminal harm posed by people with criminal records. Therefore, it should be left up to individuals to decide whether they have a 'need to know' about the information, rather than assumed by some academic sitting in their ivory tower, or worse decided on their behalf by the state. The categories I propose are, they would insist, artificially narrow. What's more, they would argue, they are narrower than is justified by my own criteria, because they deprive those best placed to prevent harm of the information needed to do so.

James Jacobs articulates this libertarian position when he argues that 'liberal access to individual criminal history information reflects the same cultural values as liberal access to firearms, that is, that the individual has the right to protect herself from possibly dangerous people based on her own assessment. She should not have to rely on government officials to decide what criminal record information she and other community members should have access to' (2015: 223). Jacobs argues that policies enforcing the publication in open fora of the details of child sex offenders in the community are 'an excellent example' of this approach because they 'reduce victimization' (p. 219). Similar arguments about the public's entitlement to information about safety have been made for the establishment of publicly searchable registries of sex offenders and of domestic abuse offenders.[14] These echo more general arguments that a

[14] To my knowledge, the only existing domestic abuse register is the Guam Family Violence Registry. It is an online portal that allows anyone to see the name, photograph, address, and conviction record of all those convicted of family violence (which equates to what we in the United Kingdom call domestic

proper concern for individual freedom requires that governments refrain from using 'legal coercion' to conceal criminal records and 'keep them in the dark' (Volokh, 2000: 36-38).

The problem with these arguments is, quite plainly, that they are wrong.[15] The analogy they rest on is accurate, but the conclusion is mistaken. Giving the public the right to bear firearms does not improve people's ability to protect themselves and their families. On the contrary, it is the reason US citizens are over three times more likely than Canadian citizens and about twenty-five times more likely than Japanese citizens to die from homicide (UNODC, 2023). Turning back to child sexual abuse, evidence shows that, far from reducing crime, sex offender notification measures that publicize criminal records to the entire community actually increase specific reoffending (Prescott and Rockoff, 2008; Hamilton and Fairfaz-Columbo, 2023). Sex offender notification also drives offenders to seek to avoid registration by going underground and off the radar, undermining the efforts of professionals such as probation and parole officers to monitor them and manage their risk. It discourages children from reporting their abusive parents and family members for fear of stigmatization and attack. And it prompts violence and harassment by members of the public.[16] Even if some people do form beliefs and behave rationally when given access to information about people's criminal histories, their numbers are dwarfed by those who abuse such information or react irrationally, in ways that have cumulatively devastating effects on individuals while also harming communities. Whatever else complete liberalization of criminal record information might achieve, it would not result in a reduction in victimization from criminal harm.[17]

abuse) in Guam. The 2011 Act establishing that registry can be found at: https://www.guamlegislature.com/Bills_Introduced_31st/Bill%20No.%20B195-31%20%28COR%29.pdf. Logan described what he calls a 'sense of informational entitlement, predicated on the idea that the public was morally entitled to registrants' information in order to self-protect, and that the failure of the government to ensure public safety made public dissemination a practical necessity' (Logan, 2009: xv to xvi).

[15] Much worse libertarian arguments have also been put forward in the past by economists. They make claims like 'stigma actually increases efficiency, because allocative efficiency increases as information is disclosed' (Rasmusen, 1996: 536) and "[i]nsofar as the stigma of conviction hurts merely because it conveys useful information to potential transactors with the convicted criminal . . . it creates social value that may offset the hurt" (Posner, 1992:226). But the assumption that more information always equals more efficient decisions is clearly fallacious and has been thoroughly discredited as such. As a result, these arguments are rarely voiced today. Corda (2016) provides further useful refutation of this position.

[16] Allen (2009) reported in the media how prison and probation staff 'are not happy . . . They believe it is leading sex offenders to stop registering with the state and go underground"; See also attacks on sex offenders whose personal details are made public under Megan's Law in the USA, reported in Levenson et al, 2007.

[17] In response it might be argued that people have a right to know *not* because giving them information leads to better outcomes like reduced criminal harm, but because the information is *true*. I deal with this objection, which is relevant beyond this specific section, in the concluding chapter.

Conclusion

I have argued in favour of a right to know about the criminal histories of people who pose a significant risk of criminal harm, especially to people and things that are vulnerable to such harm. I have sought to describe and defend such a right in detail. And I have argued that taking my proposed right seriously implies significant reductions in the sharing of criminal records with employers and providers of other services than currently occurs in most countries. In the next chapter, I show how these same criteria would permit a significant expansion in disclosures even of non-conviction records to prevent predatory crimes and crimes of abuse. As I argue in depth there, the special circumstances surrounding those kinds of harms makes disclosures both more protective and less unfairly stigmatizing than they are for other crimes.

7

Disclosing Criminal Records to Protect People from Predatory Crimes and Crimes of Abuse

Introduction 153
The Distinctiveness of Dangerousness, Predation, and Abuse 154
Protecting Sex Workers from Predatory Offenders: 'Ugly Mug' and 'Dodgy Punter' Schemes 158
Domestic Abuse Disclosure Schemes 159
Objections from the Presumption of Innocence and of 'Harmlessness' 164
Conclusion 167

Introduction

It is universally recognized that many of the most serious and serial violent crimes take place in the home and other 'caring' environments and in the context of intimate, trusted, and familial relationships. But these crime types and contexts are largely overlooked in the debate about criminal records. This chapter offers evidence about the effectiveness of criminal records disclosures to prevent exploitation and abuse and, drawing on the criteria defended in Chapter 6, argues for a significant expansion in their use in such contexts, including records of behaviour for which a person has never received a conviction.

Nowhere is public support for criminal record disclosures stronger than in relation to the protection of vulnerable people from serial perpetrators of 'hidden' and predatory crimes like sexual violence, domestic abuse, and child abuse.[1] Public support for the sharing of criminal history information about

[1] In 1993, the Home Office launched a public consultation on the sharing of criminal history information. It published a summary of the approximately 200 responses it received. The majority of respondents were in favour of continuing to release 'non-conviction information' in situations such as crimes of sexual abuse against children (Home Office, 1993: para. 10).

The Crimes of Others. Katerina Hadjimatheou, Oxford University Press. © Katerina Hadjimatheou 2026.
DOI: 10.1093/9780198925149.003.0007

such crimes has grown, along with greater awareness of the extent to which repeat and serial perpetrators have been able to attack and abuse multiple victims with impunity over many years.[2] In what follows, I draw on my own empirical research as well as research carried out by others to argue that the distinctive features of such crimes—namely, the special role of secrecy, lies, manipulation and silencing in their perpetration, their serial nature, and the widespread impunity with which they are committed—make preventive measures including criminal record disclosures more appropriate than they would be for other crime types. Focussing on case studies around violence towards sex workers and domestic abuse, I argue that patterns of behaviour exposed through non-conviction records can counter the perpetration of such crimes by revealing risk and dangerousness to those directly vulnerable to harm. I end by defending my position against the criticism that disclosing non-conviction records violates the presumption of innocence, by arguing that reliable evidence of serious risk is not reducible to criminal convictions proven in court.

The Distinctiveness of Dangerousness, Predation, and Abuse

Some readers will have noticed my switch in this section to the use of the term 'perpetration'. This is intentional. It recognizes that most people who abuse and violate others exhibit a pattern of behaviour that is calculated and persistent. This distinguishes them from other lawbreakers. The kind of behaviour I have in mind aligns with Antony Duff's definition of 'dangerous offenders' as:

> 'persistent, serious, violent offenders . . . those whose repeated crimes cannot, given the character and contexts of their commission, be seen merely as a succession of discrete aberrations in otherwise law-abiding lives; [but] rather display a *pattern* of offending, which persists despite regular convictions and punishments . . . [and which] is such that we can interpret it only as displaying his utter and continuing disregard for the values on which our community depends' (1998: 141, 161).

[2] We have all seen the recent scandals about child abuse in the church and schools, the abuse of children and young mothers in residential homes, the #MeToo movement, so-called 'revenge pornography', and anti-femicide initiatives, to name a few.

Though Duff himself does not focus on any specific crime type in particular, his description paints an accurate portrait of those who target vulnerable people for violence and abuse.

Duff's own aim in conceptualizing dangerousness is to explore why it might be justified to continue to detain some people beyond the end of their punitive imprisonment. But his reasoning can help us to understand why disclosing non-conviction records might be justified for people with histories of perpetrating predatory crimes and crimes of abuse. For Duff's purposes, dangerousness of a severity sufficient to justify preventive detention is constituted by multiple convictions. For preventive disclosure of criminal records, which is a far less serious interference with individual rights than incarceration, the threshold for dangerousness should be lower. Professionals should be given discretion to determine what constitutes dangerousness in this context, but a relevant conviction should not be a necessary requirement.

One of the reasons why I think it is legitimate to treat people with non-conviction records as dangerous enough to lose their right to privacy with respect to those records relates to the nature of predatory offending. Specifically, the serial nature of those crimes and the widespread impunity with which they are perpetrated combine to mean that an existing criminal record—whether a conviction or a police report—is most probably indicative of broader, unreported, or unprosecuted offending. Earlier, I referred to these crimes as 'hidden'. This is because they tend to take place in the context of private relationships or private spaces, meaning that they are only ever recorded as crimes if reported as such by victims or, less frequently, by third parties. Yet only a small minority of victims of abuse ever report their crimes to police. In the United Kingdom, for example, national statistics show that only one in four people sexually abused in childhood report their victimization (Office for National Statistics, 2020). A similar but not identical story can be told about domestic abuse and rape, as national statistics in England and Wales show. In 2023, only 18.9% of women who experienced partner abuse reported it to the police.[3] In 2020, around 16% of female victims of rape and 19% of males report their crime to the police (Rape Crisis, 2024).

Social narratives about the inherent unreliability, deceitfulness, and attention-seeking tendencies of women and children fuel popular but unfounded assumptions about the reliability of their testimonies of abuse and violence. Sadly, most children who do speak out about their abuse, even to

[3] For a summary of this and other useful statistics on the prevalence and reporting of domestic abuse, see Women's Aid (2024).

their parents, are not believed (Frost, 2025). But the reality is that these crimes are perpetrated through abusive power dynamics, the exploitation of trust, love, and specific vulnerabilities. The silencing of victims also plays an important role. Perpetrators take advantage of their position of relative power to manipulate and terrorize victims and to trash their credibility when they do speak out.[4] Among the most frequently cited barriers to reporting in the case of child abuse are psychological factors, such as abuse-induced shame, guilt, self-blame, and fear for self and others. Equally important factors are threats or force by the perpetrator, close victim–perpetrator relationships, and victim grooming (Winters et al., 2020: 589). Victims of all these crimes are frequently held responsible for the abuse they experience and feel shame about their victimization. Often, the criminal justice system also supports perpetrators by perpetuating victim-blaming myths and disbelieving victims.[5]

Even when they are reported to police, only a fraction of predatory and abuse crimes ever result in a conviction. In England and Wales, for reported child sexual abuse crimes the conviction rate is 6% (Karsna and Bromley, 2024). As mentioned in Chapter 5, the figures are worse for domestic and sexual violence: only 2.8% of domestic abuse crimes and 1% of rapes recorded by police result in a conviction (Cuffe and Leigh, 2024). It is no accident that London's Metropolitan Police chose to give their 2004 report on domestic abuse perpetration the title 'Getting Away With It'. The fact is that many people known to police and other authorities to be dangerous, serial abusers are never held accountable and remain entirely free to continue harming others with impunity.

Dismayingly, some academics have argued that low conviction rates for these crimes are explained by the fact that false accusations are widespread and that many of the children and women who do report their abuse are lying.[6]

[4] A 2025 scoping review which examined the evidence base on why cases are dropped by victims found that that reasons 'included the offender staying away, agreeing to seek help/counselling, agreeing to divorce or another settlement, the offender's attorney convincing the victim to drop the case, the victim not wanting more hassle/remaining uncertain, and not wanting the offender jailed'. Victimized women withdrew or minimized their statements 'when male partners were highly threatening and controlling' (Chopin et al., 2025: 12–13).

[5] In 2014, the then Association of Chief Police Officers stated in its statement on the disclosure of non-conviction records that 'the two groups that disclosure primarily seeks to protect from harm are children and vulnerable adults, both of whom, sadly, are the least likely to make good witnesses' (ACPO/DBS 2014: 9).

[6] See, for example, Thomas and Beckett who argue in relation to domestic abuse that '[t]hose who tend to have tempestuous personal relationships are particularly likely to fall foul of allegations that may be based purely on malice following a relationship breakdown or can have an ulterior motive which benefits the accuser' (2019: 46). The only evidence they cite in support of this claim is a link to a single journalistic publication in a right-wing UK tabloid newspaper well known for its misogynistic stance (The Daily Mail). They also claim that the criminal justice system should treat with scepticism 'politically sensitive areas of crime, in which allegations are more vigorously pursued for example in domestic

But the evidence demonstrates precisely the opposite.[7] A 2005 study commissioned by the Home Office analysed a database of reported rape case files and concluded that the false allegation rate was 3% (Kelly et al., 2005). Similar studies carried out in Europe and in the United States indicate rates of between 2% and 6% (Kelly, 2010).

In the rare instances in which predatory and abuse crimes are discussed in the literature on criminal records, they tend to be treated as marginal cases or rare occurrences. For example, Baldwin, in his case against the disclosure of non-conviction information to prevent child abuse, argues that disclosure 'devastate(s) the lives of tens of thousands of people for the sake of preventing a tiny handful of some of the rarest crimes'. (2012: 162). But child abuse is not rare. A study from 2013 found that 10% of children in the United States had experienced child sexual abuse (Perez-Fuentes et al., 2013). And a systematic review of evidence across twenty-four countries found that up to 31% of girls and 17% of boys had experienced child sexual abuse (Barth et al., 2013). Even greater prevalence is evident with sexual and intimate partner violence perpetrated by men towards women. In 2024, the World Health Organization (WHO) estimated that 30% of women worldwide had been subject to sexual or intimate partner violence, and 27% to intimate partner abuse (WHO, 2024). In the United Kingdom, official figures from the police in 2023 showed that, nationally, 20% of police-recorded crime was violence against women and girls.[8]

To see how sharing information about criminal records or disclosing them directly to people at risk could protect them from these kinds of criminal harm, we can consider two examples from the United Kingdom, where disclosure policies of non-conviction records have been implemented most systematically.

violence, hate crime and sexual offences' (p. 146). This is a myth, and statistics illustrating vanishingly low convictions rates demonstrate the contrary.

[7] A review of evidence by the House of Lords in 2025 entitled 'Rape: Level of Prosecutions' reports that, according to the national crime survey, which is representative of the population and relies on self-reporting rather than criminal justice system records, rape has been experienced by 7.8% of women and 0.4% of men in England and Wales. It refers to an official review by the UK Home Office which found that 'the reasons for the decline in [rape] cases reaching court are complex and wide-ranging, including an increase in personal digital data being requested, delays in investigative processes [it takes an average of 10 times longer for a charge to be laid and 100 days longer for a trial to be heard for rape than for other victim-based crimes], strained relationships between different parts of the criminal justice system, a lack of specialist resources and inconsistent support to victims'.

[8] See note 3 above.

Protecting Sex Workers from Predatory Offenders: 'Ugly Mug' and 'Dodgy Punter' Schemes

First introduced in 2006 by the UK Home Office, 'Ugly Mug' or 'Dodgy Punter' schemes were designed to help sex workers report crimes and share information with each other about the identities of dangerous customers safely, to help protect them from future attack. Sex workers have always been at a much higher risk of rape, murder, and violent crime than the general population. In the United Kingdom, two studies showed that 74% of sex workers experienced physical/sexual violence from clients and female sex workers were eighteen times more likely to be victims of homicide than the general population, respectively (Hester and Westmarland, 2004; Salfati, 2009).

The reasons lie in the stigmatization of sex work and the vulnerability of sex workers. Sex workers are often perceived as disposable. They are also treated as if they have forfeited their right to refuse consent to sex. In many countries, aspects of sex work are illegal and workers are afraid of being criminalized or stigmatized if they seek contact with criminal justice agencies. Perpetrators of abuse against sex workers often hold disparaging views about them and know that they are less likely to report crimes than other people. This is part of the reason why they view them as 'easy targets' in the first place. Several high-profile cases of serial killers targeting sex workers in the United Kingdom illustrated the dangers of such work. This eventually prompted the police to try to work more proactively with them to prevent harm.[9]

In 2004, an evaluation of Ugly Mugs information sharing schemes found that they led to improved prosecution of serial perpetrators of violence against sex workers (Hester and Westmarland, 2004; Connelly et al., 2021). In 2016, almost half of sex workers who received their alerts reported that these enabled them to avoid a dangerous offender as a result (Feis-Bryce, 2017). The scheme is now a national programme which takes the form of a web-based platform on which sex workers can confidentially report crime and receive advice on staying safe and support if they have been victimized. Reported information is collated in one central database, from which members receive email or text alerts about potentially dangerous clients. It requires registration and login which serves both to protect it from ill-intended users and to maintain the security of the information shared. Only sex workers, professionals with a relevant role in a recognized sex-worker support organization, and police can register, and verification checks are put in place to ensure the site is not subject

[9] Most notoriously, five sex workers were murdered in Ipswich in 2006–2008.

to malicious use. Members can share non-conviction information about reported crimes as well as number plates, physical descriptions, warning signs, and convictions.

The ability of police and others to share details of people's non-conviction records is essential for sex workers to be able to recognize a specific client in any potential encounter and understand the specific risk they pose. Limiting disclosures to convictions only would defeat the purpose. Convictions are rare and can take years to be achieved. And conviction records do not include the kind of detail about a perpetrator and their behaviour that a sex worker would need to be able to recognize and assess the risk reliably. To protect themselves, sex workers need to be able to physically identify dangerous punters and recognize their behaviours and *modus operandi*. Serial perpetrators of all kinds of violent and abusive crimes tend to use similar tactics with different victims. Conviction records are highly generic, giving no details about the offender and specifying merely the formal legal description of the crime, for example, 'common assault', 'harassment' or 'grievous bodily harm'. In contrast, police records specify what someone actually did and the context in which they did it, in a narrative form. Sharing the kind of detail captured in a police record is important for potential victims to be able to recognize these behaviours and to protect themselves.

Ugly Mug schemes are permitted under the criteria for a right to know that I defended in Chapter 6 because there is a close nexus between the risk posed and the purpose of the disclosure, because only those who need to know are given a right to know, and because the extent of the disclosure is limited to what is necessary—but no less than what is necessary—to prevent harm. In addition, Ugly Mug schemes provide for some rights of due process for people listed on the site. Though people are not proactively informed of their listing, as this might risk identifying the person who reported them, prompting reprisals, members of the public can use an online checker to see if they are listed, and there are avenues for them to contest this formally if they wish.

Domestic Abuse Disclosure Schemes

As mentioned above, domestic abuse is a serious problem worldwide. A systematic review from 2013 found that at least one in seven homicides globally and more than a third of female homicides are perpetrated by an intimate partner. It also found that such violence commonly represents 'the culmination of a long history of abuse' (Stöckl et al., 2013). In the United Kingdom in 2022–2023, one in five killings was a domestic homicide (Respect, 2024). Domestic abuse is to a significant extent a serial crime, with each perpetrator abusing multiple victims.[10] The harms of domestic abuse go beyond the impact on the person targeted as a victim. Witnessing abuse as a child is strongly associated with committing abuse as an adult and 20% of children in the United Kingdom have lived with an adult perpetrating domestic abuse.[11] Serial perpetrators with multiple victims sow the seeds for generations of future harm.

The aim of domestic abuse disclosure schemes (also known as Clare's Law in the United Kingdom and Canada) is to provide information to people vulnerable to abuse about the risk their current or ex-partner poses to them and their family. Better understanding of risk can save lives. A US study with over 450 victims of domestic abuse found that in situations where women were later killed by an intimate partner, only half had accurately predicted the risks they faced (Campbell, 2004).

Disclosure schemes aim to improve understanding of risk by enabling someone who has concerns about their partner or ex-partner to find out if that person has a history of using violence and abuse in previous relationships. In most countries in which they operate,[12] disclosure schemes also allow police to offer criminal record information proactively, as a way of warning a person that they are in a relationship with a dangerous, serial offender.

Under these schemes, a person at risk can apply online to police for relevant information held on police systems to be disclosed (a third party can also apply on behalf of someone else if they are concerned about a risk to their safety, but information is only shared with the person at risk). The information shared is delivered orally and in order to receive it people at risk have to sign a confidentiality agreement promising not to share it with anyone apart from a caseworker or other safeguarding professional. Subjects of disclosure are not informed that their history has been shared and recipients of disclosures are strongly urged not to tell their (ex)partners about the disclosure because this could increase the risk of abuse to them and to ex-partners whose reports police have shared. In England and Wales, disclosures have become an important

[10] For example, in a 2024 paper, colleagues and I analysed a longitudinal police dataset of over sixteen thousand domestic abuse suspects in an English region. Over a period of only five years, the average number of victims per suspect was two and the average number of reported crimes was five (Hadjimatheou et al, 2024).

[11] Systematic and other reviews of research confirm consistently that childhood exposure to domestic abuse in the home significantly increases the risks of intimate partner violence perpetration. For an overview of this literature, see Hadjimatheou and Hamid (2024:5–12).

[12] The first domestic abuse disclosure scheme was introduced in England and Wales in 2012 and has since have been replicated in New Zealand, South Australia, various provinces in Canada, Malta, Northern Ireland, Scotland, and (in law though not yet in practice) Spain.

part of how police seek to protect people at risk of domestic abuse: in the year ending March 2024, over 58,000 applications for disclosure were processed.

My own empirical research in the United Kingdom and Australia shows that disclosure schemes can be useful in helping people avoid abuse when they are starting a relationship and have concerns about a new partner's behaviour (Hadjimatheou and Seymour, 2024). But it also shows that they are frequently accessed by people who are already experiencing abuse, and those who are trying to get out of an abusive relationship. Why would someone who already knows their partner is abusive need a disclosure of their criminal history to understand the risk they face? To grasp the potential value of disclosures, one must first understand the dynamics of domestic abuse and especially the way perpetrators manipulate the truth to expand their scope for power over their victims. Abuse often takes place over years, and in many cases victims do not leave even after they have experienced serious physical and sexual violence and emotional and psychological harm. Part of the reason why such relationships persist is that perpetrators deploy self-serving narratives about why abuse happens and who is responsible for it. If a person believes the abuse is their fault, or that they can make it stop by adapting their behaviour to their partner's demands, or that their partner is trying hard to change, then they are more likely to try to endure it. A representative survey with victims in New Zealand also found that 23.8% of women who ended a relationship returned because they believed their partner would change (Fanslow and Robinson, 2009). Belief in the potential for change is also driven by the fact that many perpetrators behave wonderfully at the start of a relationship, showering a new partner with attention, affection, and care in a process known as 'love-bombing'. Victims of abuse are then motivated to try to achieve what they once had. Most often they cannot, because the shift in behaviour is a pattern played out by the perpetrator the same way in multiple relationships, and nothing to do with their own behaviour.

Research has shown that when people are manipulated to rationalize the violence or abuse they are experiencing, they are less likely to seek help and more likely to decide to stay in a relationship. Perpetrators drive such rationalization through a process of manipulation that has been conceptualized as the 'monopolisation of perception' (Jones and Schechter, 1993; Stark, 2007). To monopolize perception is to impose one's own narrative or interpretation of reality on another person, to undermine their capacity to exercise independent judgements and further entrap them in the relationship. Specific tactics include minimizing and denying past abusive conduct, blaming previous partners for past incidents of abuse and for breakdown of previous relationships, justifying violence, and gaslighting (i.e., using psychological manipulation to confuse and distort someone's sense of reality such that they must accept the perpetrator's version of the truth in place of their own 'from minor details of everyday life to their partners' entire biographies' [Sweet, 2019: 853]). If a victim already knows something of a partner's criminal history—which many do—rationalization can involve accepting a partner's claim that their record is the result of malicious allegations by a 'crazy ex' (Stark, 2007:262). The phrase 'look what you made me do' articulates one typical strategy by which perpetrators use gaslighting to shift the blame for abuse on their victims (Hill, 2020).

Evidence from my research on disclosure schemes internationally shows that the information shared in a disclosure can counter the monopolization of perception, exposing risk and empowering people in abusive relationships and helping them make more informed decisions about their safety (Hadjimatheou, 2022; Hadjimatheou and Seymour, 2024). These benefits are realized when the disclosure reveals a pattern of behaviour that undermines the perpetrator's narrative. The reason patterns are important is that incidents of violence experienced or heard about by a person at risk are often explained away, minimized, or denied by perpetrators. For example, perpetrators may explain the violence as out of character; a response to trauma, stress, a troubled childhood or mental health struggles; a symptom of alcohol or drug addiction; or the fault of the victim, children, or others. Patterns show that abusive behaviours are not out of character but rather typical of that person's conduct in a relationship. One of the police officers I interviewed for a study on disclosure schemes in the United Kingdom provided a powerful example of the power of patterns, in her description of a particular case. She was making a disclosure to a woman whose case had been flagged to police after she was admitted to hospital, and narrated:

> she was pregnant and she had a saucepan mark on her stomach where he had burnt her. And she was saying "this is a freak accident, I made him do it". But he had burnt the stomach of a previous partner who was pregnant, with an iron. It demonstrates a propensity to a certain crime . . . so I could say "this is a dangerous man, this wasn't something which had happened "by accident". This is what he does. (Hadjimatheou, 2022)

Disclosures that reveal multiple victims (as many do) can also expose as lies a perpetrator's efforts to blame previous victims for convictions or arrests. Seeing that others have received the same abusive behaviour one is experiencing can also reveal that one is not alone and reduce the shame and self-blame that has been shown to prevent people from taking steps to protect themselves. One of 250 Australian women who described the impact of a disclosure in another of my studies said: 'It helped me realise I'm not the cause of his abuse as he has done this before, and I can't change him. It gave me the strength to say I've had enough of being abused'. That research found that 98% of respondents felt they were able to make better decisions about personal safety, and 95% were able to make better decisions about other aspects of safety, including children and pets.[13]

Some have proposed a public register of domestic violence offenders as an alternative way of using criminal records to protect people from serial perpetrators. But a register would not be protective, because most countries' legal systems would rightly require the information published to be limited to convictions. Any resulting register would therefore lack the detail needed for a disclosure to effectively communicate risk. It would leave open the potential for a perpetrator to spin their own narrative on the facts included in the register. And its accessibility to any member of the public would be far more stigmatizing of those with records of abuse than a disclosure scheme operating on a need-to-know basis.

My criteria for a right to know, defended in Chapter 6, would endorse domestic abuse disclosure schemes because revealing patterns of abuse has been shown to prevent criminal harm, and patterns are only likely to become visible when police are legally empowered to disclose detailed information about *all* behaviours that indicate risk. Merely reporting convictions will neither reveal patterns nor provide the insight into a perpetrator's behaviour that makes a disclosure powerful. Research shows that disclosure schemes that limit information sharing to convictions miss important opportunities to inform people about the risk they face (Hadjimatheou and Grace, 2020). Because the non-conviction information shared under disclosure schemes is only given to the people at risk and only when there is a real risk, the intrusion into the privacy of the subject of a disclosure is limited.

Disclosure schemes also exist for child sexual offenders in some countries. In England and Wales the child sex offender disclosure scheme is called Sarah's Law after a child who was murdered by a serial offender. Perhaps surprisingly, such schemes are accessed far less often than those operating for domestic abuse. The reasons for this discrepancy are varied and illustrate the fact that sharing criminal history information is more protective in preventing some

[13] This study also underscored the value of the disclosure process itself (e.g., seeking information and receiving help from safeguarding professionals) for people at risk.

kinds of criminal harm than others. Children themselves lack the legal capacity to seek the information and, for reasons already described above, tend not to report their crimes anyway. Children would be unlikely to request a disclosure even if they could and their lack of autonomy seriously limits the extent to which they could be expected to manage their own exposure to risk. Parents and other responsible adults do not often access the scheme because they typically do not know about the abuse nor suspect the person responsible for it. This is not surprising, because child abuse typically involves the exploitation of a position of trust. In England and Wales, applications under the child sex offender disclosure scheme are a fraction of those made for domestic abuse. They most often occur in circumstances in which professionals, such as social workers, become aware that a person with a history of abuse has started a new relationship with a person who has children at home. Under my proposals, disclosing non-conviction records for the prevention of child sexual abuse is permissible, but likely to be protective in a far more limited range of circumstances than for domestic abuse.

Objections from the Presumption of Innocence and of 'Harmlessness'

Legal and philosophical theorizing about criminal records and preventive justice remains largely silent about the kinds of crimes I have just been discussing, despite the fact that these kinds of crime have always been widespread.[14] The omission reflects a much broader failure in the field of legal and political theory of punishment and criminal justice to acknowledge let alone attempt to understand crimes of abuse.[15] As a result, the arguments and positions developed in this field are largely insensitive to the distinctive features of predatory crimes and crimes of abuse. This oversight skews the focus of those arguments in ways that undermines their strength and their applicability to

[14] Barring Duff's discussion of dangerousness, none of the many important writings on criminal records and their collateral consequences discuss crimes of abuse in anything but passing reference.

[15] As Walby et al. (2014) argued in relation to the discipline of criminology, which has since made a much greater effort to catch up than penal theory: 'The scholarly neglect of domestic violence and other forms of violence against women has a long heritage. Weber (1948) thought the modern state had a monopoly of legitimate violence in its territory, even at a time when rape and violence in the domestic sphere were not crimes when committed by husbands against wives' (Walby et al, 2014: 188). A glaring omission in philosophy can be found in the numerous recently published books on the philosophy of policing such as Hunt (2018), del Pozo (2022), and Monaghan (2023). None of these even discuss predatory crimes and crimes of abuse, let alone take them seriously as an area of policework. Yet in all the authors' countries, around one fifth of police call outs relate to such incidents.

the world in which we live. This omission is worthy of a separate and deeper discussion, which I hope to explore elsewhere. For our current purposes, it is sufficient to point out that it undermines the most frequently and strongly voiced argument against sharing non-conviction records. That argument relates to the impact of disclosures on people's rights not to be labelled as criminal in the absence of sufficient evidence or proof, in other words their right to be presumed innocent.

In her 2018 review of the evidence on the disclosure of criminal records in Scotland, Weaver asks, 'Why are arrests, cautions and soft information disclosable when they are, by definition, judicially unproven?' (Weaver, 2018: 12). The idea that disclosing records of criminal behaviour not proven in court is a violation of the presumption of innocence is also voiced by Larrauri (2014a) as an objection to practices of disclosing spent convictions and non-conviction records to employers recruiting people to work with vulnerable adults and children. For Larrauri, the violation lies in the fact that disclosures endorse suspicion through official confirmation of risk and therefore 'attribute stigma to people who might (later be found to) be innocent' (Larrauri, 2014b: 385; see also Purshouse, 2018). Ashworth and Zedner argue further that merely carrying out a risk assessment that identifies someone as likely to present a danger 'constitutes a denial of the presumption of harmlessness (the equivalent of the presumption of innocence applied outside the context of a criminal trial) and that this denial cannot easily be squared with the maintenance of the right to be presumed innocent of future crimes' (2014: 130). And Thomas and Beckett claim that 'the injustice of a disclosure decision-making process in which so much weight is attached to the circumstances in which an individual happens to be accused is the perverse outcome of effectively reversing the burden of proving innocence against the applicant' (2019: 108).[16]

Thomas and Beckett claim further that as well as being unproven in court, non-conviction records are inherently unreliable. They argue that even when such records reveal a clear pattern of violence and abuse, they should be discounted as evidence of risk. This, they argue, is because 'what may appear on the face of the intelligence to be an emergence of a pattern may actually be evidence of a propensity to be suspected rather than a propensity to commit

[16] In support of their point, Thomas and Beckett make the logically tortured claim that evidence of criminal threat might 'bias' police against certain suspects: 'The merging of the police's role of investigating the crime with their role in making quasi-judicial declarations of criminal liability, or suspicious behaviour relevant to considerations of risk, is arguably sullied by their having a natural bias against suspects regarding whom they have accumulated evidence to suggest their involvement in criminality (2019: 114).

crime' (2019: 46). But there is no reason to think that people who commit the kinds of crimes we are discussing have a 'propensity to be suspected' by police. On the contrary, and as described above, such crimes take place behind closed doors as it were, meaning victims or witnesses must actively report them for the police to intervene. Thomas and Beckett's argument might make sense when applied to street crimes such as drug and knife offences, because there is strong evidence that police do proactively profile and discriminate against groups and individuals for suspicion. But it doesn't work for crimes of abuse.

The problem is partly that theorists like Thomas and Beckett wrongly take street crimes and the way they are policed to be paradigmatic of crime as such, and partly that theorists such as Larrauri take an unwarrantedly idealistic view of the way criminal justice processes work. In his 2025 article on methodological issues in academic penal ethics, Jesper Ryberg warns of the dangers of 'ideal theorising', by which he means theorizing about the justice of criminal justice measures on the assumption that they would be implemented in a world in which the rest of the system works perfectly. Ryberg's concern is that ideal theorizing leads academics to make recommendations for measures that might be just in a perfect world, but 'without addressing the question of what [they] would imply under non-ideal circumstances'. In this chapter I have sought to show how far from the ideal our criminal justice system is when it comes to preventing predatory crimes and crimes of abuse and holding their perpetrators accountable. That non-ideal reality should be factored into debates about what the presumption of innocence requires when it comes to the disclosure of criminal records. But too often it is not.

Let's have a look then at the criminal histories of people whose records are subject to disclosure, to get a real sense of the kinds of patterns and impunity we are dealing with. In 2025, in a pilot study for a much larger project, 3 English police forces shared with me a total of 16 anonymized examples of the scripts their officers had read out to recipients of a disclosure. These scripts describe the history of the suspect, listing reported crimes and providing detail of the context in which they allegedly occurred so that recipients of the disclosures can understand the behaviour their partner is capable of. Of the 16 cases, only 2 of the suspects were associated with a single victim, though the police had been called out on many separate occasions by those victims. The remaining 14 had been reported by multiple victims for multiple incidents, with few, but more often no convictions. For example, one man had been reported for one case of stalking, 31 violent assaults, and 3 sexual assaults on 'multiple' victims, none of which resulted in a conviction. Another had 33 reports across 13 victims including threats to kill, battery, kidnapping, actual bodily harm, and wounding with a weapon. A script from another force described a suspect with 'multiple' victims who had experienced physical violence at his hands, including being tied up and threatened with razors, receiving threats to kill, and being attacked with acid. Another suspect had been the subject of 42 domestic abuse investigations in relation to 10 victims over a 20-year period. In 9 of those investigations, policed assessed that the subject posed a risk of physical harm so severe it would be 'likely to be difficult or impossible [for a victim] to recover from'. Another two suspects had reports of violence from 7 and 6 separate domestic abuse victims respectively. Only a handful of all these incidents resulted in a conviction. The situation is anything but ideal.

People do have rights not to be unfairly stigmatized. But it seems a perversion (or at least a fetishization) of the presumption of innocence to insist that justice requires that we treat people with evident criminal histories of violence and abuse as if they were harmless. It is unreasonable to expect criminal justice professionals or indeed anyone to act as if there is no evidence of risk when in fact the evidence is clear. And it is negligent to act as if protecting the reputations of those who have demonstrated a propensity to serious and serial harm is more important than protecting those to whom they pose a risk.[17]

I want to insist that the stigmatization inflicted by a non-conviction disclosure is not unfair if it is grounded in evidence that is reliable and is limited to what is necessary to prevent harm, through the application of a need-to-know approach. The fact that disclosure schemes only involve sharing information with those individuals who are at risk, who have a duty of care to others, and are in a position to prevent harm means that both the severity and scope of stigmatization is significantly constrained.[18]

Conclusion

In this chapter I have argued for an expansion in the disclosure of criminal records to prevent predatory crimes and crimes of abuse. My justifications rest in part on an acknowledgement that the criminal justice system fails to hold perpetrators of these latter kinds of crime accountable. If it did, we would not need

[17] I am not the first to make these points. Hoskins (2019, ch. 6) and Duff (1998) made similar observations before me. But some philosophers and legal theorists continue to insist that this is what the presumption of innocence requires. Legislators and professionals whose role it is to protect the vulnerable and maintain public safety have long since moved on.

[18] Campbell has argued, in my view convincingly, that the stigmatization included in an official declaration of riskiness or of suspicion is qualitatively different from that of an official declaration of criminal guilt, and therefore that disclosures do not violate the presumption of innocence (Campbell, 2013).

to look to measures such as disclosures to protect people from criminal harm. The measures I have here defended are compatible with efforts to improve the effectiveness of the criminal justice system and with efforts to reform or replace that system with fairer alternatives to penal responses. Nothing I have said in this chapter suggests that criminal records disclosures should be seen as a substitute for or an alternative to efforts to increase legal and moral accountability for such crimes or for measures to address their root causes.

8
Defending a Limited Right to Know

Introduction 169
Lingering Lines of Objection to My Proposals 172
The role of the state in controlling access to criminal records 172
Social reform and rehabilitation certificates as an alternative proposal 173
Could the interests of people with criminal records be better protected by asserting a right to 're-biography'? 176
Broader Implications of My Proposal: #MeToo and the Informal Exposure of Wrongdoing 178
Conclusion 179

Introduction

This book set out to take seriously the claim that citizens have a right to know about each other's criminal records and to investigate the reasons for and against such a right. It began in Chapter 1 by defining criminal records broadly, to include official records of reported crimes, convictions, cautions, anti-social behaviour orders, restraining orders, non-molestation orders, and other prevention orders, records of fines, community service penalties, arrest, charge, prosecution and sentencing data, parole and probation records, and inclusion on registers for domestic violence, terrorism, or sex offences, amongst other things. It explained that one of the important reasons for focussing on all records created by the criminal justice system—but only such records—is that all the activities of that system are guided and regulated by a discrete set of moral norms and principles, which form a coherent framework of analysis. Chapter 2 argued that one of the reasons it is worth revisiting the question of whether we have a right to know about people's criminal records is that a public criminal record often harms individuals—and, by extension, communities—by undermining their ability to flourish. It did this by first synthesizing findings from a broad variety of empirical studies on the individual and social impacts of public criminal records, and, then, showing how the notion of flourishing articulates, unifies, and gives moral meaning to the full range of those impacts.

The Crimes of Others. Katerina Hadjimatheou, Oxford University Press. © Katerina Hadjimatheou 2026.
DOI: 10.1093/9780198925149.003.0008

Chapters 3–6 considered four distinct potential justifications for a right to know, namely the notion of crime as an intrinsically public matter (Chapter 3); the importance of transparency and openness in criminal justice (Chapter 4); publicizing criminal records as a means of punishing the guilty (Chapter 5); and the importance of preventing criminal harm (Chapter 6). Each of these chapters concluded that there is no general right of citizens to know about each other's criminal histories. Instead, there are limited rights to know, which differ based on the status or role of the person claiming such a right, the nature of the crime in question, and the purpose for which the right is asserted.

Chapter 3 argued that neither appeals to the social contract nor appeals to the notion of crime as a public wrong can justify a general right to know about people's criminal records. Appeals to the intrinsic or essential publicness of crime, it argued, do not end up taking us very far in understanding how much public access there should be to records of it. So instead of asking 'in what sense is crime properly understood as 'public'?', we should rather ask 'what public interest, if any, is served by giving citizens access to information about who has been involved or implicated in crime?'. Because people who have been wronged criminally have strong interests in knowing who is responsible, the chapter argues that citizens as such should have presumptive rights to know the identities and access the records of those who have committed crimes against the public or whose crimes relate to their role in public office.

Chapter 4 argued that proper concern for transparency and openness in criminal justice requires that public should be able to freely scrutinize the actions of criminal justice officials who act in their name. But this does not extend to scrutiny of the identities of those accused or convicted. In practice, this means that journalists, researchers, victims, and other members of the public should be free to attend trials, but not to report the identities of those involved. However presiding judges should have wide discretion to determine where the balance between openness and privacy should lie in each case, with respect to the public interest and the fair administration of justice. The chapter also argued that people accused of crimes should always have the right to publicize their cases, to expose and protect against miscarriages of justice. It closed by arguing that, unlike in courts which should be open to the public, in policing there should be an assumption of confidentiality, as this is necessary to ensure safe reporting of crime and the dignity of those involved in crisis situations.

Chapter 5 argued that making a person's criminal conviction or other criminal record public is not a legitimate form of punishment because it neither deters future offending nor ensures the proportionate and effective communication of censure to offenders. But it also argued that publicizing a person's past crimes can be justified as a means of achieving accountability for their criminal behaviour, if doing so encourages as-yet-unidentified victims come forward and seek justice. This use of exposure to facilitate justice, which I call the flypaper strategy, tends to be justified in cases relating to serial perpetrators of predatory crimes, including sexual violence, and crime of abuse, which are a theme throughout the book.

Chapter 6 argued that the need to prevent criminal harm and protect the vulnerable provides strong grounds for a right to know. It set out and defended the criteria defining the parameters of such a right and argued that it can claimed by people who can use that information to prevent criminal harm and protect the vulnerable, on a need-to-know basis. It argued that criminal justice officials should also have a right to share criminal record information proactively with those at risk, where doing so would prevent harm. The rights of those with criminal records are protected by limiting disclosure to cases in which there is a significant risk of criminal harm, and by only permitting the disclosure of information that is relevant to the prevention of that harm. It is argued that harm-prevention disclosures of criminal records are often justified when the risk relates to predatory crimes and crimes of abuse. The distinctive features of such crimes—namely their serial nature, widespread impunity, and the special role of secrecy, lies, and silencing in their perpetration—make criminal record disclosures for prevention more appropriate than they would be for other crime types.

Chapter 7 developed this latter argument further, through examination of two case studies relating to predatory crimes and crimes of abuse. The first involved a secure online platform enabling sex workers and police to share information about 'dodgy punters' or violent clients, to allow them to recognize and avoid contact with dangerous people. The second involved 'domestic abuse disclosure schemes' which allow police to share information about the criminal histories of serial abusers with people to whom they pose a risk. Here, disclosures aim to help people in or at risk of abusive relationships understand the risk they face and make better-informed decisions about their safety. This chapter explicitly endorses the sharing of criminal records which fall short of a conviction but still demonstrate significant risk of criminal harm, such as police records. In response to critics, it is argued that sharing of non-conviction records is compatible with respect for the presumption of innocence, as long as it is implemented on a strictly need-to-know basis, and as long as proper consideration is given to the rights of subjects of disclosure to contest their exposure.

Taken together, my arguments provide a coherent set of criteria for the disclosure of criminal records that can be drawn upon to answer the question: when, to whom, and on what grounds should different kinds of information about the criminality of others be available? The system I propose would practice a) a general presumption in favour of confidentiality around all kinds of criminal records, with notable exceptions described above, as well as b) significant discretion (backed up by independent oversight) afforded to criminal justice professionals including judges and the police to decide in what additional circumstances publicity or disclosure is warranted.

Lingering Lines of Objection to My Proposals

I anticipate at least three lingering lines of objection to my account and proposals, and I'll try to address them each in turn now, starting with what I take to be the strongest. All relate to concerns about my actual proposals rather than my diagnosis of the problem, specifically their potential side-effects and their arguable lack of ambition.

The role of the state in controlling access to criminal records

The first takes issue with the fact that my proposals accord such a central role to the state and its agents in managing criminal records and in making decisions about where the line between publicity and privacy should lie. I have already made some efforts to defend this position against communitarian and libertarian objections. These schools of thought place much greater faith than I do in the rationality, judgement, and effectiveness of communities and individuals to treat people with criminal records fairly and in ways that promote public safety and accountability. Throughout this book, I have drawn on empirical research to try to demonstrate that such faith is unfounded. And rather than underplaying the risks that accompany concentration of power in the state, I have acknowledged them and insisted that those subject to criminal justice processes should always have the right to publicize and contest their case. I have argued, too, that those who exploit or abuse their position as agents of the state or public officials should be publicly identified as such, because the public has a right to know when they have been directly wronged. To the criticism that my position empowers the state to control the narrative about people's criminality, and to manipulate it at will through policies of concealment and disclosure, I respond that such control should be authorized democratically and subject to independent oversight.

If we reach democratic agreement that criminal record information is, like much other personal information, to be treated as confidential, then we also have a response to those who insist that concealing a criminal history is tantamount to lying.[1] As I argued in Chapter 3 in my discussion of so-called 'public facts', that assertion involves a fallacious conflation of confidentiality with deception. Of course, recasting the 'lie' as a legitimate refusal to disclose only renders the secrecy justified if the basis for the official designation of confidentiality is itself sound. The arguments in this book have sought to provide just such a basis.

This response should also serve as a partial reply to those who argue that 'the immense value of truth will always outweigh the countervailing interest of an individual in nondisclosure of private information'. (Edelman, 1989: 1201). Unless those who support such a position are prepared to make some kind of metaphysical claim about the value of 'truth', they will need to demonstrate what earthly value disclosure generates. As I argued in Chapter 2, the available evidence shows that the harms of unfettered access to criminal records are serious for individuals and for society as a whole.

Social reform and rehabilitation certificates as an alternative proposal

Still, I want to respond to a line of potential objection challenging both the way I have framed the problem of criminal records and the kind of solutions I propose. I have implied more than once in this book that the harms and wrongs of public criminal records are inevitable and only mitigable through confidentiality. But it could be argued that this implied dichotomy between damaging exposure and mitigating concealment is false. After all, negative consequences do not *necessarily* follow from the act of state labelling of criminals as such. It is the free and voluntary individual and collective reactions to criminal records, rather than government's policies of exposure or concealment, that cause and determine those harms and wrongs, and those free and voluntary reactions

[1] Colgate Love (2011: 777). For an earlier expression of this view, see also Franklin and Johnsen (1980). Lawmakers in the South African parliament similarly objected to a proposal to introduce processes for expungement of criminal records as authorizing 'a statutory lie by trying to rewrite history and pretending that an offence never took place' (cited in Mujuzi, 2014: 280).

could be different. In which case, perhaps we should try to change those responses first, before reaching for the levers of the law to conceal or expunge.[2]

It might further be argued, along the lines proposed by 1970s US probation officers Kogon and Loughry, that failing to address social responses to criminality merely 'helps society to evade its obligation to change its views toward former offenders' (Kogon and Loughery, 1971). Proponents of such a view might point out that a society in which people do not unfairly stigmatize and discriminate against each other *only* because they are denied the information that would enable them to do so is inferior to one in which they refrain from such behaviour because they respect people, or because they believe stigmatization and discrimination to be wrong. If so, should I not aspire to more here and argue for the creation of a society in which we can be trusted with the truth about ourselves and each other? Would not proposals for a pathway to such a society be more valuable than the modest—and arguably unambitious—case for confidentiality and selective disclosure this book has put forward?[3]

An alternative proposal to my own might take the shape of what we could call a social reform approach to the problem of criminal records. For example, in some countries people with convictions can apply for and obtain 'rehabilitation certificates', 'certificates of relief', or certificates of 'good conduct'.[4] These are supposed to supersede visible or accessible criminal records, facilitating reintegration and social acceptance, and helping people access jobs and housing from which they would otherwise likely be excluded (Petersilia, 2003: 216). Those who defend this approach argue that it resolves the problem of dissonance between the person represented by a criminal record and the (reformed) person they go on to become, respecting better what some have called the individual 'right to re-biography' (Maruna, 2001: 165). They might also argue that it could service both to motivate and to empower people to achieve

[2] It has even been argued that the state should not bear responsibility for the harms of public criminal records because it is not causally responsible for them. For example, in his rejection of a legal challenge against community notification laws for sex offenders, US Judge McKeague argued that 'truthful, public information . . . may result in damage to plaintiff's reputation, or may destabilize their employment and other community relations [but] such effects . . .would appear to flow most directly from plaintiff's own convicted misconduct and from private citizens' reactions thereto, and only tangentially from state action' (Doe v. Kelley in Michigan 1997, cited in Logan, 2009: 146). Judge McKeague concluded that the state bore no legal responsibility for preventing those harms, and duly rejected the challenge to sex offender notification. McKeague's argument seems wrong in two respects. The first is its stipulation that 'directness' of causal 'flow' of harms is a proxy for legal or moral responsibility for them, though such terms are alien to assignations of liability or responsibility in civil and criminal law. The second is its claim that states cannot be legally responsible for addressing harms they did not cause directly. But of course states have many responsibilities, including national security and criminal justice, for preventing or addressing harms they did not cause.

[3] Thanks to Milena Tripkovic for raising this potential objection.

[4] New York and Illinois provide these as does France and other countries.

rehabilitative goals and change their record status. What's more, the process for obtaining such a certificate might itself express respect for an individual's moral agency by providing 'an opportunity for the individual to evidence demonstrable personal change and a recognition of the harms caused by their offences' (Henley, 2019: 334).[5] Introducing rehabilitation ceremonies and certificates is, one might argue, a win-win solution to the apparent conflict between rehabilitation and the right to know.

I have two lines of response to this argument. First, research suggests that the impact of rehabilitation certificates is likely to be mixed at best. For one thing, where opportunities to clear a record or obtain a rehabilitation certificate already exist, people do not take them up. The reasons for this have not been examined, but perhaps they are unaware of them or are reluctant to draw attention to themselves or to deal with the authorities. For example, one US study from 2021 found that less than 10% of those eligible for measures reducing the impact of their criminal record obtained them (Chien, 2020). This figure might be increased to some extent by publicizing the availability of such certificates and encouraging people to apply for them.[6] But even if some improvement were achieved, the willingness of employers to hire people with criminal records has been shown to be low. Experimental research asking employers about their hiring decisions in a range of fictional scenarios suggests that rehabilitation certificates could encourage them to employ people with records, if combined with financial incentives including tax credits of 2400 dollars per applicant (Bushway and Pickett, 2025). There is of course no guarantee that governments anywhere have the political will to invest such sums in improving the employment prospects of people with criminal records, especially considering the inevitable populist backlash and potential resentment from those without records who are also struggling to find work and may feel disadvantaged as a result.

Meanwhile, another study using similar methods found that the potential positive impact of rehabilitation certificates was much higher for White than for Black applicants, with the result that the discrimination gap widened significantly amongst those with such certificates (Leasure and Anderson, 2019). This indicates that employers hold racial prejudices about people's potential for rehabilitation and reform, which rehabilitation certificates provide an opportunity to express. The potential impact of rehabilitation certificates on

[5] Rehabilitation certificates have been introduced in Australia for people with convictions who want to work with children (Naylor, 2011).

[6] Thanks to Antony Duff for this point.

access to housing, insurance, and other social and economic benefits has not been tested.

The second, deeper concern I have with the idea that we can avoid the harms of accessible criminal records through rehabilitation certificates is that we would in the first place need to change the way we understand and view criminality, and by extension, criminal records . The assumption that 'criminality' is a durable condition that needs to be recorded has become deeply embedded in the fabric of society and our institutions. It has in Hough's words 'encouraged the view that criminality in some way inheres in the personality of offenders, so that, come what may, they will seek out their opportunities for crime' (Hough, 2014: 215). As Earle argues, today's ever-increasing access to and commodification of criminal records itself brings with it 'a corresponding degree of fetishisation, as people are persuaded that criminal records have a power far beyond their actual material potential' (Earle, 2016: 94). And the policies, regulations, and practices that make criminal records ever-more public are the very same that invest them with 'insight' or 'truth'. So I am sceptical that one can be decoupled from the other, as the proposal for rehabilitation certificates implies.

To the general objection from un-ambitiousness, I can only say that I agree that it is worth both aspiring to and actively trying to achieve a better society: one in which we do not associate acts of criminality with enduring shamefulness, and in which people with criminal records do not suffer unfair disadvantage. Efforts in that direction are entirely compatible with treating criminal records as in most cases confidential, with a significant range of exceptions as outlined above.

Could the interests of people with criminal records be better protected by asserting a right to 're-biography'?

In Chapter 2, I proposed a flourishing-based account of the morality of criminal record disclosure which justified a right to privacy with respect to criminal records in certain circumstances. A different account is proposed by Jefferson-Jones, who argues directly from the assertion of a supposed moral right to ownership over one's reputation, to a 'rebiography right' that would give people the power to control the ways in which they are represented in public (Jefferson-Jones, 2014). Unlike my right to privacy, a right to re-biography would give people power over other people's access to their criminal records as well as access to any other reputation-degrading information.

The argument for a right to re-biography seems misguided for a couple of reasons. The first relates to the idea that imposing on someone a visible criminal record is wrong *because* it is a violation of that person's property rights. This is both un-intuitive and unsupported by the evidence. None of the personal accounts of criminal stigmatization documented empirically and recounted in Chapter 2 describe the harms experienced in terms of violations of their property. Nor do the exclusions, disadvantages, and chilling effects documented empirically as suffered by those with published records correspond to anything anyone would recognize as a property violation. Second, to conceptualize reputation or social identity as *property* belittles it, because it makes it analogous to any other commodity which a person might have a right to buy and sell or transfer. Further, property rights usually convey sweeping liberties to use a thing as one wishes, including to spoil, manipulate, or even destroy it. In the case of reputation this would surely accord too much power to the property-holder. I argued in Chapter 2 that a spoiled identity has direct implications for one's self-realization and for one's dignity, and dignity and its foundational sources should surely be inalienable if anything is. Asserting a right to transfer ownership over the sources and means of one's dignity to another seems analogous therefore to asserting a right to sell oneself into slavery, which has thankfully been long rejected by moral theories and global norms.

Beyond the issue of transfer, it seems dangerous to assert that people should have such sweeping entitlements over their public representation. For if managing one's reputation includes the right to entirely misrepresent oneself or twist the truth for personal gain at the expense of others—as so many dangerous serial perpetrators do to enable them to continue to harm and abuse—why should any *moral* right be invoked in support of it?

It might be argued in response to my points just made (though Jefferson-Jones himself does not make this claim) that correspondence between certain harms and the form of the right invoked to protect against them is unnecessary; rather, the reason for asserting a property right is just that it is what is needed *in practice* to protect against those harms. But there are reasons to think a property right goes far beyond what is needed. Jefferson-Jones argues that giving people a rebiography right 'will ensure a measure of liberty and autonomy by managing the way in which she is portrayed to others—by managing her reputation' (2014: 531). But any measure of liberty and autonomy gained by asserting a right to rebiography can be equally obtained via a far more circumscribed right to privacy, without any of the attendant risks. A right to privacy entitles someone to protections against unfair discrimination or disadvantage, but does not entitle someone to unilateral control over the representation of their social identity. For these reasons at least, attempts to frame the harms and wrongs of a visible criminal record in terms of a violation of a right to rebiography will not take us far.

Broader Implications of My Proposal: #MeToo and the Informal Exposure of Wrongdoing

Throughout this book, I have sought to draw attention to the distinct considerations in favour of sharing criminal records that arise around what I call predatory crimes and crimes of abuse. As mentioned above, I have argued, especially in Chapter 7, that the distinctiveness relates to their serial nature, the widespread impunity with which they are committed, and the special role of secrecy, lies, and silencing in their perpetration. But I have not said much about the *informal* exposure and shaming of perpetrators of such crimes that is currently taking place through social media and movements such as #MeToo. In the introduction to this book, I defended my decision to focus on criminal records imposed by the criminal justice system alone, arguing that the range of reasons relevant to their disclosure or concealment is distinct enough from that applying to informal labelling of someone as criminal to necessitate a stand-alone analysis. Nevertheless, it is undeniable that some of the same considerations that I argue are relevant to the disclosure of criminal records of predatory crimes and crimes of abuse also speak in favour of these kinds of informal social exposure. For example, it might be argued that bringing 'hidden crimes' into the light makes wrongs that have historically gone unpunished—and their perpetrators—hyper-visible. This could be an important step towards changing the problematic social norms that have sustained that historic impunity. Such norms include misogyny, victim-blaming, myths around the image of an 'ideal victim', and the credibility of the testimony of women, children, and other vulnerable people (Tuerkheimer, 2019: 1175).

It is also true that many victims of such crimes actively seek exposure, the deprivation of undeserved privilege and status, and community acknowledgement of the wrong done. Indeed, many seek it *above* retribution or reconciliation. In her 2005 qualitative study with victims of such crimes, Judith Herman found that many victims wanted exposure to achieve what Maruna and Pali (2010: 38) have usefully termed 'shame-deflection'. That is, they wanted to improve their own standing relative of that of the perpetrator so that they could 'walk with their heads held high, and the perpetrators would be the ones to look down in shame' (Herman, 2005: 580). Similarly, Susan Miller's analysis of restorative justice for such crimes found that 'victims wanted offenders, "visibly and publicly", to "acknowledge the consequences of their actions"' (Miller, 2011: 178–179).

My arguments acknowledge the value of these kinds of exposure for victims, especially in terms of individual empowerment and restitution of status. But my proposals for the management of criminal records created and disclosed by public authorities do not by themselves imply any action with respect to the regulation of informal reports of criminal behaviour made by private individuals. Having said that, I agree with Maruna and Pali that the #MeToo movement has its limitations, primary amongst which is its preference for stigmatization and ostracism over reintegration. Yet I also see immense dangers with any proposals that would presumptively restrict what people can say publicly about their own lives and their own experiences of trauma and victimization.

Conclusion

This book's overarching academic inquiry has been essentially philosophical. But I have sought to pursue it in an interdisciplinary way, synthesizing and advancing research from three fields of study: philosophical work on punishment, criminological work on the collateral consequences of criminal convictions, and studies in gender violence and crimes of abuse. The aim has been to provide an empirically grounded, normative account of the purposes and just limits of public access to criminal records. The social value of this account is, I hope, its provocation of a more comprehensive debate about criminal pasts and criminal records, and its proposal for a more coherent and just approach to the management and regulation of criminal history information.

Bibliography

ACPO (Association of Chief Police Officers)/DBS (Disclosure and Barring Service). (2014). *Quality assurance framework: An applicant's introduction to the decision-making process for enhanced disclosure and barring service checks.* Standards and Compliance Unit. https://assets.publishing.service.gov.uk/government/uploads/system/uploads/attachment_data/file/295392/DBS_Applicant_s_introduction_to_QAF_March_2014.pdf

Allen, G. (2009, May 20). Sex offenders forced to live under Miami bridge. *National Public Radio.* http://www.npr.org/templates/story/story.php?storyId=104150499

Anderson, H. (2012). The mythical right to obscurity: A pragmatic defense of no privacy in public. *I/S: A Journal of Law and Policy for the Information Society*, *7*(3), 543–602.

Arneson, R. J. (2007). Shame, stigma and disgust in the decent society. *Journal of Ethics*, *11*, 31–63.

Arpaly, N. (2002). Moral worth. *Journal of Philosophy*, *99*(5), 223–245.

Ashworth, A., & Zedner, L. (2014). *Preventive justice.* Oxford University Press.

Aukerman, T. (2005). The somewhat suspect class: Towards a constitutional framework for evaluating occupational restrictions affecting people with criminal records. *Journal of Law in Society*, *7*(1), 2–65.

Austin, R. (2004). The shame of it all: Stigma and the political disenfranchisement of formerly convicted and incarcerated persons. Columbia Human Rights Law Review, *36*, 173.

Bailey, J., & Burkell, J. (2016). Revisiting the open court principle in an era of online publication: Questioning presumptive public access to parties' and witnesses' personal information. *Ottawa Law Review*, *48*(1), 143–184.

Baldwin, C. (2012). Necessary intrusion or criminalising the innocent? An exploration of modern criminal vetting. *The Journal of Criminal Law*, *76*(2), 140–163.

Barlow, C., & Weare, S. (2019). 'You're told that you're going to be raped and that it'll be my fault': Former prisoners' experiences of sexual violence and harassment in prison. *Howard Journal of Crime and Justice*, *58*(1), 86–104.

Barth, J., Bermetz, L., Heim, E., Trelle, S., & Tonia, T. (2013). The current prevalence of child sexual abuse worldwide: A systematic review and meta-analysis. *International Journal of Public Health*, *58*, 469–483.

Bauhr, M., & Grimes, M. (2014). Indignation or resignation: The implications of transparency for societal accountability. *Governance*, *27*(2), 291–320.

Beccaria, C. (2009). *On crimes and punishments* (5th ed.). Routledge. (Original work published 1764)

Becker, L. (1974). Criminal attempts and the theory of the law of crimes. *Philosophy and Public Affairs*, *3*, 272–294.

Behrens, A., Uggen, C., & Manza, J. (2012). Stigma, race, and barriers to employment. *American Sociological Review*, *77*(1), 107–129.

Bentham, J. (1790). *Draught for the organization of judicial establishments, compared with that of the National Assembly, with a commentary on the same.*

Bentham, J. (1999). *Political tactics* (M. James, C. Blamires, & C. Pease-Watkin, Eds.). Clarendon Press.

Bentham, J. (2009). *The rationale of punishment* (J. McHugh, Ed.). Prometheus Books.

Bernburg, J. G., Krohn, M. D., & Rivera, C. J. (2006). Official labelling, criminal embeddedness, and subsequent delinquency: A longitudinal test of labelling theory. *Journal of Research in Crime and Delinquency*, *43*(1), 67–88.

Birdsey, E., & Snowball, S. (2013). *Reporting violence to police: A survey of victims attending domestic violence services* (Issue Paper No. 91). NSW Bureau of Crime Statistics and Research.

Bows, H., & Westmarland, N. (2018). Older sex offenders – Managing risk in the community from a policing perspective. *Policing and Society*, *28*(1), 62–74.

Braithwaite, J. (1989). *Crime, shame and reintegration*. Cambridge University Press.

Brayne, S. (2014). Surveillance and system avoidance: Criminal justice contact and institutional attachment. *American Sociological Review*, *79*(3), 367–391.

Briscoe v. Reader's Digest Association, Inc., Defendant and Respondent. Supreme Court of California (1971).

Brooks, C. (2023). Higher education policies for applicants with criminal records in the United Kingdom: Are universities 'banning the box'? *Widening Participation and Lifelong Learning*, *25*(1), 72–98.

Brown, M. (2019). Transformative justice and new abolition in the United States. In P. Carlen & L. Ayres França (Eds.), *Justice alternatives* (pp. 73–87). Routledge.

Bushway, S. D., & Pickett, J. T. (2025). Direct incentives may increase employment of people with criminal records. *Criminology & Public Policy*, *24(2)*, 209–236.

Campbell, J. C. (2004). Helping women understand their risk in situation of intimate partner violence. *Journal of Interpersonal Violence*, *19*, 1464–1477.

Campbell, L. (2013). Criminal labels, the European Convention on Human Rights and the presumption of innocence. *The Modern Law Review*, *76*(4), 681–707.

Chiao, V. (2016). What is the criminal law for? *Law and Philosophy*, *35(2)*, 137–163.

Chien, C. (2020). America's paper prisons: The second chance gap. *Michigan Law Review*, *119*(3), 519–582.

Chin, G. J. (2012). The new civil death: Rethinking punishment in the era of mass conviction. *University of Pennsylvania Law Review*, *160*(6), 1789–1833.

Chiricos, T., Barrick, K., Bales, W., & Bontrager, S. (2007). The labeling of convicted felons and its consequences for recidivism. *Criminology*, *45*(3).

Chopin, J., Aebi, M. F., & Rigoni, C. (2025). Attrition in intimate partner violence cases through the criminal justice system: A scoping review of patterns and predictors. *International Journal of Comparative and Applied Criminal Justice*, 122.

Cohen, G. A. (2008). *Rescuing justice and equality*. Harvard University Press.

Colgate Love, M. (2011). Paying their debt to society: Forgiveness, redemption, and the Uniform Collateral Consequences of Conviction Act. *Howard Law Journal*, *54*(3), 753–793.

College of Policing. (2023). *Police information and records management code of practice*. https://www.college.police.uk/guidance/police-information-and-records-management-code-practice

Collett, N. (2023). Constructing and maintaining a 'noncriminal' identity: A psychosocial narrative inquiry into the lives of people with convictions (Doctoral dissertation). Keele University. https://keele-repository.worktribe.com/output/597588

Connelly, L., Kamerāde, D., & Sanders, T. (2021). Violent and nonviolent crimes against sex workers: The influence of the sex market on reporting practices in the United Kingdom. *Journal of Interpersonal Violence*, *36*(7–8).

Cooper, G. (2019). Open (in)justice: Privacy, open justice and human rights. *Trusts & Trustees, 25*(7), 712–721.

Corda, A. (2016). More justice and less harm: Reinventing access to criminal history records. *Howard Law Journal, 60*(1), 1–60.

Corda, A., Rovira, M., & Henley, A. (2023). Collateral consequences of criminal records from the other side of the pond: How exceptional is American penal exceptionalism? *Criminology & Criminal Justice, 23*(4), 528–548.

Cuffe, R., & Leigh, S. (2024, November 27). Domestic abuse cases rarely convicted, data shows. *BBC News*. https://www.bbc.co.uk/news/articles/c748p7wkevgo

Cullen, F. T., & Jonson, C. L. (2014). Labelling theory and correctional rehabilitation: Beyond unanticipated consequences. In D. P. Farrington & J. Murray (Eds.), *Labelling theory: Empirical tests* (pp. 63–85). Routledge. Transaction.

Cuomo, C. (1998). *Feminism and ecological communities: An ethic of flourishing*. Routledge.

Davis, M. (1991). Thinking like an engineer. *Philosophy & Public Affairs, 20*(2), 150–167.

Del Pozo, B. (2022). *The police and the state*. City University of New York.

Department for Education. (2019). *Recruiting teachers from overseas*. https://www.gov.uk/government/publications/recruit-teachers-from-overseas/recruiting-teachers-from-overseas

Department for Work and Pensions. (2024). *Labour market statistics, UK: April 2024*. https://www.gov.uk/government/statistics/labour-market-statistics-april-2024

Department of Health and Social Care. (2024). *Integration and innovation: Working together to improve health and social care for all*. https://www.gov.uk/government/publications/working-together-to-improve-health-and-social-care

Department of Justice v. Reporters Committee for Freedom of the Press, 489 U.S. 749 (1989).

Department of Justice. (2001). *Public attitudes toward uses of criminal history information* (Bureau of Justice Statistics Report). https://bjs.ojp.gov/content/pub/pdf/pauchi.pdf

Dimock, S. (1997). Retributivism and trust. *Law and Philosophy, 16*(1), 37–62.

Disclosure and Barring Service. (2024). *Statutory disclosure guidelines*, Principle 2. https://www.gov.uk/government/publications/statutory-disclosure-guidance/statutory-disclosure-guidance

Disley, E., Taylor, C., Kruithof, K., & Sim, M. (2022). *Evaluation of the domestic abuse perpetrator programme: Final report*. RAND Corporation. https://www.rand.org/pubs/research_reports/RRA1356-1.html

Doe v. Kelley, 961 F. Supp. 1105 (W.D. Mich. 1997).

Drakulich, K. (2018). Perp walks. *Criminology & Public Policy, 17*(3), 601–604.

Drapal, J. (2021). Day fines. In *Oxford bibliographies: criminology*. https://doi.org/10.1093/obo/9780195396607-0303

Duff, A. (1998). Dangerousness and citizenship. In A. Ashworth et al. (Eds.), *Fundamentals of sentencing theory: Essays in honour of Andrew von Hirsch* (pp. 141–163). Oxford University Press.

Duff, A. (2005). Punishment, communication, and community. In Matravers, D. & Pike, J. (Eds.). *Debates in contemporary political philosophy: An anthology* (1st ed.). Routledge.

Duff, R. A. (1986). *Trials and punishments*. Cambridge University Press.

Duff, R. A. (2007). *Answering for crime: Responsibility and liability in the criminal law*. Bloomsbury Publishing.

Duff, R. A. (2010). Towards a theory of criminal law? *Aristotelian Society Supplementary Volume, 84*(1), 1–28.

Duff, R. A. (2011). Responsibility, citizenship, and criminal law. In R. A. Duff & S. P. Green (Eds.), *Philosophical foundations of criminal law* (pp. 125–215). Oxford University Press.

Duff, R. A. (2020). Criminal law, civil order and public wrongs. *Law, Ethics and Philosophy, 7*, 233–270.

Duff, R. A., & Marshall, S. E. (2010). Public and private wrongs. In J. Chalmers, F. Leverick, & L. Farmer (Eds.), *Essays in criminal law in honour of Sir Gerald Gordon* (pp. 70–85). Edinburgh University Press.

Duff, R. A., & Marshall, S. E. (2024). Reporting crimes and arresting criminals: Citizens' rights and responsibilities under their criminal law. *Criminal Law and Philosophy, 18*, 557–577.

Dyzenhaus, D. (1992). John Stuart Mill and the harm of pornography. *Ethics, 102*, 534–551.

Earle, R. (2016). *Convict criminology: Inside and out.* Policy Press.

Edelman, P. B. (1989). Free press v. privacy: Haunted by the ghost of Justice Black. *Texas Law Review, 68*(6), 1195.

Edwards, J., & Simester, A. (2017). What's public about crime? *Oxford Journal of Legal Studies, 37*(1), 105–133.

Elliot, G., Ziegler, L., Altman, B., & Scott, D. (1982). Understanding stigma: Dimensions of deviance and coping. *Deviant Behavior, 3*(3), 275–280.

Ellis, A. (2003). A deterrence theory of punishment. *The Philosophical Quarterly, 53*(212), 337–351.

Elster, J. (2013). *Securities against misrule.* Cambridge University Press.

Equality and Human Rights Commission. (2021). *Public sector equality duty: Technical guidance for England.* https://www.equalityhumanrights.com/en/public-sector-equality-duty

European Commission. (2023). *Victims' rights directive: Implementation and evaluation report.* https://commission.europa.eu/publications/victims-rights-directive-report_en

Evans, D. N., & Porter, J. R. (2015). Criminal history and landlord rental decisions: A New York quasi-experimental study. *Journal of Experimental Criminology, 11*(1), 21–42.

Fanslow, J., & McIntosh, T. (2023). *Key findings and policy implications from He Koiora Matatapopore | The 2019 Family Violence Study.* University of Auckland.

Fanslow, J. L., & Robinson, E. M. (2009). Help-seeking behaviors and reasons for help seeking reported by a representative sample of women victims of intimate partner violence in New Zealand. *Journal of Interpersonal Violence, 25*(5), 929–951.

Feinberg, J. (1984). *Harm to others: Moral limits of the criminal law.* Oxford University Press.

Feis-Bryce, A. (2017, May 10). 'Ugly mugs': The technology saving the lives of sex workers. *The Guardian.* https://www.theguardian.com/voluntary-sector-network/2017/may/10/national-ugly-mugs-the-technology-saving-the-lives-of-sex-workers

Fenster, M. (2015). Transparency in search of a theory. *European Journal of Social Theory, 18*(2), 150–167.

Fields, G., & Emshwiller, J. R. (2014). As arrest records rise, Americans find consequences can last a lifetime. *Wall Street Journal, 18.*

Fiss, O. M. (1983). Against settlement. *Yale Law Journal, 93*(6) 1073–1092.

Fitzgerald O'Reilly, M. (2018). Information pertaining to released sex offenders: To disclose or not to disclose, that is the question. *The Howard Journal of Crime and Justice, 57*(2), 204–230.

Flanders, C. (2017). Punishment, liberalism, and public reason. *Criminal Justice Ethics, 36*(1), 61–77.

Fletcher, H. (2009, February). NAPO warning on high visibility vests. *NAPO (National Association of Probation Officers) News, 206.*

Fletcher, D. R. (2001). Ex-offenders, the labour market and the new public administration. *Public Administration, 79*(4), 871–891.

Franklin, M. A., & Johnsen, D. (1980). Expunging criminal records: Concealment and dishonesty in an open society. *Hofstra Law Review*, *9*(3), 733.

Friedewald, M., van Lieshout, M., Rung, S., Ooms, M., & Ypma, J. (2015). Privacy and security perceptions of European citizens: A test of the trade-off model. In J. Camenisch et al. (Eds.), *Privacy and identity 2014, IFIP advances in information and communication technology* (Vol. 457, pp. 39–53). Springer.

Frost, E. (2025). 'In silence there was a lot of suffering': The impact of child sexual abuse across the life-course (Doctoral dissertation). Essex University, https://repository.essex.ac.uk/41230/

Furst, R. T., & Evans, D. N. (2017). Renting apartments to felons: Variations in real estate agent decisions due to stigma. *Deviant Behavior*, *38*(6), 698–708.

Gardner, J. (1998). On the general part of the criminal law. *Philosophy and the Criminal Law: Principle and Critique*, 205, 244.

Globe Newspaper Co. v. Superior Court, 457 U.S. 596 (1982).

Goffman, E. (1963). *Stigma: Notes on the management of spoiled identity*. Prentice-Hall.

Government of Canada. (2024). *Intimate partner violence factsheet*. https://www.canada.ca/en/women-gender-equality/gender-based-violence/intimate-partner-violence.html

Grace, J. (2014). Old convictions never die, they just fade away: The permanency of convictions and cautions for criminal offences in the UK. *The Journal of Criminal Law*, *78*(2), 121–135.

Gray, D. (2010). Punishment as suffering. *Vanderbilt Law Review*, *63(6)*, 1617–1657.

Hadjimatheou, K. (2016). Criminal labelling, publicity, and punishment. *Law and Philosophy*, *35*(6), 567–593.

Hadjimatheou, K. (2022). Using criminal histories to empower victim–survivors of domestic abuse. *European Journal of Criminology*, *20*(3), 1106–1122.

Hadjimatheou, K., & Grace, J. (2020). 'No black and white answer about how far we can go': Police decision making under the domestic violence disclosure scheme. *Policing and Society*, *31*(7), 834–847.

Hadjimatheou, K., & Hamid, R. (2024). A register for domestic abuse and stalking offenders in England and Wales? A report to inform policy and practice. https://www.essex.ac.uk/-/media/documents/departments/sociology/da_stalkers_register_report_essex_university-accessible-appendix-final.pdf

Hadjimatheou, K., & Seymour, K. (2024). *Independent review of the South Australian domestic violence disclosure scheme*. https://repository.essex.ac.uk/39915/

Hadjimatheou, K., Quiroz Flores, A., Weir, R., & Skevington, T. (2024). Using unsupervised machine learning to find profiles of domestic abuse perpetrators. *Policing: A Journal of Policy and Practice*, *18*.

Hahn, U., & Oaksford, M. (2007). The burden of proof and its role in argumentation. *Argumentation*, *21*(1), 39–61.

Hamilton, E., & Fairfax-Columbo, J. (2023). Predicting recidivism: Psychosocial collateral consequences among registered offenders. *Journal of Sexual Aggression*, *29*(1), 160–176.

Harcourt, B. (2015, December 14). In Rahm Emanuel's Chicago surveillance state, controlling the data is key. *The Intercept*. https://theintercept.com/2015/12/14/in-rahm-emanuels-chicago-surveillance-state-controlling-the-data-is-key/

Harding, D. (2003). Jean Valjean's dilemma: The management of ex-convict identity in the search for employment. *Deviant Behavior*, *24*(6), 571–595.

Harman, G. (1983). Human flourishing, ethics, and liberty. *Philosophy & Public Affairs*, *12*(4), 307–322.

Hart, H. L. A. (1959). The presidential address: Prolegomenon to the principles of punishment. *Proceedings of the Aristotelian Society, 60*, 1–26.
Hart, H. M. (1958). The aims of the criminal law. *Law and Contemporary Problems, 23*(3), 401–441.
Henley, A. (2018). Civil and social death: Criminalisation and the loss of the self. In Read et al. (Eds.), *Loss, dying and bereavement in the criminal justice system* (pp. 76–84). Routledge.
Henley, A. (2019). Alternative approaches to criminal records: How can we achieve justice as fairness? In P. Carlen & L. Ayres França (Eds.), *Justice alternatives* (pp. 321–339). Routledge.
Herman, J. L. (2005). Justice from the victim's perspective. *Violence Against Women, 11*(5), 571–602.
Hester, M., & Westmarland, N. (2004). *Tackling street prostitution: Towards a holistic approach* (Home Office Research Study 279). Home Office.
Hill, J. (2020). *See what you made me do: Power, control and domestic abuse.* C. Hurst & Co.
Hill, T. E. (2019). *Dignity and practical reason in Kant's moral theory.* Cornell University Press.
HM Inspectorate of Probation. (2022). *A thematic inspection of the criminal justice response to adult female offenders.* https://www.justiceinspectorates.gov.uk/hmiprobation/inspections/adult-female-offenders/
Hohl, K. (2022). New scorecards on rape reports. *City, University of London.* https://www.city.ac.uk/news-and-events/news/2022/04/new-scorecards-show-under-1-of-reported-rapes-lead-to-conviction-criminologist-explains-why-englands-justice-system-continues-to-fail
Holman v. Central Arkansas Broadcasting Co., 611 S.W.2d 21 (Ark. 1979).
Holzer, H. J., Raphael, S., & Stoll, M. A. (2006). Perceived criminality, criminal background checks, and the racial hiring practices of employers. *The Journal of Law and Economics, 49*(2), 451–480.
Home Office. (1993). *Protection of children: Disclosure of criminal background of those with access to children (Home Office Circular 47/1993).*
Hoskins, Z. (2019). *Beyond punishment? A normative account of collateral legal consequences of conviction.* Oxford University Press.
Hoskins, Z. (2023). Collateral Legal Consequences and Criminal Sentencing. *American Philosophical Quarterly, 60*(2), 117–130.
Hough, M. (2014). Confessions of a recovering 'administrative criminologist': Jock Young, quantitative research and policy research. *Crime, Media, Culture, 10*(3), 215–226.
House of Commons. (2017). *Housing support for ex-offenders (England and Wales)* (Briefing Paper No. 2989). https://researchbriefings.files.parliament.uk/documents/SN02989/SN02989.pdf
House of Commons Library. (2024). *Domestic abuse: Policy developments 2020–2024* (Briefing Paper No. 09129). https://researchbriefings.files.parliament.uk/documents/CBP-9129/CBP-9129.pdf
House of Lords. (2025). *Rape: Level of prosecutions.* House of Lords Library. https://lordslibrary.parliament.uk/rape-levels-of-prosecutions
Hoye, J. M., & Monaghan, J. (2018). Surveillance, freedom and the republic. *European Journal of Political Theory, 17*(3), 343–363.
Hunt, L. W. (2018). *The retrieval of liberalism in policing.* Oxford University Press.
Husak, D. (2008). *Overcriminalization: The limits of the criminal law.* Oxford University Press.

Husak, D. (2016). "Does the State Have a Monopoly to Punish Crime?". In Chad Flanders & Zachary Hoskins (Eds.), *The new philosophy of criminal law*. Rowman & Littlefield.

In re British Broadcasting Corporation [2009] 3 WLR 142, 152, para 25.

Independent Anti-Slavery Commissioner. (2020). *Annual report 2019–2020*. https://www.antislaverycommissioner.co.uk/reports/annual-report-2019-2020/

Information Commissioner's Office. (2021). *Guide to the UK General Data Protection Regulation (UK GDPR)*. https://ico.org.uk/for-organisations/uk-gdpr-guidance-and-resources/

International Labour Organization. (2023). *Global estimates of modern slavery: Forced labour and forced marriage*. https://www.ilo.org/global/topics/forced-labour/lang--en/index.htm

Jacobs, J. B., & Larrauri, E. (2012). Are criminal convictions a public matter? The USA and Spain. *Punishment & Society*, *14*(1), 3–28.

Jacobs, J. B. (2015). *The Eternal Criminal Record*. Harvard University Press.

Jefferson-Jones, J. (2014). A good name: Applying regulatory takings analysis to reputational damage caused by criminal history. *West Virginia Law Review*, *116*(2), 497–533.

Jefferson-Jones, J. (2014a). Second chance: Rebiography as just compensation. *West Virginia Law Review*, *117*(1), 203–230.

Jones, A., & Schechter, S. (1993). *When love goes wrong: What to do when you can't do anything right*. HarperCollins.

Kahan, D. M. (2006). What's really wrong with shaming sanctions. *Texas Law Review*, *84*(7), 2075–2097.

Karsna, K., & Bromley, P. (2024). *Child sexual abuse in 2022/23: Trends in official data*. Centre of Expertise on Child Sexual Abuse. https://www.csacentre.org.uk/app/uploads/2024/02/Trends-in-Offical-Data-2022-23-FINAL.pdf

Kelly, L. (2010). The (in) credible words of women: False allegations in European rape research. *Violence Against Women*, *16*(12), 1345–1355.

Kelly, L., Lovett, J., & Regan, L. (2005). *A gap or a chasm?: Attrition in reported rape cases* (Home Office Research Study 293). Home Office.

Kemshall, H., & Wood, J. (2007). Beyond public protection: An examination of community protection and public health approaches to high-risk offenders. *Criminology & Criminal Justice*, *7*(3), 203–222.

Kennedy, J. (2021). Crimes as public wrongs. *Legal Theory*, *27*(4), 271–293.

Kleinig, J. (1998). 'The hardness of hard treatment.' In A. Ashworth and M. Wasik (Eds.), *Fundamentals of sentencing theory: Essays in honour of Andrew Von Hirsch*. Clarendon.

Kleinig, J., & Evans, N. G. (2013). Human flourishing, human dignity, and human rights. *Law and Philosophy*, *32*(5), 539–564.

Kogon, B., & Loughery, L., Jr. (1971). Sealing and expungement of criminal records—The big lie. *Journal of Criminal Law & Criminology*, *61*(3), 378–389.

Kolber, A. J. (2012). Unintentional punishment. *Legal Theory*, *18*(1), 1–29.

Kurtovic, E., & Rovira, M. (2017). Contrasts in the hidden obstacles to reentry in the labour market based on criminal records between the Netherlands and Spain. *European Journal of Criminology*, *14*(5), 505–521.

LaFollette, H. (2005). Collateral consequences of punishment: Civil penalties accompanying formal punishment. *Journal of Applied Philosophy*, *22*(3), 241–261.

Lageson, S. (2016). Found Out and Opting Out: The Consequences of Online Criminal Records for Families. *The ANNALS of the American Academy of Political and Social Science*, 665(1), 127–141.

Lageson, S. (2020). *Digital punishment: Privacy, stigma, and the harms of data-driven criminal justice.* Oxford University Press.

Lageson, S. (2023). Criminally bad data: Inaccurate criminal records, data brokers, and algorithmic injustice. *University of Illinois Law Review, 2023*(5), 1772–1810.

Lageson, S., Denver, M., & Pickett, J. T. (2018). Privatizing criminal stigma: Experience, intergroup contact, and public views about publicizing arrest records. *Punishment & Society, 21*(3), 315–341.

Lageson, S., & Maruna, S. (2018). Digital degradation: Stigma management in the Internet age. *Punishment & Society, 20*(1), 113–133. https://doi.org/10.1177/1462474517737050

Lageson, S. & Stewart, R. (2024). The problem with criminal records: Discrepancies between state reports and private sector background checks. *Criminology, 62*(1), 5–34.

Lageson, S., Vuolo, M., & Uggen, C. (2015). Legal ambiguity in managerial assessments of criminal records. *Law and Social Inquiry, 40*(1): 175–204.

Lamond, G. (2007). What is a crime? *Oxford Journal of Legal Studies, 27*(4), 609–632.

Larmore, C. E. (2008). *The autonomy of morality.* Cambridge University Press.

Larrauri, E. (2014). Legal protections against criminal background checks in Europe. *Punishment & Society, 16*(1), 50–73.

Larrauri, E. (2014a). Are police records criminal records?: Disclosure of criminal information and the presumption of innocence. *European Journal of Crime, Criminal Law and Criminal Justice, 22*(4), 377–395.

Lasher, M. P., & McGrath, R. J. (2012). The impact of community notification on sex offender reintegration: A quantitative review of the research literature. *International Journal of Offender Therapy and Comparative Criminology, 56*(1), 6–28.

Laub, J., & Sampson, R. (2003). *Shared beginnings, divergent lives: Delinquent boys to age 70.* Harvard University Press.

Law Commission. (2020). *Abusive and controlling behaviour: Proposals for law reform.* https://www.lawcom.gov.uk/project/domestic-abuse/

Leasure, P., & Andersen, T. S. (2019). Race, criminal records, and certificates of relief: An experimental pilot study. *Deviant Behavior, 41*(9), 1065–1083.

LeBel, T. P. (2011). Invisible stripes? Formerly incarcerated persons' perceptions of stigma. *Deviant Behavior, 33*(2), 89–107.

Lee, A. (2015). Public wrongs and the criminal law. *Criminal Law and Philosophy, 9*(1), 155–173.

Lee, H. W. (2017). Taking deterrence seriously: The wide scope deterrence theory of punishment. *Criminal Justice Ethics, 36*(1), 2–24.

Legal Action Group. (2023). *Access to justice for survivors of domestic abuse.* https://www.lag.org.uk/article/212826/access-to-justice-for-survivors-of-domestic-abuse

Lernestedt, C. (2014). Victim and society: Sharing wrongs, but in which roles? *Criminal Law and Philosophy, 8*(1), 187–203.

Levenson, J., Brannon, Y. N., Fortney, T., & Baker, J. (2007). Megan's law and its impact on community re-entry for sex offenders. *Behavioral Sciences and the Law, 25*(4), 587–602.

Leveson, B. (2012). *Leveson inquiry: Report into the culture, practices and ethics of the press.* https://www.gov.uk/government/publications/leveson-inquiry-report-into-the-culture-practices-and-ethics-of-the-press

Li, E. (2023). The Qianke system in China: Disorganisation, discrimination and dispersion. *Criminology & Criminal Justice, 23*(4), 568–587.

Link, B. G., & Phelan, J. C. (2001). Conceptualizing stigma. *Annual Review of Sociology, 27*(1), 363–385.

Lippke, R. L. (2018). Legal punishment and the public identification of offenders. *Res Publica, 24*(2), 199–216.

Lippke, R. L. (2025). Punishment, public safety, and collateral legal consequences. *Journal of Applied Philosophy*. (forthcoming)

Locke, J. (1993). Two treatises of government. In Goldie M. (Ed.), *Everyman*. Everyman Paperbacks (Original work published 1689).

Logan, W. A. (2009). *Knowledge as power: Criminal registration and community notification laws in America*. Stanford University Press.

Luban, D. (1998). The publicity principle. In R. E. Goodin (Ed.), *The theory of institutional design* (pp. 154–198). Cambridge University Press.

Luca, D. L. (2018). The digital scarlet letter: The effect of online criminal records on crime. *SSRN*. http://dx.doi.org/10.2139/ssrn.1939589

Magee, I. (2008). *The review of criminality information*. Everyman Paperbacks.

Mannheim, H. (2021). *The dilemma of penal reform*. Routledge. (Original work published 1939).

Markel, D. (2001). Are shaming punishments beautifully retributive: Retributivism and the implications for the alternative sanctions debate. *Vanderbilt Law Review, 54*(6), 2157–2242.

Markel, D., & Flanders, C. (2010). Bentham on stilts: The bare relevance of subjectivity to retributive justice. *California Law Review, 98*, 907–956.

Marshall, S. E., & Duff, R. A. (1998). Criminalization and sharing wrongs. *Canadian Journal of Law and Jurisprudence, 11*(1), 7–24.

Marshall, S. E., & Duff, R. A. (2010). Public and private wrongs. In J. Chalmers, F. Leverick, & L. Farmer (Eds.), *Essays in criminal law in honour of Sir Gerald Gordon* (pp. 70–85). Edinburgh University Press.

Maruna, S. (2001). *Making good* (Vol. 86). American Psychological Association.

Maruna, S. (2011). Judicial rehabilitation and the 'clean bill of health' in criminal justice. *European Journal of Probation, 3*(1), 97–117.

Maruna, S., & Pali, B. (2010). From victim blaming to reintegrative shaming: The continuing relevance of *Crime, Shame and Reintegration* in the era of #MeToo. *The International Journal of Restorative Justice, 3*(1), 38–44.

Masny, M. (2022). Wasted potential: The value of a life and the significance of what could have been. *Philosophy & Public Affairs, 51*(1), 6–32.

Matravers, M. (2017). Legitimate expectations in theory, practice, and punishment. *Moral Philosophy and Politics, 4*(2), 307–323.

Maurutto, P., Hannah-Moffat, K., & Quirouette, M. (2023). Punishing the nonconvicted through disclosure of police records. *The British Journal of Criminology, 63*(6), 1368–1383.

Mayson, S. G. (2015). Collateral consequences and the preventative state. *Notre Dame Law Review 91*(1), 301.

McElhattan, D. (2022). The exception as the rule: Negligent hiring liability, structured uncertainty, and the rise of criminal background checks in the United States. *Law & Social Inquiry, 47*(1), 132–161.

McWilliams, E. R., & Hunter, B. A. (2021). The impact of criminal record stigma on quality of life: A test of theoretical pathways. *American Journal of Community Psychology, 67*(1-2), 89–102.

Meijer, S. (2017). Rehabilitation as a positive obligation. *European Journal of Crime, Criminal Law and Criminal Justice, 25*(2), 145–162.

Mendlow, G. S. (2022). On the state's exclusive right to punish. *Law and Philosophy*, *41*(2), 243–262.

Mill, J. S. (1859). *On liberty*. Longman, Roberts, & Green.

Miller, J. R. (2021). *Halfway home: Race, punishment, and the afterlife of mass incarceration*. Little, Brown and Company.

Miller, S. L. (2011). *After the crime: The power of restorative justice dialogues between victims and violent offenders*. New York University Press.

Ministry of Justice. (2017). *The lammy review: An independent review into the treatment of, and outcomes for black, asian and minority ethnic individuals in the criminal justice system*. https://www.gov.uk/government/organisations/lammy-review

Ministry of Justice. (2024a). *Criminal court statistics 2016–24*. https://rapecrisis.org.uk/get-involved/years-too-long-dont-keep-survivors-waiting-for-justice/

Ministry of Justice. (2024b). *Criminal court statistics quarterly: January to March 2024*. https://www.gov.uk/government/statistics/criminal-court-statistics-quarterly-january-to-march-2024

Ministry of Justice. (2024c). *Outcomes by offence data tool*. https://www.gov.uk/government/statistics/criminal-justice-system-statistics-quarterly-december-2023

Mokrosinska, D. (2018). Privacy and autonomy: On some misconceptions concerning the political dimensions of privacy. *Law and Philosophy*, *37*(2), 117–143.

Monaghan, J. (2023). *Just policing*. Oxford University Press.

Moreham, N. A. (2006). Privacy in public places. *The Cambridge Law Journal*, *65*(3), 606–635.

Moore, M. H. (1989). The moral worth of retribution. In F. E. Zimring & G. Hawkins (Eds.), *The ethics of punishment* (pp. 179–200). Oxford University Press.

Moore, M. S. (2010). *Placing blame: A theory of the criminal law*. Oxford University Press.

Moore, K. E., & Tangney, J. P. (2017, June). Managing the concealable stigma of criminal justice system involvement: A longitudinal examination of anticipated stigma, social withdrawal, and post-release adjustment. *Journal of Social Issues*, *73*(2): 322–340.

Mosweu, T. (2021). Access to electronic court records in Botswana: trends, status and recommendations. *ESARBICA Journal: Journal of the Eastern and Southern Africa Regional Branch of the International Council on Archives*, 40, 87–99.

Mujuzi, J. D. (2014). The expungement of criminal records in South Africa: The drafting history of the law, the unresolved issues, and how they could be resolved. *Statute Law Review*, *35*(3), 278–303.

Mulcahy, A., & Traynor, J. (2019). Criminal histories and employment: The stigmatization of offender job seekers in the UK. *Criminology & Criminal Justice*, *19*(3), 336–354.

Mungan, M. C. (2012). Don't take the punishment seriousness requirement lightly: Assessing the seriousness of crimes in criminal law theory. *Law and Philosophy*, *31*(6), 681–705.

Murphy, J. G. (1987). Marxism and retribution. *Philosophy & Public Affairs*, *4*(3), 217–243.

Murphy, J. G., & Hampton, J. (1988). *Forgiveness and mercy*. Cambridge University Press.

Myrick, A. (2013). Facing your criminal record: Expungement and the collateral problem of wrongfully represented self. *Law & Society Review*, *47*(1), 73–104.

Nagel, T. (1998). Concealment and exposure. *Philosophy & Public Affairs*, *27*(1), 3-30.

Nash, M. (2013). Police vetting and barring: An historical account of a modern crime prevention strategy. *Policing and Society*, *23*(1), 25–43.

Nathan, C. (2022). Punishment the easy way. *Criminal law and philosophy*, *16*(1), 77–102.

National Association for People Abused in Childhood (NAPAC). (2022). *The impact of childhood sexual abuse: A rapid evidence assessment*. https://napac.org.uk/wp-content/uploads/2022/04/NAPAC_REA_2022.pdf

National Center for State Courts. (2020). *Best practices for online publication of court records.* https://www.ncsc.org/__data/assets/pdf_file/0021/40718/Online-Publication-of-Court-Records_Best-Practices.pdf

National Police Chiefs' Council. (2023). *Domestic abuse, stalking and harassment policy 2023–2025.* https://www.npcc.police.uk/

National Society for the Prevention of Cruelty to Children. (2022). *How safe are our children? An overview of data on child abuse and neglect in the UK.* https://learning.nspcc.org.uk/research-resources/how-safe-are-our-children

Naughton, M. (2007). *Rethinking miscarriages of justice: Beyond the tip of the iceberg.* Palgrave Macmillan.

Naylor, B. (2011). Criminal records and rehabilitation in Australia. *European Journal of Probation, 3*(1), 79–96.

Naylor, B., & Schmidt, C. (2010). Do prisoners have a right to privacy? Media access to prisoners and the implications for human rights. *Alternative Law Journal, 35*(4), 222–226.

Nellis, A. (2016). *The color of justice: Racial and ethnic disparity in state prisons.* The Sentencing Project. https://www.sentencingproject.org/reports/color-of-justice-racial-and-ethnic-disparity-in-state-prisons/

Newburn, T. (2017). *Criminology* (2nd ed.). Routledge.

Neyroud, P. (2020). Ethics in policing: Past, present and future. In B. Bradford, B. Jauregui, I. Loader, & J. Steinberg (Eds.), *The SAGE handbook of global policing* (pp. 457–472). SAGE.

Nicholls, J. (2018). Open justice and developments in the law on anonymity, access to material and reporting restrictions. *Judicial Review, 23*(3), 200–224.

Nozick, R. (1974). *Anarchy, state, and utopia.* Basic Books.

Nunziato, D. C. (2017). The fourth year of forgetting: The troubling expansion of the right to be forgotten. *University of Pennsylvania Journal of International Law, 39*(4), 1011.

Nussbaum, M. (2004). *Hiding from humanity: Disgust, shame, and the law.* Princeton University Press.

Nussbaum, M. (2011). *Creating Capabilities: The Human Development Approach.* Harvard University Press.

O'Hear, M. M. (2007). Barrock Lecture: The second chance gap. *Federal Sentencing Reporter, 19*(3), 125–133.

Oaten, M., Stevenson, R. J., & Case, T. I. (2011, December 12). Disease avoidance as a functional basis for stigmatization. *Philosophical Transactions of the Royal Society, 366*(1583), 3433–3452.

O'Neill, O. (2002). *A question of trust: The BBC Reith lectures 2002.* Cambridge University Press.

Office for National Statistics. (2020). *Child abuse in England and Wales: January 2020.* https://www.ons.gov.uk/peoplepopulationandcommunity/crimeandjustice/bulletins/childabuseinenglandandwales/january2020

Office for National Statistics. (2023). *Sexual offences prevalence and victim characteristics, England and Wales: Year ending March 2022.* https://www.ons.gov.uk/peoplepopulationandcommunity/crimeandjustice/bulletins/sexualoffencesprevalenceandvictimcharacteristics/appendixyearendingmarch2022

Office for National Statistics. (2024). *Crime in England and Wales: Annual trend and demographic tables.* https://www.ons.gov.uk/peoplepopulationandcommunity/crimeandjustice/datasets/crimeinenglandandwalesappendixtables

Office for Standards in Education (Ofsted). (2021). *Review of sexual abuse in schools and colleges.* https://www.gov.uk/government/publications/review-of-sexual-abuse-in-schools-and-colleges

Office of the Privacy Commissioner of Canada. (2014). *Police information checks: Consultation report.* https://www.priv.gc.ca/en/opc-actions-and-decisions/research/explore-privacy-research/2014/pic_201403/

Padfield, N. (2019). Risk and the parole process. *European Journal of Probation, 11*(2), 75–91.

Pager, D. (2003). The mark of a criminal record. *American Journal of Sociology, 108*(5), 937–975.

Pager, D., Western, B., & Sugie, N. (2009). Sequencing disadvantage: Barriers to employment facing young black and white men with criminal records. *Annals of the American Academy of Political and Social Science, 623*(1), 195–213.

Parole Board for England and Wales. (2024). *Annual report and accounts 2023–2024.* https://www.gov.uk/government/organisations/parole-board

Parsons, S., & Radford, L. (2021). *The prevalence and nature of sexual violence against children in the UK.* National Society for the Prevention of Cruelty to Children. https://learning.nspcc.org.uk/research-resources/prevalence-nature-child-sexual-abuse

Patterson, K. (2008). Shaming the constitutional order: Burdens on expression and dignity in sexually violent predator legislation. *Northwestern University Law Review, 102*(3), 1271–1298.

Peay, J. (2010). Tribunals and truth. *Criminal Law Review, 2010*(4), 347–362.

Peay, J. (2017). *Mental health and criminal justice: A review of the relationship between mental disorder and offending behaviours.* Routledge.

Peay, J., & Ashworth, A. (2013). The future of sentencing: Towards principled sentencing reform. *Oxford Journal of Legal Studies, 33*(2), 269–295.

Peck, J. H., & Jennings, W. G. (2016). A review of the empirical research on sex offender registration and notification. *Criminal Justice Policy Review, 27*(4), 355–371.

Pérez-Fuentes, G., Olfson, M., Villegas, L., Morcillo, C., Wang, S., & Blanco, C. (2013). Prevalence and correlates of child sexual abuse: A national study. *Comprehensive Psychiatry, 54*(1), 16–27.

Perlin, M. L. (2003). Therapeutic jurisprudence: Understanding the sanist and pretextual bases of mental disability law. *New York Law School Journal of Human Rights, 10*(1), 9–31.

Petersilia, J. (2003). *When prisoners come home: Parole and prisoner reentry.* Oxford University Press.

Pickett, J. T., & Bushway, S. D. (2023). Can public safety incentives overcome bias against people with criminal records? Evidence from a survey experiment. *Criminology & Public Policy, 22*(3), 415–448.

Pickett, J. T., Graham, A., Cullen, F. T., & Bushway, S. D. (2023). Does knowing a person with a criminal record reduce punitive attitudes? Evidence from a national survey experiment. *Criminology, 61*(2), 232–258.

Pimentel, D. (2010). Fearing the bogeyman: How the sex offender registry turns participants into victims. *Cardozo Law Review, 31*(2), 867–887.

Pleskach, P. (2008). The right to know versus the right to privacy: Ethical and legal dilemmas in the publication of criminal records. *Criminal Justice Ethics, 27*(2), 26–41.

Police Act. (1997). https://www.legislation.gov.uk/ukpga/1997/50/contents

Posner, R. A. (1992). *Economic analysis of law* (4th ed.). Aspen.

Prah Ruger, J. (2020). Positive public health ethics: Toward flourishing and resilient communities and individuals. *The American Journal of Bioethics, 20*(7), 44–54.

Prescott, J. J., & Rockoff, J. E. (2008). Do sex offender registration and notification laws affect criminal behavior? *Law & Economics Working Papers Archive: 2003–2009*, 85.

Prescott, J. J., & Starr, S. B. (2020). Expungement of criminal convictions: An empirical study. *Harvard Law Review, 133*(8), 2460–2556.

Prison Reform Trust. (2017). *Counted out: Black, Asian and minority ethnic women in the criminal justice system*. https://prisonreformtrust.org.uk/wp-content/uploads/old_files/Documents/Counted%20Out.pdf

Purshouse, J. (2018). Non-conviction disclosure as part of an enhanced criminal record certificate: Assessing the legal framework from a fundamental human rights perspective. *Public Law, 2018*(4), 668–686.

Quong, J. (2011). *Liberalism without perfection*. Oxford University Press.

R (on the application of P) (Appellant) v. Secretary of State for the Home Department and others (Respondents). UKSC/2017/0170.

R (on the application of C) (Appellant) v. Secretary of State for Justice (Respondent), Supreme Court of the United Kingdom (27 Jan 2016) https://www.supremecourt.uk/cases/uksc-2014-0210

Rape Crisis (2024). Rape Statistics. At: https://rapecrisis.org.uk/get-informed/statistics-sexual-violence/

Rasmusen, E. (1996). Stigma and self-fulfilling expectations of criminality. *Journal of Law and Economics, 39*(2), 519–536.

Rawls, J. (1971). *A theory of justice*. Belknap Press of Harvard University Press.

Rawls, J. (1993). *Political liberalism*. Columbia University Press.

Refuge. (2024). *The economic cost of domestic abuse*. https://refuge.org.uk/wp-content/uploads/2024/03/EconomicCostofDA_Refuge.pdf

Reiter, K., Selbin, J., & Hersh, E. (2014, December 28). Should a shoplifting conviction be an indelible scarlet letter? *Los Angeles Times*. http://www.latimes.com/opinion/op-ed/la-oe-selbin-prop-47-criminal-records-20141229-story.html

Respect. (2024). *Respect manifesto*. https://hubble-live-assets.s3.eu-west-1.amazonaws.com/respect/file_asset/file/2148/Respect_Manifesto.pdf

Roberts, A. (2012). (Re)forming the jury: Detection and disinfection of implicit juror bias. *Connecticut Law Review* 44(1). 827–833.

Roberts, J. (2015). Expunging America's rap sheet in the information age. *Wisconsin Law Review*, 1, 321–348.

Robinson, J., & Yoshida, K. (2024). *Silenced women: Why the law fails women and how to fight back*. Allen & Unwin.

Rovira, M. (2022). The next Pandora's box of criminal background checks. *European Journal of Criminology, 19*(6), 1386–1402.

Rovira, M. (2023). The global rise of criminal background checks. *International Criminology, 3*(1), 1–11.

Ryberg, J. (2004). *The ethics of proportionate punishment*. Kluwer Academic Publishers.

Ryberg, J. (2025). How should we work as penal ethicists? In J. Ryberg (Ed.), *The Oxford handbook of the philosophy of punishment* (pp. 707–724). Oxford University Press.

SafeLives. (2022). *The whole picture: SafeLives strategy 2022–2027*. https://safelives.org.uk/the_whole_picture

Sakiyama, M. (2011). Reintegrative shaming and juvenile delinquency in Japan. *UNLV Theses, Dissertations, Professional Papers, and Capstones, 995*, 1–72.

Salfati, C. G. (2009). *Safer sex in the city: The experience and management of street prostitution*. Routledge.

Scorza, J. (2013). Civic friendship. In H. LaFollette (Ed.), *The internet encyclopedia of philosophy*. Blackwell Publishing.

Selbin, J., McCrary, J., & Epstein, J. (2018). Unmarked? Criminal record clearing and employment outcomes. *Journal of Criminal Law & Criminology, 108*(1), 1–72.

Sentencing Council. (2023). *Overarching principles: Domestic abuse*. https://www.sentencingcouncil.org.uk/

Shklar, J. (1989). The liberalism of fear. In N. L. Rosenblum (Ed.), *Liberalism and the moral life* (pp. 21–38). Harvard University Press.

Siddique, H. (2021, February 25). Rapist John Worboys loses appeal against two life sentences. *The Guardian.* https://www.theguardian.com/uk-news/2021/feb/24/john-worboys-rapist-loses-appeal-against-life-sentence

Silverman, G. (2004). Rise of the machines: Justice information systems and the question of public access to court records over the internet. *Washington Law Review, 79*, 175–222.

Simester, A. (2021). *Fundamentals of criminal law: Responsibility, culpability, and wrongdoing.* Oxford University Press.

Skardhamar, T., & Savolainen, J. (2014). Changes in criminal offending around the time of job entry: A study of employment and desistance. *Criminology, 52*(2), 263–291.

Smith, A. (2002). *The theory of moral sentiments* (K. Haakonssen, Ed.). Cambridge University Press. (Original work published 1759)

Solove, D. (2002). Access and aggregation: Privacy, public records, and the Constitution. *Minnesota Law Review, 86*, 1137–1184.

Stark, E. (2007). *Coercive control: How men entrap women in personal life.* Oxford University Press.

Stewart, R., & Uggen, C. (2020). Criminal records and college admissions: A modified experimental audit. *Criminology, 58*(1), 156–188.

Stewart, S., Willmott, D., Murphy, A., & Phillips, C. (2024). 'I thought I'm better off just trying to put this behind me' – A contemporary approach to understanding why women decide not to report sexual violence. *The Journal of Forensic Psychiatry, 35*(1), 85–101.

Stöckl, H., Devries, K., Rotstein, A., Abrahams, N., Campbell, J., Watts, C., & Moreno, C. G. (2013). The global prevalence of intimate partner homicide: A systematic review. *The Lancet, 382*(9895), 859–865.

Stoll, M. A., & Bushway, S. D. (2008). The effect of criminal background checks on hiring ex-offenders. *Criminology & Public Policy, 7*, 371–404.

Sudbeck, L. (2005). Placing court records online: Balancing judicial accountability with public trust and confidence. *Justice System Journal, 27*(3), 268–286.

Survivors Trust. (2023). *Support for victims of sexual violence: A national survey.* https://www.thesurvivorstrust.org/research

Sweet, P. L. (2019). The sociology of gaslighting. *American Sociological Review, 84*(5), 851–875.

Taslitz, A. (2009). 'Judging Jena's DNA: The Prosecutor and Racial Esteem'. *Harvard Civil Rights and Civil Liberties Review, 44*(2), 1–53.

Thacher, D. (2008). The rise of criminal background screening in rental housing. *Law & Social Inquiry, 33*(1), 5–30.

Thomas, T., & Beckett, K. (2019). *Employment screening and non-conviction information: A human rights perspective.* Palgrave Macmillan.

Thompson, D. F. (1999). Democratic secrecy. *Political Science Quarterly, 114*(2), 181–193.

Tonry, M. H. (Ed.). (2011). *Why punish? How much?: A reader on punishment.* Oxford University Press.

Travis, A. (2008, November 22, Friday). *High-visibility offenders face reprisal attacks, union warns.* The Guardian Newspaper. http://www.theguardian.com/uk/2008/nov/28/community-payback-high-visibiity-vests

Tripkovic, M. (2019). *Punishment and citizenship: A theory of criminal disenfranchisement.* Oxford University Press.

Tuerkheimer, D. (2019). Beyond #MeToo. *New York University Law Review, 94*(5), 1146–1208.

Tunick, M. (2015). *Balancing privacy and free speech: Unwanted attention in the age of social media*. Routledge.

Uggen, C., Manza, J., & Behrens, A. (2014). The edge of stigma: An experimental audit of the effects of low-level criminal records on employment. *Criminology*, *52*(4), 627–654.

UK Government. (2024). *Violence Against Women and Girls (VAWG) Strategy: Progress update*. https://www.gov.uk/government/publications/vawg-strategy-progress-report-2024

United Nations. (2023). *Convention on the elimination of all forms of discrimination against women (CEDAW): UK implementation report*. https://www.un.org/womenwatch/daw/cedaw/

Unlock. (2021). *Angels or witches? The impact of criminal records on women*. https://unlock.org.uk/wp-content/uploads/2021/10/The-impact-of-criminal-records-on-women.pdf

Unlock. (2023). *Problems accessing insurance with a criminal record*. https://unlock.org.uk/wp-content/uploads/2023/04/Unlock-briefing-on-impact-of-a-criminal-record-on-insurance-April-2023-1-1.pdf

Unlock. (2023a). *Why we need reform of the criminal records system*. https://unlock.org.uk/wp-content/uploads/2023/02/Why-we-need-reform-of-the-criminal-records-system.-Unlock-briefing-February-2023.pdf

Unlock. (2024). *Briefing on people with criminal records who are also victims of crime*. https://unlock.org.uk/wp-content/uploads/2024/05/Crossover-of-people-with-criminal-records-and-victims-Unlock-Briefing-May-24.pdf

UNODC (United Nations Office on Drugs and Crime). (2023). *Intentional homicide statistics*. https://dataunodc.un.org/dp-intentional-homicide-victims

Vallas, R., & Dietrich, S. (2014). *One strike and you're out: How we can eliminate barriers to economic security and mobility for people with criminal records*. Center for American Progress. https://cdn.americanprogress.org/wp-content/uploads/2014/12/VallasCriminalRecordsReport.pdf

Van der Geest, V., Bijleveld, C., & Blkland, A. (2011). The effects of employment on longitudinal trajectories of offending: A follow up of high-risk youth from 18 to 32 years of age. *Criminology*, *49*(4), 1195–1234.

Victim Support. (2024). *Understanding victims' experiences of the criminal justice system*. https://www.victimsupport.org.uk/research-and-insight

Victims' Commissioner for England and Wales. (2020). *Annual report of the Victims' Commissioner, 2019 to 2020*. https://victimscommissioner.org.uk/document/annual-report-of-the-victims-commissioner-2019-to-2020/

Volokh, E. (2000). Freedom of speech and information privacy: The troubling implications of a right to stop people from speaking about you. *Stanford Law Review*, *52*(5), 1–65.

Von Hirsch, A. (1993) *Censure and sanctions*. Oxford University Press.

Walby, S., Towers, J., & Francis, B. (2014). Mainstreaming domestic and gender-based violence into sociology and the criminology of violence. *The Sociological Review*, *62*(2), 187–214.

Waldron, J. (2016). *Political political theory: Essays on institutions*. Harvard University Press.

Walker, N. (1980). *Punishment, danger and stigma: The morality of criminal justice*. Rowman & Littlefield.

Walzer, M. (2015). *Just and unjust wars: A moral argument with historical illustrations*. Basic Books.

Weaver, B. (2018). *Time for policy redemption? A review of the evidence on disclosure of criminal records*. Scottish Centre for Crime and Justice Research.

Weber, M. (1948). *From Max Weber: Essays in sociology* (H. H. Gerth & C. W. Mills, Eds.). Routledge and Kegan Paul.

Williams, A. (1998). Incentives, inequality, and publicity. *Philosophy & Public Affairs, 27*(3), 225–247.

Winter, J. (2024, December 13). Luigi Mangione and the making of a modern antihero. *The New Yorker*. https://www.newyorker.com/news/the-lede/luigi-mangione-and-the-making-of-a-modern-antihero

Winters, G. M., Colombino, N., Schaaf, S., Laake, A. L. W., Jeglic, E. L., & Calkins, C. (2020). Why do child sexual abuse victims not tell anyone about their abuse? An exploration of factors that prevent and promote disclosure. *Behavioral Sciences and the Law, 38*(6), 586–611.

Winnick, T. A., & Bodkin, M. (2008). Anticipated stigma and stigma management among those to be labeled 'ex-con'. *Deviant Behaviour, 29*(4), 295–333.

Wolff, J., & Leopold, D. (2020). Karl Marx. In E. N. Zalta (Ed.), *The Stanford encyclopedia of philosophy* (Spring 2021 Edition). https://plato.stanford.edu/archives/spr2021/entries/marx/

Women's Aid. (2024). *How common is domestic abuse?* https://www.womensaid.org.uk/information-support/what-is-domestic-abuse/how-common-is-domestic-abuse/

Women's Budget Group. (2023). *Cost of living crisis: Impact on women survivors of abuse*. https://wbg.org.uk/analysis/cost-of-living-crisis-impact-on-women/

Women's Resource Centre. (2023). *The state of the women's sector: 2023 report*. https://www.wrc.org.uk/resources

Working Chance. (2022). *Progress & prejudice: Shifts in employer attitudes to hiring people with convictions*. https://workingchance.org/about-us/our-policy-focus/progress-prejudice/

World Health Organisation. (2024). *Violence against women: Key facts*. https://www.who.int/news-room/fact-sheets/detail/violence-against-women

Yukhnenko, D., Farouki, L., & Fazel, S. (2023). Criminal recidivism rates globally: A 6-year systematic review update. *Journal of Criminal Justice, 88(Sept–Oct)*, 1–15.

Zand Kurtovic, E. (2017). Invisible bars: The impact of having a criminal record on young adults' position in the labour market (Doctoral dissertation). Leiden University, https://www.universiteitleiden.nl/binaries/content/assets/rechtsgeleerdheid/instituut-voor-strafrecht-en-criminologie/elina-van-het-t-zand---dissertatie-invisible-bars-2017.pdf

Zand Kurtovic, E., & Boone, M. (2023). Privacy, promotionalism and the proliferation of state-performed criminal record screening in the Netherlands: How a restrictive legal framework can still result in a steep increase of criminal background checks. *Criminology & Criminal Justice, 23*(4), 549–567.

Zevitz, R. G., & Farkas, M. A. (2000). Sex offender community notification: Managing high risk criminals or exacting further vengeance?. *Behavioral Sciences & the Law, 18*(2–3), 375–391.

Zhang, X. (2024). Labor market reentry among white-collar female ex-prisoners in China: A feminist desistance perspective. *Feminist Criminology. 20*(3), 285–306.

Zimmerman, A. (2019). Criminal disenfranchisement and the concept of political wrongdoing. *Philosophy and Public Affairs, 47*(4), 378–411.

Index

For the benefit of digital users, indexed terms that span two pages (e.g., 52–53) may, on occasion, appear on only one of those pages.

accountability 73–97, 127–30

Bentham:
  on the principle of less eligibility 17–20
  on publicity 80–82
  on deterrence 123–24

censure 65, 99–130
  and communicative theories of punishment 112–15
  and stigma 104
communicative theory of punishment
  as a justification for public labelling of criminals 107–23
court records:
  confidentiality of, in different countries 89–90
  disclosure of historic 88
  and the doctrine of public fact 85–90
  publicity of 151

deterrence 99–130
  as a justification for public labelling of criminals 100, 123–27
dignity:
  as an element of human flourishing 45–47
disclosure schemes 153–68
domestic abuse 10, 27–29, 61–62, 79
  low rates of conviction 129
  registries of perpetrators of 149–50
  reluctance of victims to report 128–29
domestic violence disclosure schemes 159–64
Duff 5, 14–15
  and the communicative theory of punishment 53–54, 58–59, 63–64, 69–70
  on dangerousness 154, 155
  on public wrongs 107–8, 109–10

employers:
  and criminal record checks 11
  Dutch approach to disclosures to 145
  and fear of being stigmatised by association when hiring people with convictions 34–35
  as gatekeepers to vulnerability 137–38, 148
  legality of disclosing minor historic convictions to 142
  proposals for a system of disclosures to 151
  responses to a candidate's criminal record 27, 33, 141
employment:
  exclusion from, with a criminal record 26–30
  relevance of a criminal record to 131–32

flourishing 23–48
  and dignity 45–47
  and the harms of a public criminal record 44–45

Hoskins, Z.:
  on collateral consequences that express contempt for people with convictions 46
  on dangerousness 143

Lageson 8–9
  on the harms of a public criminal record 28–29, 30, 37n.23, 38, 39–40, 42n.29
Larrauri 92–93

Maruna 28–29, 174–75
  on the #MeToo movement 178–79
Megan's Law 111n.17, 124
Mill, J. S. 43–44, 80–81

non-conviction records
of child sexual abuse 157
and crimes of abuse 153–68
disclosing, to prevent harm 131–51
and employer discrimination 27
as indicators of a person's criminal risk 153–54
as indicators of dangerousness 10
as more indicative of risk than conviction records 159
and predatory criminals 155
and the presumption of innocence 164–67
reasons to include in category of criminal records 10
trends in recording and storing of 25–26

open justice 73–97
and interference with privacy 90
legal judgement of interference with 89
openness 73–97

police records 1–3, 9–10
digitization and storing of 134
importance of sharing to prevent harm to sex workers 159
inapplicability of social contract arguments to 52
mistakes in and ways of contesting 30
presumptive confidentiality of 96, 134
and reasonable grounds for belief that a person poses harm 136–37
and reoffending 34–35
presumption of innocence 15, 136–37
and objections to disclosing criminal records 164–67
prevention 14n.14, 171
of harm, as a justification for disclosing criminal records 131–51
privacy:
and the 85–97
as a ground for objecting to public criminal records 11–16
and the legal right to know 75–79
professional ethics:
as analogous to public ethics 63–66
proportionality 101–2, 106, 107–23, 133, 137, 139
public fact 85–90
public wrongs 49–71
as analogous to acts of professional misconduct 63–66
as crimes that threaten the civic order 60–63
as crimes that victimize the public 58–60
as crimes that wrong the public causally 66–68
in legal theory 58
punishment:
as disproportionate in response to public criminal record 11–12, 14–15

right to be forgotten 11

sexual offences 31–33, 145–46
shame
experienced by those with public criminal records 37–38
as something desired for offenders by victims of abuse crimes 178–79
threat of, as a deterrent to crime 123–24
threat of, as a deterrent to wrongdoing in public office 80
shaming sanctions as just 32–33
as the exclusive right of the state to inflict 54
as a justification for public labelling of criminals 99–130
as a justified response to breaches of the social contract 51n.2
unjust, as prevented by openness of courts 84, 88–89
stigma 18–19, 24, 32–40, 99–106, 125, 139–40, 150, 158, 167
stigmatization
as a process 33–35

transparency 73–97
Tunick 4–5, 11, 14–15, 136–37, 166

Ugly Mugs 158–59